DATE DUE

Feb 18, 2011	

THE BIG BOOK OF
PAIN

TORTURE & PUNISHMENT THROUGH HISTORY

MARK P. DONNELLY & DANIEL DIEHL

ALSO BY THE AUTHORS:

I Thought Edison Invented That
Management Secrets from History
Eat Thy Neighbour: A History of Cannibalism
Tales From the Tower of London
Elbert Hubbard: Common Sense Revolutionary
How Did They Manage?
Siege: Castles at War
Medieval Furniture: Plans & Instructions
Medieval Celebrations
Constructing Medieval Furniture

The past is like a foreign country, they do things differently there.

L.P. Hartley (from *The Go-Between*)

When reason sleeps monsters are born.

Francisco Goya

Within this gibbet, the condemned would be forced to sit and wait for starvation, dehydration and exposure to take their inevitable effect. It was a slow and public death.

The coward wretch whose hand and heart
Can bear to torture aught below,
Is ever first to quail and start
From the slightest pain or equal foe.

Bertrand Russell

First published in the United Kingdom in 2008 by
The History Press · Cirencester Road · Chalford · Stroud
Gloucestershire · GL6 8PE

British Library Cataloguing in Publication Data
A catalogue record for this book is available from the British Library.

Hardback ISBN 978-0-7509-4583-7

Typeset in Photina.
Typesetting and origination by
The History Press.
Printed and bound in the United Kingdom.

CONTENTS

ACKNOWLEDGEMENTS

The authors extend their thanks and gratitude to our editor at Sutton Publishing, Mr Jim Crawley, for his continued patience and assistance. Thanks are also due to Paul Hares for additional information on the Spanish Inquisition; to Mr Matteo Cantini of the Mueseo della Tortura e della Pena di morte di San Gimignano (via San Giovanni 123, 10a) and the Museo della Tortura di Volterra (piazza XX settembre 3/5) for allowing us to photograph items from their collection; to Miss Samantha Acciuffi (www.acciuffidesign.eu) for her photographic and translation work, and finally to Kevin Duncan for debugging Dan's computer.

AUTHORS' INTRODUCTION

Over the many months required to compile this book we have been repeatedly queried as to why, over the past few years, our work has taken such a macabre turn. Undoubtedly the fact that this book has come out so soon after our work on cannibalism, *Eat Thy Neighbour* (Sutton, 2006), has fuelled these questions. One pundit went so far as to suggest that we might have done well to entitle this work 'Beat Thy Neighbour'. Humour aside, as historians we believe that the most important lessons history has to teach us are not all pleasant ones. As Dr Benjamin Franklin once said: 'Those who will not learn from the mistakes of the past are doomed to repeat them'. With this simple dictum in mind we have once again set out to write a book that not only provides an interesting and informative journey into mankind's darker nature, but which also tries to analyse the 'whys' and 'hows' of the subject at hand without becoming bogged down in political jargon or scientific double talk. Since learning that *Eat Thy Neighbour* has been adopted as required reading by a number of American University courses in aberrant human psychology, we feel justified in taking this approach to our subject and hope that *The Big Book of Pain* is as well received as its predecessor.

One of the greatest challenges we have faced in writing this book has been to find agreement on precisely what constitutes torture. According to the United Nations Convention Against Torture, no distinction can be made between actual, physical torture and what they term 'cruel and degrading treatment', which the UN interprets as any form of interrogation which results in prolonged mental harm; what is sometimes referred to as 'post traumatic stress syndrome'. Amnesty International seems to feel that nearly any deprivation of freedom of action, be it chaining a victim to a wall or simple incarceration, is an abuse of basic human rights and therefore constitutes torture. The United States government, on the other hand, seems to feel that torture only qualifies as torture if it was inflicted with the specific intent of inflicting long-term physical or mental damage. Even by comparing and contrasting these few definitions it becomes obvious that opinion varies greatly as to what does, and does not, constitute torture. Unlike the learned men and women who compile such official reports for the press and public studies, we are not psychologists, psychiatrists, human rights campaigners nor members of a governmental or military organisation trying to justify our methods of interrogation. We are historians. Therefore, like any good historian, we have decided to take a completely objective and pragmatic approach when deciding what punishments and forms of physical abuse to include in this book; if it walks like a duck and quacks like a duck it is, in all probability, a duck.

We have also made the conscious decision not to include the vast variety of torture methods invented during the twentieth century in this work. The horrors of Nazi Germany's gas chambers and the all-too-common use of cattle prods and automobile batteries to inflict pain on human beings are well enough known to almost any socially aware reader for us to need to recount them between these covers. Rather, we have undertaken an examination of the various methods and approaches to torture which varying societies have engaged in over the centuries. Working within these broad parameters we have come to understand that there are two basic reasons why governments inflict torture on supposed criminals and enemies of the state. First is the extraction of information. This information may take the form of a personal confession or, just as often, be related to forcing a prisoner to reveal the names of co-conspirators in some real or imagined plot. Second is the use of torture as a form of punishment. While torture as punishment is not as prevalent as it was two centuries ago, it remains alive and unwell in many countries and cultures around the world. In the words of Peter Benenson (founder of Amnesty International): 'Torture is banned, but in two-thirds of the world's countries it is still being committed in secret. Too many governments still allow wrongful imprisonment, murder or "disappearance" to be carried out by their officials with impunity.'

Torture, however you choose to define it, is still used to some greater, or lesser, extent almost everywhere and will probably remain so for as long as the cops have to beat confessions out of the bad guys. If we are to be completely honest, without at least the threat of physical violence and/or imprisonment, virtually no perpetrator would confess to their crime, or crimes, and society would break down completely.

While we offer no solutions to the problems presented in this book, it is our earnest hope that our efforts will allow you, the reader, to gain a better understanding of the many reasons why the human race has steadfastly clung to the practice of torture since we first stood erect and organised ourselves into the earliest, primitive societies. That mankind has done so is a fact. That we have known for more than 2,000 years that confessions extracted under severe torture are virtually worthless and that torture as punishment does nothing to deter crime, makes this fact all the more tragic and appalling.

Having stated our small justification for, yet again, taking on such a grim topic we will leave you to enjoy the rest of the book in peace. Like most of you, we find over-extended introductions to be a most egregious and uncivilised form of torture. As you pick your way through the catalogue of horrors recounted in the upcoming pages, please bear in mind that the torture masters whose handiwork we describe were highly skilled professionals: do not try this at home.

Mark P. Donnelly and Daniel Diehl

TORTURE: MOTIVES, METHODS AND MADNESS

T he word torture is used so often and so inappropriately that it seems necessary to define exactly what it means before entering into any serious investigation of its uses; or more specifically to extricate the term from the confused jumble of multiple definitions in order to determine precisely what *we* mean by 'torture'. Contrary to popular belief all forms of punishment, even when it involves physical abuse, do not qualify as torture. The thirteenth edition of the *Encyclopedia Britannica* describes torture as follows: 'Torture (from Latin "torquere", to twist), the general name for innumerable modes of inflicting pain which have been from time to time devised by the perverted ingenuity of man, and especially for those employed in a legal aspect by the civilised nations of antiquity and modern Europe.' From this point of view, torture was always inflicted for one of two purposes:

(1)   as a means of eliciting evidence from a witness or from an accused person either before or after condemnation;
(2)   as a part of punishment.

The second was the earlier use, its functions as a means of evidence arising when rules were gradually formulated by the experience of legal experts. Webster's *New Collegiate Dictionary* describes it more briefly, but more succinctly, in this manner:

1.   The infliction of intense pain (as from burning, crushing or wounding) to punish, coerce or afford sadistic pleasure.
2.   An anguish of body or mind.
3.   To punish or coerce by inflicting excruciating pain.
4.   To cause intense suffering, to torment.

Using these basic premises as a starting point, we can immediately say that before physical brutality can qualify as torture it must be inflicted with very specific goals in mind. If a street gang attacks, beats and systematically abuses someone they are not, strictly speaking, torturing their victim. They are certainly assaulting them and may cause grievous bodily harm, but because they are not acting under any kind of governmental, military or judicial authority the assault is not technically torture. On the other hand, a gang of revolutionary guerrilla fighters who commit the same atrocities are, in fact, committing torture. The main difference then between a simple act of barbarism and full-blown torture is the influence of a higher, sanctioning authority. Inherent, but seldom stated, in this definition is the implication that when torture is carried out at the behest of governmental authority it is somehow justified. By bringing a legal sanction into the equation those involved in ordering, or administering, torture provide themselves with the advantage of removing the taint of personal guilt: 'I was only following orders'.

As we shall see time and time again, those governments that have sanctioned the use of torture tend to be either weak and fearful (as in the case of most early, primitive societies and modern, third world dictatorships), or paranoid. In the later case there is almost always the belief, either sincerely held or merely a cynical ploy to keep the masses in line, that there is some massive conspiracy at work which is bent on the destruction of the 'system' and that it must be stopped before society is overthrown. Such claims of imminent destruction are always a good way to keep the population in a constant state of fear and thereby make them easier to control. It also provides a convenient means to make the leader popular; first he institutes a climate of fear by describing this vague, often nameless threat, and then sets out to destroy that threat by arresting, torturing and executing as many of the 'conspirators' as possible. Naturally the threat can never truly be eliminated; either because it never existed in the first place or because if the 'enemy' ceased to exist the leader might lose his grip on power.

In its earliest form, however, torture – in some greater or lesser form, as befits the crime – was usually practiced as a means of punishing actual wrongdoers. In a primitive world, where all life was short, brutish and cruel, we could hardly expect legal or penal punishment to be any different. When a criminal, or transgressor against the prevailing moral code, was publicly whipped, crucified, or otherwise horribly killed or maimed, it provided a graphic example that the law was being upheld, society was being kept safe and that good, law abiding people could sleep safe in their beds. Such graphic examples of the law taking its due course always pleased the mob, giving them a nice comforting sense as to the 'rightness' of things. It also provided a form of cheap entertainment and, unless the leader was unusually stupid, offered a convenient way of doing away with political enemies in a way that sent out a clear message to anyone else who might decide to voice opposition to the powers that be.

Over the millennia, thousands of civilisations have risen and fallen, but the use of torture and the reasoning behind it, remain pretty much constant. The earliest use of torture, that of punishment, tended to be psychologically unsophisticated. The party in question, or the conquered group, was adjudged guilty and then taken out and punished. But as time went on, and as the motive behind torture evolved from simple punishment to the need to extract information, the approach to the process of torture evolved. Victims were first taken to the torture chamber and shown the tools of their forthcoming anguish. To get the victim's attention, the entire process was described in lurid detail. Then they were sent back to their cell and given some time to think things over. Unless the poor wretch had no more imagination than a cow, the mere contemplation of what was about to happen to them was often enough to make them spill everything they knew and a whole lot they didn't know. Sometimes, however, the victim was unusually strong-willed or it had already been decided that they were going to be tortured no matter what they said.

In 1307 King Phillip IV of France (with the whole-hearted support of the Pope) ordered the mass arrest of the Knights Templars on charges of heresy. Did he really believe them to be heretics? Probably not. Did he owe them huge sums of money that he had no intention of repaying? Absolutely, but it would not have looked good if he had been honest about his motives. Instead, Phillip had thousands of Templars rounded up, thrown into prison, put to the rack, roped, starved and beaten to within an inch of their lives. Eventually they confessed to the most absurd charges imaginable. Once in possession of their confessions, Phillip was free to convict, sentence and burn them at the stake. Then he confiscated their land and property. The fact that nearly all of the Templars later refuted their forced confessions made no difference. This single example of confessions forced through pain is only one of hundreds we will examine in this book but it serves as a workable, introductory illustration to both the advantages and drawbacks of torture. Torture can always be used to extract a confession or other information – almost anyone will confess to nearly anything if they think it is going to make the pain stop. Conversely, torture cannot be used to establish innocence – possibly because it would be a sorry sort of torture master who mutilated his victims while repeatedly asking 'Have you been a good boy?'

The point we are making is that torture has only one conceivable end – to extract the information, or punishment, demanded by the system. In the case of obtaining information, the torture will continue until the victim has provided whatever information they are instructed to provide or dies. It does not take a genius to realise that this is an ultimately flawed process. Indeed, if what the inquisitors are really looking for is the truth, then torture is demonstrably counter-productive. The sad truth of this fact has been realised and admitted to by law-givers, philosophers and clerics since time immemorial and still, by and large, they approved of, and used, torture to extract confessions as well as inflict punishment. Why? Because the true object of torture is not to discover the truth but to secure a conviction; and therein lies its greatest limitation. A person under torture will, sooner or later, confess but this is no assurance that a) they actually committed the crime and b) if they did not, and an actual crime has been committed, then the real culprit is still at large. Occasionally, someone being subjected to torture has been able to overcome their terror and pain long enough to throw this fact back in the face of their persecutor.

During the height of the Spanish Inquisition in the sixteenth century, a Portuguese woman named Maria de Coceicao was arrested on charges of heresy and sent to the torture chamber where she was racked. To avoid having her arms and legs ripped from their sockets, Senora Coceicao immediately confessed but as soon as she was released from the rack she refuted her confession. A second turn on the rack brought an identical response. It was a familiar pattern: Confess anything to make the pain stop and then recant when released. In her case, Coceicao was both clever enough, and brave enough, to tell her tormentors: 'As soon as I am released from the rack I shall deny whatever was extorted from me by pain.' Maria de Coceicao was far more lucky than tens of thousands of other victims of the Spanish Inquisition. She was publicly flogged and sentenced to ten years in exile but the courage of her convictions had saved her from being burned at the stake. So, had she brought some revelation to the local inquisitor? Probably not. We can readily assume he already knew that torture did not discover the truth. So why did he and hundreds of others employ it over thousands of years of history? Because it was part of a workable system that kept the established powers securely in their place and the peasants safely in theirs.

Curiously, since the signing of the Magna Carta in 1215, England has considered the use of torture for the purpose of extracting information or a confession to be illegal. We say 'curiously' because throughout the Middle Ages and Renaissance, England was as guilty of torturing its subjects as any other country in Europe – they simply never admitted this small fact to themselves. In 1583, Sir Thomas Smith, then serving as Secretary of State under Queen Elizabeth I, wrote:

> Torment or question, which is used by the order of the civil law and custom of other countries, to put a malefactor to excessive pain, to make him confess of himself, or of his fellows or accomplices, is not used in England ... [as] the nature of our country is free ... and beatings, servitude, servile torment and punishment it will not abide.

Sir Thomas wrote this – undoubtedly in all honesty – despite the fact that at no time, nor in any place, in history has torture been more commonly in use than in sixteenth-century England. So how did it come to pass that a long string of English monarchs, and their governments, tortured their subjects while steadfastly denying that they did so? Simple. Torture was only allowed when the reigning monarch approved of it and since monarchs were technically above the law, their word superseded any and all written laws. An interesting example of how one man tried to overcome this technical 'glitch' in English law, and at the same time foil his torturer, took place during the reign of King Charles I (1625–49).

In April, 1628, John Felton stabbed the Duke of Buckingham to death, was arrested and, as the English politely put it, 'put to the question'. There was no doubt of Felton's guilt; he committed the act in full view of a large crowd which subdued him after the murder and held him until he could be formally arrested. The question facing the court was whether or not Felton had acted alone or as part of a larger conspiracy. As was usual in such cases, the court assumed that while Felton had acted alone in carrying out the deed, he must have had help in the planning. During his initial questioning by the Earl of Dorset, Felton was threatened with the rack unless he named his accomplices. Felton then told the Earl: 'I do not believe, my Lord, that it is the King's wish for he is a just and gracious prince and will not have his subjects to be tortured against the law.' Then, with more courage than most people could have mustered in his tenuous situation, he added: 'Yet this I must tell you, by the way, that if I be put upon the rack, I will accuse you, my Lord Dorset, and none but yourself as my accomplice.' Obviously Dorset was faced with a terrifying dilemma; confessions under torture were accepted as absolute truth and he had no desire to join Felton in his meeting with the executioner. Still, he approached King Charles who immediately grasped the situation and ordered Felton to be 'tortured to the furthest extent allowed by law'. Since His Majesty had not specifically approved of torture, the matter was referred to a panel of twelve jurists who ruled: 'Felton ought not by the law to be tortured on the rack, for no such punishment is known or allowed by our law'. Felton had pointed out one of the great fallacies of life in Merry Old England and saved himself from a horrible torture but it did not save his life. On 28 November 1628 he was hanged for his crime.

Despite the fact that it was useless in discovering the truth, torture nearly always loosened people's tongues. The side effect this process may have had on a person accused of committing a criminal act, or even a perfectly innocent bystander who might have information concerning some crime, was completely irrelevant. It is results that count. What the ancient and medieval torture masters may have been unaware of is how the psychology behind the process of torture actually works. As we have already seen, one of the first steps in convincing a prospective victim to talk is to show them the instruments with which they will be tormented. This, along with the actual process of torture, and the fact that the presiding authority – be it a civil judge or a clergyman of the Inquisition – always remains one step removed from the application of torture, have become recognised as integral parts of what has become known as the 'Stockholm Syndrome'. Named for a hostage situation which took place in Stockholm, Sweden in 1973, when two bank robbers held four people hostage for a period of six days, the Stockholm Syndrome has identified the process by which an individual's will is broken down to the point whereby the victims come to cooperate with their captors. This process involves two distinct steps, the first of which rearranges the normal mind-set of the prisoner as follows:

The captive comes to believe that escape is impossible and they are made to believe – rightly or wrongly – that their survival depends on the whims of their captors.
The captor gains the confidence of their captive by showing them small, often irrelevant acts of kindness.
The prisoner is kept isolated from all contact with the outside world.

Once the victim has been sufficiently disoriented and realises that their life depends on the good graces of their tormentor, they are subjected to the next level of the interrogation process; the one intended to make them confess or provide whatever information their captors desire.

The victim is subjected to physical (or sometimes sexual) abuse, thus making them feel still more vulnerable.

The captive is deprived of a proper sense of time and place; usually by keeping them in a dark dungeon or cell.

The victim is deprived of privacy. Their guards can walk in on them at any moment for whatever reason.

The prisoner is only fed and given water when, and if, their captor feels like it.

Thus having lost all sense of control over their own life, the prisoner is kept in these conditions and tortured at unpredictable intervals. Always standing off to one side, ready to listen to their 'confession' is the person who controls both the prisoner and the torture masters. This individual is not only the source of all pain, but also the only means through which the pain can be made to stop. As soon as the victim is willing to answer the inquisitor's questions, the torture master will be told to stop inflicting pain.

By slowly building on this process, from capture through imprisonment and being shown the process by which a person's body will be slowly crushed, burned, boiled or torn to shreds, it is often unnecessary to actually subject the victim to torture. Their fear does what it might, theoretically, be impossible for the torture master to do. A personal account of how this process works comes to us from the journal of Fr. John Gerard, a Jesuit priest who was arrested as a subversive in 1605 in connection with Guy Fawkes' failed gunpowder plot to blow up the Houses of Parliament and kill the entire government of England and the royal family of King James I. It was not Gerard's first brush with the law; in 1597 he had been arrested on similar charges during the reign of Queen Elizabeth I, so he was already familiar with the official interrogation process. His description of how suspects were first encouraged to tell what they knew is one of the best surviving first-hand accounts of the torture chamber in the Tower of London during that era.

This image depicts the interior of a late medieval torture chamber. Tortures of the rack, the pulley, the stocks, the funnel, and the bilboes are visible among other objects. This is probably intended to depict an Inquisition chamber owing to the two prominent crucifixes on display and the ledger for recording confessions.

We went to the torture room in a kind of solemn procession, the guards walking ahead with lighted candles. The chamber was underground and dark, particularly near the entrance. It was a vast shadowy place and every device and instrument of human torture was there. They pointed out some of them to me and said that I [w]ould have to taste of them. Then they asked me again if I would confess. 'I cannot', I said.

For his obstinacy, Father Gerard was racked and tortured but he managed to escape and make his way to the safety of the continent.

Only five years after Father Gerard's adventure, King Henry IV of France was murdered by a man named François Ravaillac. Like his predecessors, Felton and Gerard, Ravaillac was automatically assumed to be a part of a larger conspiracy. In this case, however, Ravaillac was tried and sentenced to death before the names of his suspected accomplices were tortured out of him. As he was already condemned to death, he had no hope that naming his associates would spare him from execution. Lacking any incentive to speak, the only reasonable course of action was to subject him to enough pain to loosen his tongue. Despite swearing before the court that he had acted alone, Ravaillac was taken to the torture chamber and subjected to a torture known as the 'brodequin' – an excruciating procedure where heavy

Some implements of torture. Both commonplace and exotic these inert objects seem impotent in their state of disuse. Clockwise from top left we can see what appear to be a flail or scourge, a 'cat's paw', a chastity belt (upside down) a dismembering axe, funnels, rope, shackles, pincers, knee splitter, shears, a spiked ball and chain, galley shackles, and a spiked belt or barbed flail.

This scene depicts the torture of peine et forte en dure. The victim is forced to lie across a sharp rigid edge which is placed just below his shoulder blades. A board is then placed upon his chest and more and more weight is added until he tells his torturers what they wish to hear. Note also the chap in the background with his feet in the stocks or inversion chair – perhaps awaiting his turn under the crushing weights.

wooden wedges were driven into the muscles of the legs with mallets. According to the records of the court, when the second wedge was driven into place, Ravaillac screamed: 'I am a sinner, I know no more than I have declared, by the oath I have taken, and by the truth I owe to God and the court: all I have said was to the little Franciscan [Priest, in the confessional], which I have already declared . . . I beseech the court not to drive my soul to despair.' The torture continued, but Ravaillac steadfastly insisted he had acted alone. Finally, too crippled to walk to his execution, Francois Ravaillac was put to death for the crime of regicide.

Once the process of actual, physical torture had begun, only those with an unimaginably strong will, the deranged mind of a fanatic, or a masochist who enjoyed becoming a martyr to their particular cause, could prevent themselves from admitting to anything the inquisitor wanted to hear. In societies where torture was routine, everyone knew that if arrested they would, sooner or later, confess. When Baron Scanaw was arrested in the mid-sixteenth century, in Bohemia, on charges of heresy, he was told that if he did not willingly offer up the names of his confederates he would be racked until he decided to talk.

When the guards came to haul Scanaw to the torture chamber they found that he had cut out his own tongue. Beside his unconscious body was a note which read: 'I did this extraordinary action because I would not, by any means, or any tortures, be brought to accuse myself, or others, as I might, through the excruciating torments of the rack, be impelled to utter falsehoods.' The brave Scanaw might have saved his friends from meeting a similar fate, but he could not save himself. Since he could no longer talk, he was simply racked to death.

One of the simplest, and most bizarre, forms of torture designed specifically to induce a suspect to talk was that of 'pressing'. According to medieval and renaissance law, a suspect could only be properly tried if they openly confessed to their crime. Instances where prisoners refused to enter a plea were particularly galling because only once they admitted their guilt could their property be confiscated by the state. If they simply refused to plea, there was always enough possibility of innocence that their property would pass on to their legitimate heir. For the government to get as much satisfaction (and profit) as possible out of executing an enemy, they must confess their guilt. To this end the practice of pressing was introduced. It was extremely simple. A subject was laid on the floor of their cell or the torture chamber, a door was laid on top of them and more and more stones (or other weights) were piled on top of the door. In less than a minute breathing became difficult, then nearly impossible. As this was specifically a torture of inducement, the weight was increased very slowly: if the victim died before confessing, their estate remained in the family. Smothering is a terrible death and only the strongest willed could withstand both the crushing weight, the inability to breathe and the sure knowledge that all they had to do to make it all go away was talk. The last recorded case of pressing to extract a confession took place during the Salem, Massachusetts witch trials in 1692; in that case, like so many others before it, the victim chose not to confess to a crime of which they were wholly innocent.

No matter how effective, or ineffectual, torture might be at making a person confess their guilt or betray their accomplices, real or imagined, torture when used as a means of punishment was guaranteed 100 per cent effective. It may not have deterred other criminals, slowed a constantly rising crime rate or even reformed the person being punished, but it was completely effective in the sense that punishment had been extracted as prescribed by law and, in almost every case, the punishment had been carried out in full view of a public who demanded constant reassurance that their government was 'getting tough on crime'.

Defining precisely which forms of punishment qualify as torture, and which do not, is slightly more problematic than when dealing with torture as a means of extracting a confession or information. Any time information is forcibly extracted from a prisoner there is a high probability that some form of torture has been involved because the innocent have no information to give and the guilty are unlikely to willingly offer whatever information they possess. Punishment, on the other hand, by its very nature, implies that the convict is being disciplined to some greater, or lesser, extent; the degree of punishment being determined by the severity of the crime. No matter what the crime, when the rules of the society in question have been broken, some form of retribution must be exacted if the law of the land is to be satisfied and the public is going to be reassured that their government is doing its job. Failure to follow this simple concept would lead to a state of chaos and, inevitably, to the collapse of society.

So when does punishment become torture? Undoubtedly, when a convict is executed slowly and in an excruciatingly painful manner, it is safe to say that they are being tortured to death. Whether lesser punishments can be legitimately considered torture can only be judged by the prevailing mores of the society. In the ancient world, where life was harsh and brutal even in its quietest moments, there were only three primary kinds of punishments: whippings, imposed for minor

Here we see a public flogging taking place. This would have been a fairly commonplace scene throughout Europe until well into the eighteenth century. The victim here (apparently a woman) is being flogged with bundles of sticks (although being hung by the wrists is certainly unpleasant enough). It could well be that the man flogging her is in fact her husband and that he was legally entitled to this recourse for her shrewish behaviour or infidelity, but only if the flogging was administered publicly.

crimes; 'an eye for an eye' retributionary punishments for more serious, but not capital, crimes and finally, at the top of the list, execution. Since petty crime is always more prevalent than serious crime, whippings were the most common form of punishment meted out in almost all ancient societies. Whether the whipping was inflicted with a stick, a heavy rod, a simple leather whip or a cat-o-nine tails with sharp slivers of metal braided into the thongs, were determined by the seriousness of the crime and how brutal the standards of the society were.

Hand-in-hand with the concept of whippings and other minor, public punishments was the concept of shame and humiliation which inevitably accompanied the punishment. The whole concept of shame has virtually disappeared from modern society, due largely to the anonymity of overpopulated cities and the breakdown of community and family life. Things were different in the past. Small communities, where everyone knows everyone else and knows all about their business, are a perfect platform for imposing soul-crushing levels of shame. In the tiny, isolated communities that existed from the dawn of civilization through the late eighteenth century, when friends, neighbours and family refuse to talk to, or do business with, someone who had stepped beyond the bounds of acceptable behaviour, it was a truly shattering experience. Add to this the fact that the offender had been whipped, or otherwise punished, in full view of the entire community and they would have probably been more than happy to exchange the experience for a few months in a nice gloomy prison where they could suffer in private.

As was true with minor crimes, the punishment for more serious offences was determined largely by how civilised, or how barbaric, the individual society happened to be. The time period in which the society existed had surprisingly little to do with how 'civilised' the punishments were. As we shall discover in the next section of this book, ancient Egypt was fairly civilised but 4,000 or 5,000 years later the punishments imposed during the Dark Ages and early medieval period were unbelievably horrific. Branding, dismemberment, scalping, ripping tongues out by their roots, throwing people from cliffs, skinning them alive and ripping their entrails from their still-living bodies were all commonly imposed punishments used in early European societies. So why did society seemingly deteriorate? In reality, it did not deteriorate at all. As we saw earlier, stable societies are less likely to fall victim to the paranoia that creates brutal punishments than are unstable societies. The Egyptians had a stable, well-organised society ruled by an ancient system of royalty and priests who were not in constant fear of being

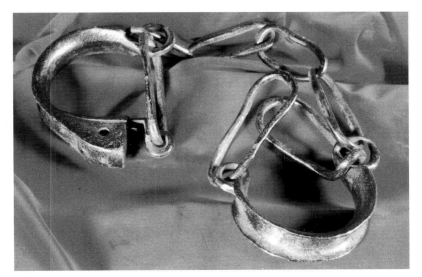

These ankle restraints are from the eighteenth or nineteenth century when somewhat more humanitarian concerns affected attitudes towards imprisonment or incarceration. These have obviously been designed for prolonged use as they have been shaped to make them more comfortable and less irritating, and yet maintain restraint.

toppled. The societies of the dark and early Middle Ages, on the other hand, were tremendously unstable and tended to be led by whichever warrior had the biggest sword at the time. To such fearful leaders every lawbreaker offered a perfect opportunity to set an unmistakable example. As late as the Renaissance, punishment throughout Europe was at least as brutal as it had been under the yoke of the Roman Empire 1,500 years earlier. A single example should serve to illustrate this point.

During the late tenth century, a bell maker from Winchester, England, named Teothic was arrested and convicted of what the church records (where the case is recorded) only refer to as 'a slight offence'. Under the rules of Anglo-Saxon England – which was one of the more stable societies in northern Europe at the time – the wretched Teothic was shackled and hung up by his hands and feet. The following morning he was taken down long enough to be whipped unmercifully before again being hung up like a side of beef. How long this horrific punishment might have continued we do not know because somehow Teothic escaped captivity and took sanctuary at a local monastery.

When the crime is more serious than the one poor Teothic was convicted of – serious enough to demand the death of the prisoner, and bear in mind that as late as the eighteenth century, stealing a loaf of bread was a capital offence – the most unspeakable tortures can be justified under the concept that once a person has committed a serious crime they surrender every protection and comfort society extends to its law-abiding citizens. Once publicly placed outside the

This engraving of a public hanging serves to illustrate what public spectacles these executions grew to be. Though we might assume by the presence of the masked executioner with the axe on the right, that this was not going to be a simple death by strangulation, but was, more likely, to have been a case of hanging, drawing and quartering as described later in this book.

parameters of society, the malefactor could be legally dealt with – either swiftly and cleanly or in the most unspeakable manner imaginable. If his end was to come swiftly – relatively speaking – the most popular form of execution has always been by hanging.

Despite the fact that until well into the nineteenth century – when a trapdoor was installed in the scaffold allowing the condemned to be 'dropped' to a nearly instantaneous death – hangings were carried out by placing a noose around the prisoner's neck and hoisting him into the air where he dangled, kicked and choked himself to death over the next ten to twenty minutes, hanging has never been considered torture. So if hanging was cheap, easy, relatively quick and never considered a form of torture, why were so many strange, bloody and painful executions devised for so many different crimes? Before answering this question, it might be well to recount the more popular forms of execution – and the concomitant crimes – still in use as late as the sixteenth century. The following list comes from 1578 when it was compiled by the English chronicler, Ralph Hollinshed.

If a woman poisons her husband she is burned alive; if a servant kills his master he is to be executed for petty treason; he that poisons a man is to be boiled to death in water or [molten] lead, even if the party did not die from the attempted poisoning; in cases of murder all the accessories [before and after the fact] are to suffer the pain of death. Trespass is punished by the cutting [off] of one or both ears . . . Sheep thieves are to have both hands cut off. Heretics are burned alive [at the stake].

Not included on this list are simple hangings; beheading in cases where noblemen were convicted of treason and hanging, drawing and quartering imposed on commoners found guilty of the same offence. Burning at the stake – that ever-popular horror – took several forms. When the person in question had been convicted of heresy, if they recanted their sin they were usually strangled to death, or hanged, before being consigned to the flames. If they clung to their heretical belief they were condemned to be slowly roasted alive. Simple cases of murder would lead a man to the gallows but a woman was more likely to be burnt. Why? Because the corpse was routinely stripped naked and left to twist in the wind after the execution and it was considered disgraceful to expose a woman's bare body to the curious stares of the public.

Before we condemn all the long-lost kings, princes, judges and churchmen who imposed such horrific tortures as barbarians, it is well to remember that, unless a nation had been overrun by a foreign power, governments generally keep their hold on power by pandering to the needs, beliefs and tastes of their people. Torture, at least when carried out in public, and public executions were not only accepted by the general populace but demanded by them. Any king who denied his subjects the thrill of an occasional flogging or hanging, risked being toppled from his throne by one of his fellow noblemen who knew how to keep the masses happy.

So far we have only considered torture as a means of punishment, or coercion, judicially inflicted by governments on their more disobedient subjects or hapless victims. Before moving on to a more complete history of torture we should look at another aspect which sometimes creeps into the already horrific annals of torture; the overall mind-set of those involved in the process at whatever remove. That is to say, the preconceptions and expectations of the individual being tortured, the person or persons inflicting the torture and, finally, on the public, which so often gathered to enjoy the spectacle of another human being subjected to unimaginable torment.

Since humanity's earliest realization that there are greater powers in the universe than our own little selves, humans have had the sneaking suspicion that the gods – and later even God, Himself – demanded sacrifices in the form of human suffering. At first it was a way to make the gods take away the thunder. Next it was a way to ensure that the crops grew, or the upcoming battle was won and last of all it just became a way to make the gods happy. In many primitive societies, this sacrificial suffering took the form of human sacrifice – the Aztecs ripped out the hearts of prisoners of war by the thousands. In more advanced societies the sacrificial pain became a more personal matter: 'If I have committed a wrong, then I must be the one to pay for it'. This concept of accepting personal responsibility may have originated among the ancient Egyptians. Records show that Egyptian priests in the service of the goddess Isis flagellated themselves during specific festivals. Similarly

In this illustration by Francisco Goya we see an execution by garrotte. This method rose to popularity in Spain during the years of the Inquisition and continued in use as late as the eighteenth century. The condemned is sat in a chair with a strap about his neck. The executioner slowly tightens the strap by way of a mechanism on the back of the 'chair' and slowly strangles the condemned to death. In some versions we find the presence of a spike at the back of the neck designed to pierce and sever the cervical vertebra thereby paralyzing the victim through the process.

This is a European depiction of methods of execution among tribes in Guinea. The kneeling victim is presumably a prisoner of war and is either going to be dispatched by the spear or the primitive axe/ sword/club held by the second tribesman. In the background we can see a decapitated body, but it is uncertain whether this was the means of execution or a result of butchering. You may note that the decapitated man's legs are missing and are being carried away by two other tribesmen – presumably for dinner.

painful self-punishments have been practiced by Hindu holy men who inflict a staggering array of painful experiences on themselves as a demonstration of their faith in their gods and control over their own bodies. It is not surprising then, to find that early Christians engaged in a variety of spiritually cleansing acts; all of which were designed to show the penitent's remorse, their desire for forgiveness and submission to the power of God.

In the early Christian Church the only universal punishment was excommunication – that is to say being expelled from the body of the Church. Slowly, an elaborate system of penances was devised so as to allow a person to cleanse themselves of their sin while remaining a member of the Church. Among the more common methods of penance was fasting, prayer and going on pilgrimage to some holy place. The length and severity of the penance naturally depended on the severity of the transgression. There was yet another form of penance which rapidly became the most common form of punishment among those in ecclesiastic orders (monks, priests and nuns) who ran afoul of the rules of their order or the precepts of Holy Mother Church – flogging. By the end of the ninth century the practice of flagellation had become such a common means of atoning for sins and transgressions that rules had been laid down as to precisely how a monk, or nun, was to be whipped, how many lashes were appropriate for which transgression and what other penances might go along with the flogging. When flagellation was to take place, the penitent was to remove all of their clothes prior to being disciplined, and the punishment was to be carried out before the entire assembled company of their house. The severity of the punishment varied vastly depending upon the seriousness of the offence, but the intent behind ritualizing the punishment was the same in all cases – by witnessing the suffering of their fellow cleric, the other members of the community would be taught a lesson in humility and discipline and, unless they were complete dullards, understood the fact that life is filled with suffering, most of which we have brought upon ourselves through our sinful ways. Medieval Christian clerics also tended to view everything in life as an allegory for something else. Hence, when they witnessed one of their brothers or sisters being whipped they were likely to think about the pain Jesus suffered on the cross and how much He sacrificed to save the souls of a sinful humanity. Being reminded of such a thing was good even if a member of the community had to suffer to make the point clear.

The problem with the practice of dwelling on the suffering of Jesus, and its concomitant reflection in inflicting pain on members of the religious community, was that pain itself – either inflicting it or experiencing it – eventually came to be seen as an act of faith. Suffering – as an act of redemption – became a religious act. While this fact may never have been actively understood, it became so tacitly accepted that even the most revered saints, such as St Francis of Assisi (now best remembered as a man so holy that he could communicate with animals) spent much of his time flogging himself to a bloody pulp and advocating the same act for others who would follow in his footsteps. Obviously, when men as revered as St Francis indulged in self-inflicted pain, others came to believe that whippings were good for the soul. The great mass of medieval people never joined monasteries or convents, but this was an age of faith and nearly everyone desired to be as pious as those who devoted their lives to God. Consequently, accepting a good flogging from the local priest, or inflicting self-flagellation, became nearly as common a means of expiating one's sins as going on pilgrimage or fasting.

In 1424, an Englishman named John Florence was accused of heresy and given the choice of being excommunicated or to submit to an appropriate punishment. A true heretic would undoubtedly have chosen excommunication but Florence presented himself for discipline. On three successive Sundays, he was whipped in front of his congregation at Norwich Parish Church and suffered the same punishment at a neighbouring church. Such punishment was not reserved for the common man; even the most exalted members of lay society were willing to suffer the pains of the lash if it would remove the stain of whatever sin they might have committed. The most famous case may well be that of England's King Henry II. In the year 1170, Henry had, either by intent or by saying the wrong thing at the wrong time, caused the murder of his good friend, the Archbishop of

Whips, flails, floggers, quirts, cat-o-nine tails, etc. all come in a variety of shapes, sizes, types and severities. This one, while it may have been intended for use as corporal or judicial punishment, is of a type which we would categorize as a 'scourge'. This may well have been made by an overly devout flagellant for the purposes of self-mortification. It was believed that through their suffering they would find redemption – both for themselves and the rest of humanity.

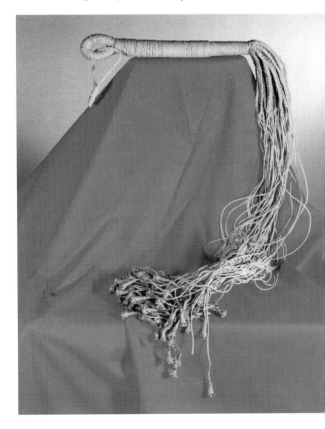

Canterbury, Thomas Becket. Outraged by Becket's killing, the pope excommunicated King Henry and told him to think things over for a while and get back to him. Knowing that an excommunicated king could never hold the throne – and probably truly remorseful over Becket's brutal death – Henry walked barefoot, in the middle of winter, from London to Canterbury. There, he submitted himself to a monumental flogging. Each of the five prelates of Canterbury Cathedral administered five lashes to the King's bare back and then each of the eighty monks gave him three more lashes. After receiving 265 lashes, the King was dressed in sackcloth, anointed with ashes and led to the altar of Canterbury Cathedral (the place where Becket had been murdered) where he knelt in prayer for an entire day and night.

Considering how socially acceptable and wide-spread the concept of flagellation as a means of penance had become, it is hardly surprising to learn that entire fraternities grew up to cater to those who chose this painful form of personal redemption.

In 1259, a plague broke out in Italy. With the country already wracked by internal wars and political corruption, society nearly broke down and itinerant priests and monks began warning that the end of the world was coming and that the arrival of the Antichrist was nigh. Terrified, one of the flagellant fraternities, known as the 'Disciplinarians of Jesus Christ', began wandering across the countryside, whipping themselves to expiate the sins of the world, and picking up masses of followers in every town and village they passed through. Men, women and even children joined their ranks and within months, parades of up to 10,000 bleeding bodies were stumbling down the roadways of Italy; chanting hymns and canticles, their faces covered against the shame of the world and their backs bared to accommodate the self-administered floggings. The sight was so terrifying that entire warring armies laid down their weapons and stood aside to let the sad procession make its way unmolested.

This might have been seen as an isolated incidence of mass hysteria except for the fact that almost 100 years later, in 1447, the Black Plague broke out in Europe. In a matter of two-and-a-half years it wiped out nearly one third of the population. As the plague spread – and with it the belief that the disease was God's punishment for mankind's sins – an army of flagellants reappeared. The events of a century earlier were repeated but this time the flagellants had assumed a truly militant attitude. Where priests spoke out against their self-abuse, they broke into church services. When they wandered through Jewish ghettos they persecuted the Jews. In a matter of months, the flagellants spread out of Italy and into Switzerland, Hungary, Bohemia, Poland, the German states, Denmark, Holland and Flanders and the farther they spread the more aggressive they became. Terrified, in 1349, Pope Clement VI outlawed the flagellant sects, insisting that such extreme actions were nothing less than heresy.

Eventually the Black Death died out and with it so did the flagellants. What no one at the time could have understood is that pain, like drugs or alcohol, can become addictive; particularly when imposed under conditions of great emotional excitement or stress. The more troubled the times, the greater the need for demonstrative emotional release. Amid the terror of war and plagues, the flagellants, who purportedly sought to mitigate mankind's sin, had embraced a new sin – sado-masochism (though that was a term which would not come in to existence for centuries). The same condition existed where corporal floggings were administered in the sexually repressed atmosphere of monasteries and convents; the whippings – either administering them or accepting them – became a substitute for sexual gratification.

This particular aspect of punishment and torture – the concept of inflicting, or accepting, pain because it provided emotional or sexual gratification is too intimately involved with the overall concept of this book not to bear at least a brief investigation. In the instances described above – that of corporal punishment in the form of religious scourging – it is self-evident that the pleasure/pain syndrome could, and undoubtedly often did, become confused. In a more general context, the infliction of pain on a helpless victim may not have been intended to be a sexually or emotionally exciting experience, but torture master is precisely the type of job that would appeal to someone of a depraved disposition. Likewise, those who oversaw the administration of such torture, be they judges, clerics or other authority figures, were in a perfect position to experience vicarious thrills by watching someone have the flesh flayed from their back or their arms and legs ripped from their sockets. Examples of men who quite obviously enjoyed their work will not be difficult to find in the next section of this book. As is true with most addictions, those who become addicted to inflicting – or in the case of the flagellants, receiving – pain, eventually develop a tolerance to their accustomed jolt and require ever stronger doses of the medicine. This may well account for the increasing levels of terror imposed by particular kings, dictators, jurists, or clerics, particularly those like Thomas de Torquemada, the first Grand Inquisitor of the Spanish Inquisition.

Evidence that the Spanish Inquisition attracted far more sadists than religious fanatics is evident when we look at the latitude which the Inquisition allowed the guards in administering whippings to prisoners, even when they were not immediately being subjected to torture. If a prisoner was heard to speak (unless they were at prayer) they were whipped; if they sang they were whipped; if they spoke to their guards they were whipped, and so on and so on. Considering such draconian rules, and the associated opportunities for sadists to indulge their whims, it would stretch credulity to breaking point not to suggest that many of the daily practices of the Spanish Inquisition were more about the emotional high seemingly brought on by crushing the spirit and body of powerless human beings than about routing out heretics and suspected enemies of the state. There has never been anything in the history of mankind more terrifying than self-righteous fanatics, convinced of their own infallibility, and with the power and authority to exercise their will.

This same principal of sadism in ever-increasing doses applies equally to the mob as it does to torture masters and Inquisitors General. From civilization's earliest hangings through the mass executions of the Spanish Inquisition to the chop, chop, chop of the guillotine during the French Revolution and the cheering, jeering, heaving crowds who brought picnic lunches to see the hangings at London's Tyburn Tree, crowds love a good display of power and 'justice'. Satisfying the desire of the masses to see social misfits strung-up or dismembered was the motivating factor in making executions public in the first place – if 'the people' didn't want to witness these things they would have been carried out in private. But the fact is, the multitudes are at least as barbaric as the torture masters, the judges, the Inquisitors and the criminals. The sight of watching people choke on the end of a rope or have their entrails ripped out excites people. When the Duke of Monmouth was beheaded in 1685 for plotting to overthrow his tyrannical uncle, England's King James II, a crowd of thousands shrieked, screamed and dipped their handkerchiefs in his blood as though he were a holy martyr. They did this because they loved him. Slightly over a century later, when the French Reign of Terror ordered that King Louis XVI and Queen Marie Antoinette be led to the guillotine, the reaction was almost identical, but for precisely the opposite reason – Louis they hated, Monmouth they loved, but both executions sent the mob into an ecstatic fervour. Why? For exactly the same reason that torture masters enjoyed their job – pain is both exciting and

addictive, and it is this specific aspect of torture and punishment that makes it both so dangerous and so prevalent throughout history. No matter how much societies and governments insist that torture is a legitimate tool for discovering the truth, or for exacting retribution from convicted criminals or imposing the law of God on religious transgressors, the fact remains that it makes both individuals and the state feel good to exercise the ultimate power over those who do not quite fit into society's accepted mould.

The public execution of the Duke of Monmouth in 1685. This was a ghastly spectacle in which the headsman (Jack Ketch) did a very poor job. According to an eyewitness, 'the butcherly dog did so barbarously act his part that he could not, at five strokes [of the axe] sever the head from the body.' Finally, Ketch used his belt knife to sever the Duke's head from his body.

A HISTORY OF TORTURE

1
TORTURE IN THE ANCIENT AND CLASSICAL WORLD

I n the preceding section we saw that torture can be a common by-product of weak, frightened, paranoid regimes. It would be logical then, to assume that early, primitive cultures would be more prone to the use of torture than more modern, sociologically advanced cultures. But this is simply not the case. While no one can say with certainty which society invented the concept of torture, we can examine those cultures which first kept judicial records and compare the ways in which they dealt with malefactors, transgressors, and enemies.

Most early record-keeping societies – primarily those around the eastern rim of the Mediterranean Sea and in the Tigris and Euphrates basin – shared certain standards as to which crimes were worthy of extreme physical punishment. Patricide (the killing of one's father), adultery and the dishonour of being taken as a prisoner of war were all considered unforgivable and worthy of severe punishment. Beyond these few common factors, how these societies dealt with other crimes seems to have depended on the particular culture.

Egypt under the Pharaohs was, by and large, a pretty enlightened place. Neither did the Egyptians impose unconscionable punishments on those convicted of crimes. Capital crimes, such as murder, were generally dealt with by hanging. One of the few exceptions to this rule came into play when a parent was convicted of having murdered a child. In this case, the parent was condemned to have the body of their dead child tied around their neck and left there until it decomposed: nasty and unhygienic, no doubt, but hardly excessive considering the crime. Another exception to hanging was when the murder victim was the killer's father. Those convicted of patricide were subjected to creatively slow and painful ends, including having the flesh whipped from their body with bundles of reeds, being thrown into thorns and rolled back and forth until they were nearly flayed and then being tossed, still living, into a roaring fire. Lesser crimes were accompanied by lesser punishments.

For most non-capital crimes, both civil and criminal, the standard punishment was a public whipping. Curiously, the manner of the whipping differed with the sex of the offender. Women were whipped while in a kneeling position, but men were laid on the ground, face down, in a spread-eagle posture. In both cases the condemned's garment was stripped from their back before punishment commenced. Logically, the severity of the whipping increased with the severity of the crime. When a man was convicted of having committed adultery with a slave (who was recognised as having no way to protect themselves from such advances) he could be sentenced to as many as 1,000 lashes. Now either this number was not meant to be taken literally, or the whipping was administered with something less than a bundle of sharp reeds or a heavy whip, as such devices would have literally torn the corpse to pieces to no possible end beyond exhausting the torture master. Curiously, when a woman was convicted of adultery she was not executed. Instead, her nose was cut off. Such a punishment would not

This image depicts the flogging of Egyptian prisoners of war or criminals. Whether the figure on the right is pleading for clemency or is participating in the flogging is uncertain.

This image shows two prisoners of war being flayed alive by the Assyrians while staked out on the ground and a third has been decapitated. This sort of image was important propaganda for its time. It showed the harsh and severe consequences for opposing Assyrian might and served as a warning to neighbouring kingdoms.

have prevented her from bearing children, but would undoubtedly have made her less than attractive to future lovers. Physical mutilation was not unique to female adulterers and a number of other crimes carried various forms of mutilation as their punishment. Interestingly, when a person was found to have falsely accused another of any type of crime they were sentenced to the same punishment that their intended victim had, or would have, received. One can reasonably assume that perjury in Pharonic courts was a fairly rare occurrence.

The Egyptians were a proud people, and one of the greatest humiliations they could experience was being taken prisoner in battle. Death was preferable to such dishonour. Consequently, when Egyptian armies captured enemy soldiers, their treatment of the vanquished was unpleasant at best. When being marched to captivity, prisoners were bound neck-to-neck, by a series of nooses, kept tight enough to be galling, but not tight enough to cause strangulation. To make the prisoners still more uncomfortable, their elbows were bound tightly together behind their backs. Sometimes, if Pharaoh's army had had a particularly hard time of it, the prisoners' agony was intensified by having a cord run from their bound wrists, up their back and around their already bound neck. The more the victim struggled to ease the pain in his elbows and wrists, the more likely he was to strangle himself. Those prisoners who survived the long march back to captivity were generally sold as slaves – after having their eyes, or tongues, cut out. The moral is obvious: don't make war on the Pharaoh.

A slightly later middle-Eastern civilization, from which a scant few judicial records survive, was the city-state of Eshunna, which flourished between 2000 BC and 1720 BC, and was located only about 30 miles (50km) north of present-day Baghdad, Iraq. Eshunna seems to have had a law covering almost every aspect of daily life and its judicial code includes such familiar offences as theft, burglary, kidnapping, murder, bodily injuries, sex crimes and injury purposefully inflicted on animals. For lesser offences, the judges of Eshunna may have been the first to impose fines rather than inflict bodily punishment – at least a fine would have gone further toward real compensation than the small satisfaction of watching a criminal having the hide flogged from his back. Curiously, when crimes were committed at night they inevitably brought a heavier sentence than when committed during daylight hours. When the crime involved stealing another man's crops, if the act was carried out during the day the sentence was a fine of ten silver shekels, if it took place during the night the sentence was death.

Similarly, there is a problem determining how the Eshunnans dealt with female criminals as opposed to males, because their written language seems not to have been sexually differentiated – he and she appear to be interchangeable. Hence, the law stating: 'The day a woman will be seized in the lap of a man, [he/she] shall die, [he/she] shall not live', leaves us in no doubt that adultery was a very serious crime, but uncertain as to which of the offenders was executed. All things considered, it is reasonable to assume that it was the woman who got the short end of the stick.

The problem with assessing institutionalised torture in early societies is that justice, and the punishment accompanying conviction, were random things, handed out at the whim of a local judge or tribunal. One of the earliest known attempts to codify laws and specify particular punishments for particular crimes came about in Babylon toward the end of the reign of King Hammurabi (reigned 1792–1759 BC). To make his 282 laws, and their associated punishments, understandable by all, Hammurabi had them carved on a 6ft-tall (2m) stone column, copies of which were erected in major cities throughout the empire. While many of the punishments might seem barbaric by modern standards, personal vendettas were outlawed as was the mistreatment of both slaves and women. In many cases, punishments were in the 'eye for an eye' tradition known as the *talio*; if a person broke another person's bones, they were to have the same bones broken or if he purposefully put out another man's eye, his own eye would be put out. Of particular interest is a law stating that if a physician killed, or maimed, a patient during an operation the doctor would have his hands cut off – obviously preventing such malpractice in the future. Worthy of note in Hammurabi's code were specific rights given to women, such as no-fault divorces and protection from rape; the punishment for sexual assault being castration for the guilty party. If a man accused his wife of adultery he was required to provide absolute proof of her guilt before casting her off, but if she were found guilty she was to be thrown into the Euphrates River. Should the gods deem her innocent, she would safely find her way to the opposite bank; if guilty she would undoubtedly drown. This watery trial by ordeal would find an echo millennia later in the persecution of women accused of witchcraft.

Slaves were also given protection from unwarranted abuse by their owners, but not surprisingly slaves had fewer rights than free men and women, particularly in regards to how serious an offence had to be in order to demand the death penalty. The death penalty could be incurred for a vast array of crimes including theft, knowingly receiving stolen goods, arson, kidnapping, harbouring run-away slaves, murder, adultery – surprisingly applicable to both men and women – and keeping a disreputable tavern. Of particular interest are such eye-for-an-eye punishments as being convicted of arson or robbing a house after a fire. In both cases the miscreant was to be thrown into a fire.

For all of its primitive qualities, Babylonian justice under King Hammurabi was surprisingly even handed. No one could be convicted

This image, albeit depicting a late medieval scene, shows the sort of 'swimming' prescribed by Hammurabi's Code. The accused is bound hand and foot and thrown into the river. If they successfully manage to cross the open expanse of deep water and somehow crawl out on the opposite bank, they are deemed innocent. If they drown (as most surely did) then they were righteously found guilty.

Opposite: We think it would be fair to say that everyone (certainly in the western world) is familiar with the concept of crucifixion. There were varying methods of crucifixion which could be employed depending on how long the executioners intended to prolong the agony. Condemned criminals could be tied to the cross, nailed to the cross, or both. They could be given a platform on which to stand or not. They could be whipped, cut, etc. If one is simply staked out to die of exposure and suffocation it will take far longer than if one is beaten, flogged and stabbed and dying of blood loss.

Opposite: In this image, the figure labeled "B" is being sawn in half. Little explanation is necessary here to convey how agonizing and slow this would have been. Obviously this is a death sentence, but even once separated from his lower half like some horrid, grizzly, ancient magician's trick, he would still have lived for some time until he eventually died of blood loss. Meanwhile, the figured labeled "A" is about to receive the comparatively merciful sentence of decapitation.

on less than rock-solid proof, perjurers were punished by having their tongue ripped out, and false-accusers were sentenced to the same punishment as their victim would have received had they been found guilty. Also well advanced for its time was the right of appeal; a right provided to all convicts regardless of their crime, and the appellate process went not only from local courts to higher courts, but could even be taken to the king himself and numerous surviving records show that Hammurabi often heard cases brought to him by common men and women of all walks of life.

Like their Egyptian and Babylonian neighbours, the ancient Hebrews codified their laws and tried to ensure that punishment remained within reasonable bounds. The Mosaic Code (the laws of Moses and his immediate successors) was laid down around 1200 BC and provided an elaborate system of punishment which included almost every type of torture known at the time. Like the Egyptians, with whom the Hebrews had a long and uneasy relationship, the most common form of civil punishment was flogging, but the number of lashes could never exceed forty. Among the list of capital crimes unique to Hebraic law were eating meat that still had blood in it, blasphemy, sacrificing children to pagan gods, pregnancy outside wedlock and sons refusing to obey their fathers' commands.

While Hebrew law included such methods of execution as burning, being thrown from a high cliff and crucifixion, the most common form of judicially sanctioned death was stoning. All executions in early cultures were public affairs; the elaborate ceremonies and pain that accompanied them being intended to sufficiently impress the crowd that it would deter others from committing similar offences. Stoning was a particularly ceremonial affair. The condemned was taken to a place, beyond the city walls, reserved for this macabre spectacle. There, a pile of stones was always kept at the ready, presumably to remind passers-by of the serious import of the spot. The person who had brought the original charge against the condemned wore a white, fringed robe and was required to throw the first stone. Once the first rock had been cast, the rest of the crowd followed suit until the condemned was not only battered to death, but their body had completely disappeared beneath the mound of rocks.

Amazingly, although it has become almost uniquely associated with the Romans, crucifixion was a fairly common means of capital punishment among the early Jews, and there are numerous crucifixions – often referred to as 'hanging from a tree' – described in the Old Testament. The language of the Bible makes it difficult to decide whether some of these incidences included traditional hanging, or simply tying the victim to a tree and allowing them to die of exposure.

One of the more bizarre, and rarer, forms of capital punishment among the Hebrew people was being buried alive; a particularly sadistic variant on this practice was to toss the victim into a tower of ashes. The tower in question had to be tall enough so the victim could be tossed into it and allowed to sink slowly into the choking ash, smothering to death in the process. Presumably there was some sort of ladder and platform allowing access to the tower and from which the death of the condemned could be viewed by the officials involved in the case, if not by the general public. During their long and turbulent history, the Hebrew tribes seem to have tried a vast variety of creative tortures. Prostitutes were routinely burned alive as were the daughters of priests found guilty of adultery. When King David (reigned 1005–965 BC) finally captured the city of Rabbah after a long and costly siege, he ordered the citizenry to be either sawn in half or buried up to their necks in the earth and have plows driven over them. Such incidents as David's subjugation of Rabbah and tossing condemned criminals into towers of ash should not be viewed as generally accepted forms of punishment in ancient Judea. These were aberrations more akin to crimes of passion, or simple acts of sadism, than to the enforcement of the Mosaic Code.

These few grotesque instances aside, the Hebrews considered their system of justice and punishment as enlightened as their belief in

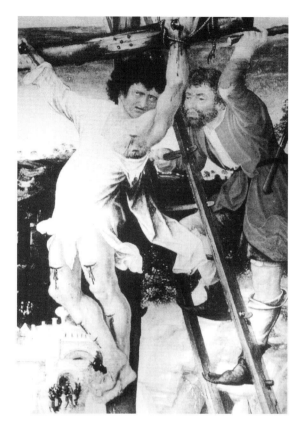

one all-powerful God. Certainly, when relations with their neighbours broke down, as they often did, the punishments inflicted on the defeated Jews by their conquerors were at least as barbaric as those the Hebrews inflicted on their own criminals; but the outcome was not always as their persecutors intended.

Opposite: This method of torture and execution took many forms. Sometimes the victims were staked out on the ground and a large wheel would be used to smash each of their limbs and joints including the hips and shoulders. In other cases, the victim was tied upon a wheel and the executioner would use bars, clubs or hammers to accomplish the same result. The idea was to break all of the bones in the body without breaking the skin or causing lethal injury. In either case, the shattered limbs of the victim were usually 'laced' through the spokes of the wheel and then mounted on a pole and displayed to the populace, where they would slowly and agonizingly die of hunger thirst and exposure (and presumably, internal bleeding).

When Nebuchadnezzar II of Babylon invaded, and destroyed, the Hebrew Kingdom of Judea in 589 BC, he treated the Jews as a subjugated people. He did, however, raise a few of them to positions of responsibility in his government. Among those few were three men named Shadrach, Meshach and Abednego. When Nebuchadnezzar built a golden idol (probably representing either Moloch or Baal) and commanded his subjects to worship it, these three civil servants refused and were subsequently hauled before the king. Their punishment for blasphemy was to be thrown into a furnace so hot that the guards assigned to stoke it were killed by the heat. According to the story, as related in the book of Daniel, an angel of the Lord saved the three Hebrews from being burnt and thereby causing Nebuchadnezzar to recognise the power of God. Only a generation later, Darius I of Persia had overrun Babylon, taken control of the displaced Hebrews and raised the prophet Daniel to a position of power in his court. When Daniel's enemies at court spread seditious rumours against him, Darius believed the gossip and had Daniel thrown into a den of lions. The next day, Darius came to view the remains and found that Daniel had made friends with his feline companions, apparently thanks to God's intervention. Realizing that a terrible mistake had been made, Darius released Daniel and had the man who brought the accusations against him driven into the lion's den where, presumably, he was torn to shreds.

If ancient Judaic heroes like King David, King Saul, Gideon and Joshuah were warriors of great renown, the greatest warrior clan ever assembled by the Hebrews was undoubtedly the Maccabees. Between 165 and 63 BC the Maccabees attempted to re-establish the Kingdom of Judea by revolting against one of the most nefarious states of the Old Testament era, the Assyrians. To give you an idea of how fierce and barbaric a people the Assyrians were, consider that only a few centuries earlier, under the rule of Ashurbanipal (reigned 669–627 BC) the Assyrian army flayed captured enemy soldiers alive, and marked its trail of conquest with pyramids of decomposing human heads. Cities conquered by Ashurbanipal were subject to having their children burned alive and the (presumably few) surviving adults being blinded, flayed alive, impaled or having their hands, feet, ears and/or noses hacked off. Five centuries later, by the time of the Maccabeean uprising, the Assyrians were a bit more civilised but no more tolerant.

The Jews hated the Assyrians because they were a constant threat; the Assyrians hated the Jews because they stubbornly refused to be subjugated even in defeat. Finally, the Assyrian king, Antiochus

Epiphanies, had had enough. He sacked Jerusalem, erected a statue of Jupiter in the inner sanctum of Solomon's temple, turned the rest of the building into a brothel and ordered anyone observing the Sabbath to be burned alive. Instead of accepting their defeat, the Jews revolted; raising a rebel army under Judas Maccabaeus. These were the Maccabees.

Antiochus took exception to all this; after all, all he wanted was for the Jews to become docile slaves like the rest of his vanquished empire. It seemed obvious to Antiochus that what the Jews needed were a few graphic examples of just how powerful their new king was, and how silly their own beliefs were. Particularly galling to Antiochus was the Jewish dietary law which forbade the eating of pork. In one instance, a boy who refused to eat pork was tied to a wheel where his joints were dislocated, his bones broken and his flesh torn with red-hot pincers. A bed of coals that had been built beneath the wheel, to increase the boy's pain, was extinguished by the boy's own, flowing blood. On another occasion, seven brothers and their aged mother were hauled before Antiochus for the same offence. The king assured them that their God would understand if they ate pork under duress and forgive for the sin, pointing out that if they refused to eat, they would all be horribly executed in front of their mother. Neither the lads, nor their mother, were having any of it. After the eldest boy had been broken on the wheel and his limbs had been cut off, the king said he would reprieve the remaining six boys if they would share a succulent pork dinner with him. Again they refused. The second youth had his limbs severed and his still-living trunk cooked in a gigantic frying pan. The third brother was skinned alive and disembowelled, the fourth had his tongue ripped out before being roasted alive on a spit and the fifth was burned at the stake. When the sixth was tossed into a cauldron of boiling water, the youngest simply threw himself into the cauldron to die with his brother. Frustrated, Antiochus accused the mother of forcing her sons to their deaths by not permitting them to transgress against their religion, and sentenced her to be burnt alive. By 63 BC the Maccabeean revolt had collapsed and the Jews remained stateless, but the power of the Assyrians was also waning. A new, more advanced civilization had taken centre stage in the world, and with them they brought new and more advanced forms of torture.

The Classical Greeks were a civilised people. Well, they certainly believed they were, and we generally accept it as fact. As early as 1179 BC there were Greek laws prohibiting murder but, in a typically enlightened way, a death sentence could only be passed by an officially sanctioned court of law. This would seem to have been a good start, but unfortunately things went rapidly downhill from there. In the decades around 700 BC the Tyrant Draco (Tyrant then being an official title as was Dictator) decided that if a little capital punishment was good then a lot of it would be all that much better. Thus he declared that administering the law would become vastly easier if there was only one punishment for all crimes – death. Everything from stealing a loaf of bread to murder was punished by death. When asked why he imposed such a law, Draco quipped: 'The poor deserve to die and I can think of no greater punishment to inflict upon the rich'. Draco – which, interestingly, translates as 'serpent' – may not have lasted long, but his name is still attached to harsh laws, or measures, in the term 'draconian'.

The Greeks, in general, seemed to have had a difficult time striking a happy medium in their judicial system. Three and a half centuries after Draco, the Athenian lawgiver Charondas came up with a slate of laws known as the Thurian Code. We are not here to take issue with the code itself – which was the basic 'eye for an eye' approach to juris prudence common among early societies – but rather with how it was administered. In order to prevent any ambitious reformers from arbitrarily altering his new laws, Charondas decreed that anyone proposing a change to the code would be forced to wear a noose around his neck until the matter was fully debated among the assembly of lawgivers. Should the change be rejected, the man was to be immediately strangled with the noose already so conveniently in place. It is hardly surprising that while Charondas remained in power only three such changes were proposed. Worth mentioning is the fact that even the hard-nosed Charondas was completely dedicated to adhering to his laws. When he inadvertently appeared at a public assembly wearing a sword (an act outlawed

Most readers will be familiar with this device. Far more than being a simple mode of imprisonment, it served to trap the victim's head and hands in a position where they could not protect or defend themselves against assaults, thrown objects or molestations by the jeering populace of the city.

by the Thurian Code) he drew the offending blade and plunged it into his own heart.

In their more enlightened moments, the Greeks introduced some of the first punishments designed to cause no physical harm to the convicted. Among these was the pillory, a device still in common use at the end of the eighteenth century, in which the condemned had their head and arms locked into a wooden frame mounted on a pole. It was an uncomfortable thing, no doubt, and made all the more so by the fact that the malefactor was displayed in a public place and subjected to the taunts and harangues of passers-by, but there was no long-term damage to their body (at least not any inflicted by the pillory itself). The most common offence which led to the pillory was public drunkenness. Curiously, when an individual committed a crime while drunk they were charged and tried twice – once for being drunk and a second time for the associated crime. Evidently the Greek legal system did not necessarily agree with Aristotle when he said: '*In vino veritas*' – 'In wine there is truth'.

Here we witness an unfortunate victim being stuffed within the brazen bull and a great fire being lit beneath. This would of course function much like a cast bronze oven and would quickly become unbearably hot to touch. The howls and screams of the roasting culprit would be heard to issue forth from the mouth of the bull like snorts and grunts, much to the amusement of the torturers and assembled court.

Not all Greek tortures were designed as punishment and the use of torture to extract confessions may well have originated in Classical Greece. To this end they employed both the rack and a version of the wheel. In Greek wheel torture, the victim was simply tied to a cart wheel and spun around until they offered up the required information. More severe 'turns' on the wheel could, and often did, lead to death, probably through asphyxiation, choking on one's own vomit, cerebral haemorrhage or heart attack. Surprisingly, even such 'enlightened' Greek philosophers as Aristotle and Demosthenes were fully in favour of torture as a means of obtaining information. Aristotle wrote that he approved of such methods because they provided: 'a sort of evidence that appears to carry with it absolute credibility'. Evidently he failed to consider the fact that almost anyone will confess to anything if subjected to enough pain. One wonders what Aristotle might have thought of that ingenious Greek device known as the 'Brazen Bull'?

The Brazen Bull was supposedly invented by a man named Perillus in an attempt to curry favour with the dictator Phalaris of Agigentum. The device was no more than a hollow, life-sized bronze figure of a bull with a door in one side and holes at its nostrils and mouth. In application, a person convicted of a capital crime was stuffed into the bull, through the door in its side, and a blazing fire was then lit beneath the statue. As the bronze heated to red-hot, the victim's screams echoed from its nostrils and mouth, much like the cries of a maddened bull. While he seems to have been delighted with the device itself, Phalaris had no time for fawning sycophants and promptly condemned Perillus, its inventor, to be its first victim. Evidently Phalaris' subjects had no more time for their dictator than he had for Perillus. After enduring all they could of his tyrannies, in the year 563 BC, the mob stuffed the dictator himself into the Brazen Bull.

Classical Greece had no coherent political system. Rather, it was a collection of culturally diverse and geographically scattered city states; some of which, like Athens, were a bit more civilised than others (such as Agigentum over which Phalaris ruled). The more remote and less civilised of these city states seemed to invent impossibly creative tortures. According to Greek historian Lucian, on one occasion a young woman was sewn inside the carcass of a freshly slaughtered donkey with only her head remaining exposed. As the Mediterranean sun beat down on the victim, the carcass shrank and began to rot. In addition to the tortures of hunger, thirst and exposure, as the carcass decomposed it attracted worms and insects which attacked the flesh of the victim as well as the carcass of the animal. How long the victim survived is not related. Another similarly grim torture comes from the pen of Aristophanes. In this account, the condemned was locked in a pillory and smeared with milk and honey as an enticement to insects. If he managed to survive hunger, thirst, exposure and insect attacks for twenty days, he was released. That is to say, he was released in order to be hauled to a cliff and thrown to his death.

Among the more hardy and individualistic of the Ancient Greeks were the Spartans. Tough, bold and decidedly war-like, the Spartans had no time for the soft-living ways of people like

This is an example of a branding iron of the type which would have been used on Spartan males found guilty of being dedicated 'bachelors'.

the Athenians. If a Spartan man became overly fat, he was publicly whipped; if he remained unmarried for too long (and thereby suspected of preferring men to women) he was publicly branded with a hot iron. The Tyrant Nabis, who ruled Sparta from 205–194 BC, invented a very personal, and personally amusing, means of torturing those who annoyed him. It seems that Nabis commissioned an iron statue in the shape of his wife, Apega. This statue was built so its arms would open on hinges, the inner face of the arms and chest being set with numerous, long, sharp spikes. When Nabis personally questioned an accused malefactor and did not like the answers he got, he is said to have quipped: 'If I have not talent enough to prevail upon you, perhaps my good wife Apega may persuade you'. One fatal embrace from the iron Apega may have ended the interrogation, but Nabis enjoyed his little jokes.

The Greeks, like the Babylonians and Assyrians before them, eventually went into decline, to be replaced by a newer and more efficient culture; in this particular case, it was the Romans who became the dominant power in the area. Roman civilisation, and its associated views on torture, must be divided into two distinct categories; the first being the Roman Republic and the second the Roman Empire (the periods before, and after, Julius Caesar).

Early Romans, like the Greeks whose culture they co-opted, tried to construct a relatively ecumenical society. As early as the fifth century BC, Servius Tullius, the sixth king of Rome, distinguished civil crimes from criminal offences. Under this new, more enlightened approach to justice, capital punishment and the horrible pain that so often accompanied it, were reserved for offences such as murder, treason, arson, perjury and temple virgins who engaged in sex. In some cases, such as arson, the punishment remained 'an eye for an eye' – arsonists being burnt to death. Perjurers were thrown from a cliff and non-virgin virgins were buried alive. Even serious civil crimes, such as physical assault or robbery, were usually punishable only by heavy fines, although theft of a farmer's crops was

While we do not have an actual depiction of Apega, this image of the Iron Maiden of Nuremburg should serve to illustrate the dangerous result of her cold embrace. There were various versions of this device. Some of which were designed to be lethal, and some were merely intended to be injurious.

occasionally punishable by hanging. Exempt from all forms of torture were priests, children under fourteen years of age and pregnant women. Throughout this period – that is to say, during the days of the Roman Republic – justice was relatively even-handed and free citizens of Rome had no more fear of random acts of judicial violence than most of us do today. All that changed around 50 BC.

Julius Caesar was no saint, but as he only held power for about six months, he had little opportunity to change things for better or worse. What he did do, however, was pave the way for a string of emperors who were, to say the very least, less than pleasant people. Immediately after Caesar's assassination, power fell into the hands of three men: Mark Anthony, Octavius Caesar and Marcus Lepidus. Partly due to the fact that this was a time of civil war, and partly due to their natures, none of these men trusted anyone, including each other. For the first time in Roman history it became a crime to speak out against the government. When the philosopher Cicero denounced Mark Anthony, he was summarily arrested, tried and executed. Not a good start for the new Roman Empire and things swiftly went from bad to worse. As with almost all dictatorships, the Roman Empire was governed by men who doubted their ability to retain power and feared anyone and everyone who might conceivably snatch that power away from them. The only way for such men to maintain power is to establish a climate of terror: all plots, both real and imagined, must be uncovered and examples must be made of any suspected conspirators. And as we discussed in the first chapter, it is precisely within this paranoid climate of fear and suspicion that tortures proliferate.

The first group to come under the harsh boot of Imperial tyranny was the Roman army. Not surprising, really, it was Julius Caesar's legions which had overthrown the old Republic and it simply would not do to have soldiers thinking they could change the government at will. Under the Empire it became a dictum that a legionnaire should fear his officers more than the enemy.

In Roman military life, as well as civilian life, the most common punishment was whipping. Whipping was certainly nothing new; the Romans adapted it, like so much else, from the

In this scene we are shown a man who is being flogged by two other men using what appear to be knotted ropes or perhaps chains with weights. To their right a victim is having molten lead dripped onto the skin of his back while in the background we see a man being lowered into a hole for some unknown reason and another man is on fire and being beaten with a club.

On the right-hand side of this woodcut, we can see the application of the torture of the pulley (also known as Squassation) the weights attached to his ankles serving to further dislocate his shoulders. On the left side of the image, another man is having his armpits burned with a torch (despite the fact that the rendering appears somewhat more like a feather duster). And in the background a criminal is having his hand chopped off or broken. Note the clerk judiciously taking note of any utterance made by the victim on the pulley while the torturer asks demanding questions.

Greeks, but in the process managed to raise the humble whip to a torture device of impressive versatility. For mild offences they used a simple, flat strap – painful, but not life threatening by any means. The next step up was a whip made from plaited strips of parchment designed to flay the flesh from a victim's back. Then there was a multi-thonged whip, the *plumbatae*, with small lead balls on the ends of the thongs, and also a version of the cat-o-nine-tails, known as the *ungulae*, that had either thorns or bits of sharp metal braided into the thongs; in a few strokes it could slice to the bone. Finally there was a bullwhip-like beast specifically intended to kill. Amazing how much can be done with a few pieces of leather and a little ingenuity.

The Romans were, if nothing else, an inventive people. Their engineers were the envy of the ancient world and many of the devices the engineer corps used to build roads and mount military sieges were equally adaptable to torture. Among these was the humble pulley. With pulleys, a man could be hoisted high into the air before being dropped suddenly to the ground. If he was particularly bad, he could be dropped onto a pile of sharp rocks again, and again, and again, until his flesh was ripped to shreds and his bones shattered. Alternatively, pulleys could be used to make an improvised rack on which a man's limbs could be pulled from the sockets. Four simple pulleys, four small winches and some rope attached to a person's limbs and a suspect could be torn limb from limb in a matter of minutes. All these devices, and more, were used by the Romans – not as a form of execution, but as a means to extract information from 'suspects' and even from potential witnesses. Under a string of increasingly paranoid Caesars, torture (and the state of fear that accompanies it) became a routine way of maintaining order in the empire. As devices once used for execution became tools for extracting information, new and more creative methods of execution had to be invented. Again, as they had always done, the Romans adapted, and improved upon, pre-existing techniques.

One of the more nefarious devices adapted by the Romans was the wheel, mentioned earlier. Unlike the Greek wheel, the Roman version was more like a drum than a cart wheel. In the simplest version, the victim was simply strapped to the outer face, or rim, of the wheel and rolled downhill until they were crushed to death. An alternative version had the wheel mounted on an axle and suspended over a fire pit, allowing the condemned to be cranked around, again and again, slowly being burnt to death – not much different than being spit-roasted, but a lot slower. For a more direct approach, there was yet another version of the wheel where the outer surface of the rim was set with spikes and it was across these that the victim was tied. On the ground beneath the wheel was another bed of spikes. When the wheel was turned the poor wretch was literally ground to pieces.

Possibly unique to the Romans was the sentence imposed on those who murdered their father. Patricides were tossed into a large canvas sack. Before the bag was sewn shut a handful of poisonous snakes were tossed in and the entire package was then thrown into a convenient river, lake or the Mediterranean.

All these creative tortures not withstanding, the method of execution most identified with the Romans will always be crucifixion. As early as the late Republic, crucifixion was adopted as a means of executing slaves convicted of capital offences, but it was not until the Empire that people other than slaves could be condemned to this particularly nasty fate. Because crucifixion was such a slow, painful death, and because it made such a grand public spectacle (particularly when large groups of victims were crucified together), it became a favourite method of disposing of 'enemies of the state'. It was crucifixion that would eventually become the execution of choice for disposing of both the recalcitrant Jewish population in Palestine and the proliferating number of bothersome Christians who began infesting the Empire during the second and third centuries after Jesus.

At the time of Jesus's crucifixion, around 27 or 28 AD, wholesale terror in the provinces was still in its infancy; Emperor Tiberius was too busy wreaking havoc back home. A half century later, when the Jews rose against Rome, Emperor Vespasian had plenty of time on his hands to crush the life out of them. When General Titus besieged Jerusalem in 70 AD, he crucified Jews at the rate of 500 a day. The problem was never finding enough Jews to murder, but finding enough wood in that arid land to build all those crosses.

Here we witness the execution of four women by crucifixion. Note that the women are merely tied to the crosses and left to die of hunger, thirst and exposure. The woman on the left has been pieced through by lances and as such will die fairly quickly. It is uncertain whether the other three women will be granted a similar 'mercy'.

Tiberius, mentioned above, reigned from 14–37 AD and was a paranoid misanthrope who hated his subjects nearly as much as they hated him. Never being a hands-on kind of ruler, he spent much of his later years isolated on the Isle of Capri and left the brutalising of Roman citizens to his henchmen. To wile away his idle hours, Tiberius had a constant string of prisoners brought to his island where he enjoyed thinking up particularly inventive ways of murdering them. Most of these victims were his political enemies, or at least he thought they were, and they were seized and hauled to Capri without either a trial or an arrest warrant. They simply disappeared. It was an amazingly subtle method of terrorising his opponents and one that would be used again and again over later centuries – specifically by dictators in Africa, South America and by one particularly vicious German despot. As was true under dictators in all time periods, there were a few who spoke out against the Roman use of torture. One of these was the philosopher Seneca (4 BC–65 AD), who recognised that torture was not only unjust but a terribly flawed way to discover the truth. Fortunately, Seneca never pointed a finger directly at the emperor and was never invited to spend a weekend on Capri: his message, if it ever reached Tiberius' ears, went unheeded. As a last insult to the Roman people, Tiberius selected his insane nephew to succeed him – his name was Caius Caesar. We know him better as Caligula.

Like his uncle, Caligula preferred torturing people in private (such as in the same room where he was throwing dinner parties) over imposing terror on the population as a whole. Indeed, Caligula knew how to curry favour with the people of Rome and it was he who changed the Roman Games from true athletic competitions into the orgies of blood and death for which they are remembered. Fortunately, Caligula only ruled for four years before being murdered at the age of twenty-nine. Although his successor, Claudius, strove to return Rome to some semblance of sanity, his efforts were doomed. When his wife poisoned him in 54 AD, after a reign of thirteen years, she installed as emperor her son by a previous marriage – Nero.

Fat, stupid, spoiled and vain, Nero may not have been as psychotically murderous as either Tiberius or Caligula, but the results were much the same. In mid-July, 64 AD, while Nero was holidaying in the country, a fire swept through Rome, nearly destroying the city. Contrary to legend there is no evidence linking Nero to the disaster, but people love to gossip, particularly about their government. When rumours of his possible involvement reached Nero he knew he had to find a scapegoat. There didn't seem to be any Jews handy, so he picked on the equally troublesome Christians and instituted one of the most brutally public purges in recorded history. Hundreds of Christians were tortured into confessing to arson and thousands more were rounded up on suspicion of complicity.

For months, Christian victims were sacrificed in the Coliseum. Dozens of new and cruel ways were thought up to kill Rome's 'enemies' and delight the bloodthirsty crowd. They were dressed in the skins of animals and set upon by packs of dogs; they were sent unarmed against trained gladiators; they were hung by their thumbs and roasted over a slow fire, beaten to death or skinned alive. Some were crushed in wine presses; shoved into suits of chain mail that had been heated

In this image we can see how two early Christian martyrs met their deaths by boiling oil. It shows how they were not only forced to suffer a bath of boiling oil but were also showered with it simultaneously adding to their unimaginable torment.

to red-hot; impaled on stakes or had their stomachs ripped open only to have their entrails eaten by wild animals while they were still alive. According to chronicler Magentus Rabanus Maurus:

> Some were slain with swords; some burnt with fire; some scourged with whips; some stabbed with [tridents]; some fastened to the cross; some drowned in the sea; some flayed alive; some had their tongues cut out; some were stoned to death; some had their hands cut off or were otherwise dismembered.

Some were even roasted in great frying pans – much like Darius had used to fry the Hebrew boy centuries earlier. A description of this particular torture comes down to us from the chronicler Gallonio, who wrote:

> The frying pan ... was filled with oil, pitch or resin, and then set over a fire; and when it began to boil and bubble, then were the Christians of either sex thrown into it, such as had persisted steadfastly and boldly in the profession of Christ's faith, to the end that they might be roasted and fried like fishes ...

When these brutal games were held at night, Christians were tied to stakes, doused with oil and lighted, serving as human torches to illuminate the playing field. Even the Roman historian, Tacitus, who was no particular friend of the Christians, wrote: 'they were put to death, not for the public good, but to satisfy the lustful rage of an individual'. Possibly for the first time in human history torture was being carried out specifically for the purpose of public sport.

And thus it went until the final, ignoble collapse of Rome during the fifth century, but the fact is, none of these ancient people understood how to use torture effectively. Brutal tortures and bloody executions were carried out without the least thought to the psychological aspect of pain. What the ancients failed to realise is that the anticipation of torture can be just as devastating, and produce far more confessions, than the immediate and uncontrolled application of brute force ever can. Torture a man for a little while, give him a few days in a filthy cell to think it over, and he is far more likely to confess the next time he is dragged into the dungeon than if he is simply torn to bits during the first round of questioning. Would their descendants learn more effective uses of torture than these ancient people ever did? In the next chapter we will examine the techniques of torture used in the medieval world to find out just how sophisticated the application of pain became over the next thousand years.

2
TORTURE IN THE MEDIEVAL WORLD

After the final collapse of Rome in the early fifth century the centre of power shifted to Constantinople, leaving Western Europe at the mercy of the Germanic tribes, the Goths and Vandals. Common sense dictates that no matter how brutal things might have been under the Romans they probably got a lot worse. The truth is that many of the so-called 'barbarian' tribes had a more enlightened approach to justice than the Empire ever had. Writing three and a half centuries earlier, the Roman historian Tacitus recorded that the only crimes the Germanic people considered worthy of execution were desertion on the battlefield, cowardice in battle, consorting with the enemy and homosexuality. Other, lesser crimes, including robbery and murder, were punished with a fine which could be paid in cattle or other property – half of the fine being paid to the family of the victim, the remainder to the local chieftain or king. It would seem the Germanic tribes were more concerned with keeping every possible man ready for battle than in extracting judiciary retribution. Apparently, they took an equally enlightened view of religion. In 410 AD, the year Alaric, King of the Vandals, sacked Rome, he declared that any Roman who sought sanctuary inside a church was to be spared – a far cry from the treatment the Christians had received at the hands of the Romans.

As followers of the gentle teachings of Jesus, it is not surprising that the early Western Church and the Christianised Eastern Roman Empire, based in Constantinople, had progressive views on crime and punishment. The legal codes of Emperors Theodosius and Justinian confined capital punishment to murder, treason, adultery and counterfeiting if it was carried out by a slave. Under pressure from the Church, the Germans, who now controlled the remnants of the Western Roman Empire, grudgingly included murder in their slate of capital crimes. Generally, under Church law, lesser crimes were punishable by a variety of penances, the severity of the penance being in line with the severity of the crime. In many cases, the Church decreed that when the facts in a case were less than clear, punishment should be left in God's hands; thus preventing human judges from making mistakes which God might construe as grievous sins. In the year 865 Pope Nicholas I wrote to the ruler of the Bulgar people insisting that forced confessions (extracted through the prolonged use of torture) violated the basic concept of Christianity. Considering the times it was a truly enlightened approach.

Elsewhere, punishments were not always imposed with such wisdom. In Britain and Gaul (now France) criminals, slaves and those captured in battle were still sacrificed and personal disputes and criminal proceedings were settled by trial by combat (where the accused engaged in one-to-one battle with their accuser), or trial by ordeal, (where the accused might be forced to plunge their hands into scalding water or grab a bar of red-hot iron). If you won the battle or came away unscathed by the boiling water, you were presumed innocent. If these seem as harsh and unenlightened as Roman punishments, it is well to consider that much of Great Britain and Western Europe was about to fall under the domination of a group whose concept of justice and punishment were even more basic and frightening: the Vikings.

The first major Viking raid on the British Isles took place at Lindisfarne Abbey, located on a small island near the Scots/English border, in the year 763 AD and was carried out with a brutality that became the hallmark of these intrepid warriors. As primitive as they may now be considered, Viking raids were carefully planned affairs, designed to provide the greatest possible psychological impact. When a Viking war party landed in their terrifying, dragon-headed ships, they swarmed toward their chosen target, killing anyone who put up the least resistance and many who did not. Men were routinely murdered, women were murdered – or raped and murdered – and babies impaled on spear points. When the object of their attention was a monastery, as it so often was, the goal was the plunder of coinage and any church ornament that could be hauled away. But the Vikings also knew that the clergy were part of a political infrastructure, capable of spreading the word that 'the Vikings are coming and they were not to be trifled with'. The more people feared them, the easier the next conquest was likely to be. It was as clever a campaign of terror as any devised before or since.

But Vikings were not only raiders. After conquering an area, they generally established a colony and made themselves lords over the local population, imposing harsh punishments and stiff fines on all who ran afoul of Viking law. To make clear that they meant business, when local chieftains or kings were defeated by a Viking army, they could be publicly executed by a method known as the Blood Eagle. This particularly decorative form of butchery involved hacking open the back of the victim with an axe and dragging his lungs through the gaping wound so it looked as though the poor wretch had sprouted a pair of bloody wings. In the words of one of the Viking Sagas: '. . . and [they] made them to carve an eagle on his back with a sword, and cut the ribs all from the backbone, and draw the lungs out there, and gave him to Odin for the victory they had won'. The same punishment was inflicted on any of their new subjects who dared kill a Viking.

There were, of course, other punishments for other crimes. Murder and robbery were routinely punished by throwing the victim from a cliff and lesser crimes were punished by the imposition of a fine – sometimes as high as confiscation of all of a man's property. Such fines, including those imposed on neighbouring, non-Viking, political entities to buy-off any possible Viking attack, were known as Wergild. For those petty kings and chieftains who refused to submit to this Dark Age protection racket there was always the option of going to war.

Two men sentenced to death by starvation in a stock inside an isolated cave.

In 870, King Edmund of East Anglia (soon to be known as Edmund the Martyr) refused to knuckle-under to these outrageous, pagan demands, took to the field of battle – and lost. As punishment for his effrontery, and for refusing to renounce Christ, the Vikings tied King Edmund to a tree, whipped him mercilessly, shot him full of arrows and hacked off his head.

As northern England slowly collapsed under the Viking onslaught, the southern kingdoms, inhabited by the Anglo-Saxons, were making far better progress toward becoming

Whether this device was intended to restrain a victim whilst plunging them beneath the surface of a lake or river or was intended to hold them aloft and captive for public display and ridicule is uncertain. It is likely that it probably served both purposes. This fine example can today be found in the Museum of Torture in San Gimignano, Italy.

civilised. Curiously, the only crime in Anglo-Saxon England generally punished by death was theft; in this harsh, primitive world stealing a person's possessions was considered crueller and more malicious than simply killing them. When arson was involved, that is to say when one person deprived another of their home or crops by burning, the culprit himself was burnt. Most other crimes, including murder and rape, were punished by a stiff fine. When a fine did not seem sufficient to the degree of the crime, or when the public demanded some visible punishment, a turn in the pillory (called the *healfang*, or half-hang) was often added to the sentence. When the miscreant was a woman she might be subjected to the *scealding* (or scolding) stool; a device similar to the ducking stool of later years, wherein the condemned was tied to a chair and subjected to a good dousing in the local pond. There is no evidence that any of these duckings lasted long enough to cause any more damage than serious embarrassment. In general, the overriding concept in Anglo-Saxon justice was one of mutual responsibility, everyone was equally responsible for helping to keep their neighbour on the straight and narrow: peer pressure can exert a considerable force in small, isolated communities. Sometimes, when an offender continued to commit crimes over and over, rather than imprison or execute them, they were simply banished from the kingdom. What they did elsewhere was someone else's problem.

In an effort to codify, and thereby equalise, the laws of his kingdom, the seventh-century king of Kent, Ethelbert I, became the first English ruler to write down his laws. Like those of his contemporaries, Ethelbert's laws relied far more on a sliding system of fines (peppered with the occasional public humiliation) than on physical punishment or execution – the need for soldiers to fight off the Vikings was too great to allow the death of any but the most hardened criminals. Women, on the other hand, did not fight and were therefore expendable. Women found guilty of theft or murder were executed. To make his concept of crime and punishment clear, Ethelbert even assigned values to specific parts of the human body and to life itself. Murder was punished by a fine of 100s. Should one person cause another to lose an eye, they were to pay the victim 50s or an equal value in goods. Should the damaged part be a toenail, the fine was 6d; the same fine being imposed if a man's reproductive organs were damaged. Naturally, the fines increased if the injured party was a person of great social standing: rank hath its privileges. What all this shows us is that the power of the Church (at this period in time at least) played an important part in civilising the laws of those nations that had accepted Christianity. Inevitably, a share of all fines collected as punishment for a crime found its way into the coffers of the local church; a small price to pay for dragging society away from blood feuds and barbaric tortures.

The impact of religion on the justice system also changed the list of acts which were considered socially unacceptable. For the first time, fornication (that is to say, sex outside of wedlock) and adultery both became punishable offences, as did eating meat during proscribed periods of fasting, working on Sunday and worshiping the old (pagan) gods. Predictably, rules governing the clergy were slightly different than those governing laymen and men of the cloth were frequently provided with neat loopholes by which they could escape punishment. The word of a bishop, like that of a king, needed no second-party confirmation to be accepted as fact. If a priest was accused of a crime he could absolve himself by swearing his innocence before the altar. The system may have had its flaws, but it was a vast improvement over what had gone before and, equally, over what was yet to come.

With the death of Alfred the Great, King of the West Saxons, in 901 the trend toward leniency slowly began to reverse itself. It was a lawless time in a lawless world and the general public insisted that criminals be soundly, and publicly, made to pay for their crimes. Within a generation whipping came back into fashion, as did physical mutilation. Capital punishment took on new and novel forms: free men and women were thrown from cliffs; male slaves who stole were stoned to death by fellow slaves (presumably as a hands-on lesson in proper behaviour) and thieving female slaves were either stoned or drowned. For the first time witches were punished, the practitioners of these dark arts being confined to prison for four months – unless they had caused a death by their conjurations, in which case they were executed.

Three-quarters of a century later, King Ethelred tried to reverse this disturbing back-sliding. Late in his reign, around the year 1000, he said: '... that Christian men for all too little be not condemned to death; but in general let mild punishment be decreed; and let not for a little God's handiwork and his own purchase be destroyed ...' Surprisingly, this more lenient policy was adopted by another English monarch of about the same period, King Canute. Canute, a Christianised Viking and King of southern England, Denmark, Norway and parts of Sweden, stated his opposition to harsh punishment with the words: '... rather let gentle punishments be decreed for the benefit of the people'. It sounds good, but bear in mind that deep down, Canute was still a Viking and Vikings had a long history of mutilating people. Under Canute's laws routine punishments included cutting off ears, noses and upper lips: a woman convicted of adultery lost both ears and her nose. Eyes were gouged out and scalping was brought into fashion. To his credit, Canute tried to take all aspects of a person's life into consideration when judging them, and was notably lenient when the criminal was a teenager, elderly, desperately poor or ill and he took into account whether they were free or a slave – presumably slaves were given less latitude than free men and women. Accidental transgressions were also judged less harshly than premeditated ones. All in all, life under Canute was relatively good and crime was at a low ebb. Sadly, Canute died in 1035 and although his laws survived him by three decades – being made even more palatable by his descendant, the pious King Edward the Confessor – all progress was lost in the autumn of 1066 when England was invaded by a group of ex-Vikings who had recently seized Northern France and begun calling themselves Normans.

Duke William of Normandy was a bastard. That much is an historical and biological fact; it was also an opinion shared by nearly all of his subjects and most of his followers. For nearly two centuries prior to the Norman invasion of England a few continental powers, including the French, Burgundians and Normans, had been following a new political system known today as feudalism. Under the feudal system, great lords owed obedience to the king, knights owed obedience to their lords, the peasants owed obedience to everyone above them and everybody owed obedience to the Church. In theory, feudalism was meant to protect the poor, the helpless and Holy Mother Church. It was a good idea but, like so many good ideas, it went wrong almost from the start. Somehow, when anything unpleasant happened, the peasants were blamed and suffered mightily under the pernicious greed of their overlords. Because the feudal system did not develop in England, but was imposed on it following the Norman Conquest of October, 1066, it is a perfect case study in how the system worked – or failed to work.

William, now known alternately as William the Conqueror and William I of England, treated his subjects like the enemy. To ensure that they would never contemplate revolting he 'harried' the countryside. In this case, harrying meant burning the fields, homesteads, villages and towns, leaving the peasants and villagers

Beheading by sword or axe was a public entertainment in central and northern Europe until as recently as 150 years ago. The axe was preferred in Gallic and Mediterranean Europe. A long apprenticeship is needed for perfecting aim and force; executioners kept in trim by practicing on animals in slaughter houses.

homeless and starving and creating a famine that lasted a decade. Even William's own chronicler, Ordericus, was appalled at the devastation. 'William, in the fullness of his wrath, ordered that the corn and cattle, with all the farming implements and provisions, [were] to be collected on heaps and set on fire.' To make certain the point was not lost on his subjects, William instituted a program of castle building

Beheading was an 'easy' death if carried out with skill and as such was reserved for noblemen. Plebeians tended to be executed by slower, more painful means such as slow hanging. This device, known as a 'fallbrett' (literally a falling board) was an ancestor of the guillotine. But unlike its later French descendant, the fallbrett would not remove the head in a single swift stroke, but rather, the wooden 'edge' would rip and chew its way through the flesh and vertebrae under the impact of the sledge blows.

intended to intimidate any of the English who survived his arrival. The Anglo-Saxon Chronicles described this program of public works with the words: 'He built him castles as a place to annoy his enemies from . . . And they oppressed the people greatly with castle building'. Obviously, as punishment for losing the war, the English were used as slave labour in the building of the very castles which would ensure their future good behaviour.

Needing all the labourers he could round up, and always believing that lasting, public examples should be made of transgressors, William preferred maiming law-breakers rather than simply executing them. In his inaugural speech, after being crowned king on Christmas day 1066, William said: 'I forbid that any person be killed or hanged for any cause.' Then he added: 'Let their eyes be torn out and their testicles be cut off'. Naturally, the 'no killing' part of this speech did not apply if a Norman was killed; in that case, Anglo-Saxon suspects were rounded up and hanged by the score. If one Norman was murdered by another it would have set a bad example for William to execute one of his own people in the same manner as a common peasant, so he devised a death sentence reserved for noblemen: beheading. It was a tradition that would outlive him by centuries.

Being a delicate and chivalrous sort, William never sentenced a woman to the humiliation of the gallows or headsman's block; for them, the only socially acceptable death was the burning post. For lesser crimes there was also a nice selection of brand-new castle dungeons now available. In a concerted attempt to keep local Church officials out of his way, the king decreed that ecclesiastic courts would, henceforth, only be allowed to try ecclesiastic crimes. Civil cases, which had previously been overseen by Church officials and carried out according to Church law, were now the Crown's own private domain.

Somehow, all these harsh measures did more to propagate crime than to end it. By the time William's second son, Henry I (reigned 1100–1135) came to the throne, not only were the old crimes still flourishing, but new ones were being invented every day and almost no witnesses could be found who were willing to testify against anybody. Knowing that he simply could not execute every possible suspect, and neither could he allow every miscreant to escape punishment, Henry decided the best thing to do was to let God decide guilt or innocence and, after convincing the Church to support him, he re-instituted trial by ordeal. There was trial by water (in which the suspect was thrown into a pool and if they sunk were deemed innocent), trial by fire (in which the suspect had to grab a hot iron bar while he walked nine paces and prayed that no blisters appeared after three days) and trial by fire and water (in which the suspect plunged their hands into a cauldron of boiling water, picked up a stone and again prayed that no blisters developed). For priests accused of civil crimes these particular atrocities were replaced with the ordeal of coarsened bread, in which the accused was made to eat bread containing feathers; if they choked, they were presumed guilty.

Such grotesque public displays were not the sole province of England. Even such an exalted personage as Holy Roman Emperor Henry IV, when excommunicated by the Pope, travelled to Rome, lay face down in the snow for two days, praying and fasting, until the Holy Father finally relented and forgave him. It did not do much good; in 1105 Emperor Henry was still forced to abdicate. Curiously, as barbaric as these punishments seem, as the Normans' fierce grip on England relaxed at the dawn of the twelfth century, it was the common people who objected to the demise of trial by ordeal. Even England's penultimate Norman ruler, Henry I, tried to reform his family's harsh, earlier laws, relying more on prisons and short turns in a dungeon than on corporal punishment. Simultaneously he increased the number of capital crimes. By 1124 death had become the standard punishment for

Here we see the accused has had his hands bound to his ankles and is being thrown off a bridge in the fast flowing currents of the river below. This is a version of the trial by ordeal. If the water rejects him (he floats) then he will be declared guilty by his accusers. But if the water accepts him (he sinks to the bottom) he will be judged innocent and presumably hauled out of the water by the attached rope. How many individuals were found innocent but died as a result of this method of assessment is unknowable.

murder, treason, burglary, arson, robbery and simple theft, and more and more people convicted of lesser crimes were simply being detained behind bars for various lengths of time. It is hardly surprising that during the protracted Civil War (1139–1148) between England's King Stephen and his cousin, Empress Matilda, the dungeons of England overflowed and by 1155 London's first purpose-built prison, The Fleet, had been erected by the new king, Henry II.

It is worth noting here, that the central fortified secure tower of a castle was known as a 'keep' in English, but as all of the castles in England were owned by the Normans at this period, they were frequently referred to by their Norman French name, 'donjon', from which the term dungeon is derived.

As Henry (the French-born son of Empress Matilda) was an outsider to England, he was not made to feel any more welcome than the Normans had been a century earlier. Rather than 'harry' his new kingdom, however, he filled it with prisons. Every town and borough was ordered to have some kind of prison facility – preferably inside a nice, secure castle – and these were to be used, in Henry's words, 'to confine tight, presumptive evil-doers'. This meant that anyone accused, or suspected, of a crime was to be locked up until the circuit judge showed up and then returned to the cells to serve their sentence. Henry also proved himself just as fond of maiming his subjects as William the Conqueror had ever been. Murder, armed robbery and counterfeiting were all punishable by having the right hand cut off. Giving in to local demands for gaudy judicial displays, he allowed trial by ordeal for any crime

The unfortunate culprit on the left-hand side of this image is about to have his left hand chopped off. Corporal punishment such as this dismemberment was commonplace throughout medieval Europe for petty crimes, while the capital punishment on the right-hand side of the image was reserved for somewhat more serious offences.

This somewhat comical image shows what appears to be a poet or balladeer (based on the lute hung upon the post) who has probably been sentenced to the stocks for seditious verses. How frustrating it must have been to see the dog making off with his stash of food from his satchel so tantalizingly out of reach. But this is of course nothing when compared to the other tortures endured by his contemporaries.

worth less than 5s; but those found guilty were not executed. Instead, they had a foot hacked off. It would take more than a century before trial by ordeal was finally abolished throughout Europe, and then only because Pope Innocent III refused to allow the clergy to assist in such divine judgments. In 1215, the same year Pope Innocent forbade the clergy from taking part in trials by ordeal, King John of England was forced into signing the Magna Charta, the closest England had ever come to a written constitution. In the Magna Charta are specific prohibitions against the use of torture and any and all legal procedures that may involve torture as being contrary to the basic concept of English Common Law. Curiously, both the abolition of trial by ordeal and the signing of Magna Charta did nothing more than throw the entire English and European legal systems into a tail-spin. Without the presence of a priest, trial by ordeal did not have the sanction of God and without trial by ordeal, how could God's will, and the truth, possibly be discovered? Judicial torture may not have involved God's will, but without the threat of torture, how could guilt ever be satisfactorily proven? It was not an enlightened age but there were voices of reason popping up here and there. In far-off Germany, Abbess Hildegarde von Bingen (1098–1179, now known as St Hildegarde) not only spoke up in favour of leniency toward those convicted of capital crimes, but even defended the un-Godly, when she insisted that those convicted of heresy should not be executed. Sometimes, voices of reason are heard, even if only temporarily.

England was already moving away from the cruellest forms of mutilation and execution and toward public humiliation that marked criminals as social pariahs without causing them any permanent, physical damage. The public aspect of punishment was important because people demanded that they be allowed to witness a criminal's punishment – how else could they know that justice had been served? Toward this end, the stocks were introduced.

Less physically painful than the pillory, the stocks only locked a person's feet in a wooden frame, the rest of their body remained free. To make this a punishment rather than just an afternoon in a public place, the convict was forced to sit on the narrow edge of a board with their legs extended in front of them and locked in the stocks. Thus secured, they were still subjected to taunts and thrown objects, but could at least fend off large objects and rocks with their arms. Still, the stocks were humiliating and seemed to satisfy the demand for public punishment. This new concept in punishment seemed so enlightened that at one point, the entirety of the House of Commons knelt and prayed that stocks would be erected in every town and village in England.

Other forms of punishment for all manner of offences were also popular. Among these was the custom of 'outlawing'. Declaring a person an outlaw (specifically meaning that the guilty party was to remain at large but were no longer afforded any protection by the law) had been introduced by the Normans, but, for several reasons, became more popular as time went on. First, it cost nothing to declare a person an outlaw and, second, it was immensely profitable for the government. An outlaw lost not only the title to his, or her, land but forfeited all personal possessions and wealth to the crown. Further, as the convicted was no longer under any form of legal protection, they could be murdered by anyone, at any time, without any consequences. An idea of just how popular a practice this was can be seen by a quick look at the judicial records for the county of Gloucestershire, England for the year 1221. Of 330 cases of murder tried that year, only fourteen of the convicted were hanged while 100 were declared outlaw and turned loose; the remaining 216 either being given alternative sentences or found innocent of the charges. Outlawing may seem like a relatively easy punishment, but consider that when a man was executed for a crime his family retained the rights to his estate, if he was declared outlaw, they were dispossessed when the land reverted to the government.

Playing on this easy method of accumulating land and money, in 1255 King Henry III outlawed more than seventy murderers, adding whatever wealth they had to his own coffers. The next year, out of seventy-seven suspected murderers five were acquitted and seventy-two were outlawed. In 1279, the Northumbrian courts heard sixty-eight cases of murder, released four of the accused and outlawed the rest. Outlawry was good business, not only for the courts, but for the convicted. If an outlaw discovered evidence that would clear them, they could apply to have their case retried. Should the new evidence convince the judges, the convict would have his sentence revoked. Of course this made him, or her, essentially a new person, and therefore not entitled

This is an example of a baker's cart. There were many variations on this punishment. A baker, having been found guilty of selling underweight loaves of bread or of 'weighting' his loaves with the inclusion of sawdust, etc, would be chained to this cart filled with heavy weights and be paraded through the streets with a loaf of bread around his neck. Baker's guild ordinances tried to mandate against such 'mistakes' and frequently, in an effort to avoid this outcome even accidentally, we find that bakers would give an extra loaf of bread away for free with every dozen purchased (just in case there was any shortfall). This then, is the origin of the baker's dozen.

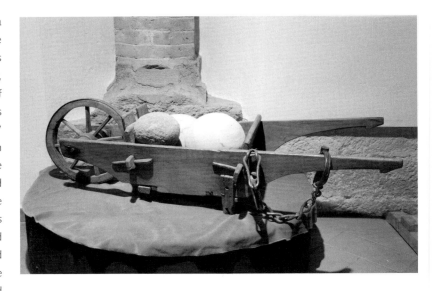

to reclaim any property which may have been the possession of the 'old' person; but at least they had their life back. Other crimes that had once been punished by harsh, physical tortures were also treated in a humiliating but harmless manner. Bakers found guilty of selling loaves smaller than regulation size, or of adulterating their flour with chaff, sand or sawdust were either displayed in the stocks or dragged through the streets of town on a section of woven fence (known as a hurdle) with a loaf of bread tied around their neck. It may not have been the best advertisement for their business, but it was a lot less grim than having a hand chopped off.

This is not to assume that harsh, and sometimes grotesquely novel, punishments did not take place in the realm of England. In 1241, Henry III – that otherwise enlightened monarch, more concerned with making a fast buck than torturing his subjects – introduced the highly creative form of terminal torture known as being hanged, drawn and quartered. The victim was first pulled from the ground by a noose and left to dangle until they lost consciousness. They were then brought down and revived only to be castrated before having their stomach ripped open, their entrails drawn out and tossed onto a fire before their still-living eyes. Only then was the victim's head struck off, ending their unspeakable suffering. The various bits and pieces of the carcass were subsequently displayed around the countryside as an example to others who might have been contemplating treason. But it hardly seemed to matter what Henry did, be it gentle or cruel, the crime rate skyrocketed. What was needed was a total reformer, a man who cared nothing for what people thought and was willing to whip society into shape at any cost. What was needed was Henry III's son Edward.

Edward I – also known as Longshanks, Hammer of the Scots and probably a lot less savoury things – ruled from 1272 until 1307 and spent every waking minute (at least those minutes when he was not busy slaughtering the Scots or the Welsh) reshaping the English legal system. He gathered the smartest lawyers and prelates in the realm and augmented their numbers by importing still more lawyers from Rome. Slowly, methodically, Henry and his advisors disassembled the feudal system and built a new system of justice. One of the first issues they tackled was the right of a prisoner to refuse to plead to charges levied against them. Under Edward's rules, anyone who refused to answer charges were chained, face down, to a dungeon floor and fed a small piece of stale bread one day and given a small cup of brackish water the next. If a week or so of this failed to loosen their tongues, they were pressed beneath an increasing amount of weight; they either lodged a plea or were slowly crushed to death.

Known as *peine forte et dure* (long-lasting, intense pain) this new approach to juris prudence was not only like Edward himself – strong and hard – but became the standard, judicial operating procedure for the next three centuries. It must be understood that such measures were not considered torture. Torture was technically illegal in England under the terms of Magna Charta. Being chained to a dungeon floor, fed

Here we see an image of three poor souls being hanged, drawn and quartered. On the right we see the hanging (though he will be cut down while still alive), then the drawing out of the entrails, evisceration and castration is shown center. This would be followed by decapitation and then the 'quartering' of the body into segments which would be boiled in tar for preservation (shown left) to be displayed in different parts of the kingdom as a warning to others. Note how the executioner with the knife holds up the heart of the victim for the approval and satisfaction of the assembled crowd.

garbage and slowly pressed to death was just a method of convincing a person to make a plea – after all, if a person was innocent, why would they hesitate to plead their case? For all his harsh treatment of accused felons, Edward was truly and deeply concerned with the corruption permeating the English court system. The main charge levied against local judges was that they arrested innocent men, threw them into prison and only released them after they had paid an exorbitant fine. It was a natural outgrowth of the eminently profitable outlawry system. When witnesses could not be found to support the system's pre-determined verdicts, totally uninvolved people were dragged off the streets and tortured until they offered evidence against innocent people and complete strangers. Juries were 'packed' with friends of the judges and sheriffs who shared in the ill-gotten booty of rigged trials. The predictable result of such corruption was that virtually no one had the least respect for either the law or those who enforced it; when juries were not coerced into bringing in the verdict, which the judge or sheriff wanted, they routinely let guilty men go free simply because they hated the system more than they hated the criminals. Furious that his kingdom had become so debased, Edward threw out everyone accused of bribe-taking, coercion, blackmail and influence peddling and replaced them only to find that after a few years the new officials had become just as corrupt as the old ones.

There were places, outside England, where the system ran more efficiently; if not the judicial system itself, then at least the mechanism for dealing with lawbreakers. In twelfth-century Russia anyone tortured without the specific approval of the local prince was allowed redress for his pain and was even able to sue for compensation; the moral being that if you wanted to torture someone you had to go through proper channels first. By 1300, those mechanical innovators, the Germans, had invented a machine capable of lopping off a criminal's head with frightening efficiency. What this guillotine-like device looked like is unknown, but in its first year it was used to cleanly, swiftly and bloodily do away

This image shows the process of pressing (*peine et forte en dure*) but does little to convey the true agony of the experience. The victim here seems almost relaxed. But in reality as more and more weight is added it becomes increasingly difficult to breathe. Eventually the ribcage will collapse and the lungs will be compressed resulting in slow suffocation.

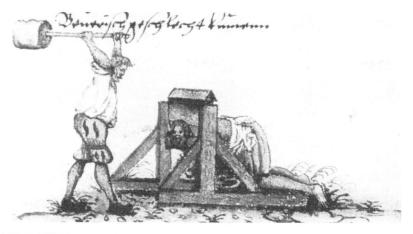

Here we find two illustrations of early medieval beheading machines sometimes known as 'fallbrett' (or falling board). These ancestors of the guillotine were slow and gruesome affairs which took a distant third to the guillotine or the headsman's axe in terms of efficiency. As the 'board' would frequently chew slowly through the victim's neck, it was hoped that the first hit might paralyze the condemned to keep them still throughout the process.

with five men in the town of Zittau. Naples, in Italy may have used such a device slightly earlier, and only seven years later a similar machine was in use in Ireland. It did not take long for the English to catch on and by the middle of the 1300s a beheading machine was in constant use in the Yorkshire town of Halifax. There, on market days, the excitement of buying, selling and general merrymaking was added to by the steady chop, chop, chop of the Halifax gibbet.

We know that as late as the mid-sixteenth century, the Halifax gibbet was still in use because in 1565 the Earl of Morton, regent of Scotland, watched it at work and was impressed enough with its efficiency that he carried the idea back across the border with him and had a similar device built in Scotland. Adding a novel twist to what could well have become stale entertainment, if a man stole a farm animal the object of his heist was used to haul in the rope attached to the Halifax gibbet's blade. When the axe, or blade, was drawn to the proper height, the rope was released and thus even God's lesser creatures could extract vengeance on their abductors. Occasionally, however, animals wound up on the wrong end of the rope. Literally. Throughout Europe, if an animal attacked a human it could be tried and, if found guilty, duly executed for its 'crime'. In France, in 1386, a sow convicted of biting a child was dressed in women's clothing and hanged. Only three years later a horse was hanged for kicking a man. So it was that the public execution of criminals, both human and animal, became as much a form of public entertainment as a judicial punishment.

If public humiliation and execution failed to change the habits of medieval Europe, the Black Death (1347–50) changed things beyond all imagining. As two out of every five individuals, regardless of age, sex or social class, fell victim to the ubiquitous and pervasive disease, the political and social glue that held society together slowly dissolved. Fields and shops went untended, cities and towns became mass graveyards and crime skyrocketed. Groups of religious fanatics accepted this as God's punishment on a sinful mankind and took it upon themselves to expiate the sins of the world by punishing themselves for all of humanity's wrongdoing. These were the flagellants, and they wandered across the face of this devastated world, whipping themselves

Saxon flagellation. From the Harleian MS. 603.

mercilessly, in the hope that their pain might ensure the salvation of all Christian souls at the final day of judgment.

If the flagellants and their self-imposed punishment had no lasting effect on the social order, the Black Death certainly did. As civilisation buried the dead and tried to reassemble the shattered pieces of civilisation, it became obvious that there were no longer enough workers (either simple peasants or skilled craftsmen) to fill the endless number of job openings. And those who did remain alive quickly realised that they could virtually name their own price for their services. Terrified of the effects of unchecked inflation and of losing their hold on power, kings, noblemen and local authorities scrambled to keep the lower classes, and the economy, under control. Laws were passed declaring that wages and prices were to be frozen at pre-1346 levels. All able-bodied men and women under the age of sixty were required to take any job offered to them and anyone demanding, or paying, increased

Used for the marking of convicted criminals, usually on the shoulder or shoulder blade but often also on the cheek or forehead (depending on the culture and the crime). His or her crime was specified by a code of letters or symbols which would have been easily recognizable to everyone in the land.

wages was to be fined or imprisoned. If a worker left one job to seek a higher-paying one elsewhere, they were to be confined, chained, beaten and given only bread and water until they learned their lesson. A second such offence carried a sentence of being branded on the chest with the letter 'V', for vagabond or 'F' for falsehood. Even giving charity (either food or money) to the poor was outlawed. Additional laws were passed to keep the old social structure securely in place. Sumptuary laws, decreeing that no one could wear clothing of a better quality than befitted their station in life, were passed throughout Europe. Both the quality and colour of cloth a person was allowed to wear were tightly regulated. All of society, at least those lower than the noble classes, was being publicly punished for trying to better themselves. It did not work.

When one plan fails, another is always devised to take its place. In 1381, when both the Statute of Labourers and the sumptuary laws failed to keep

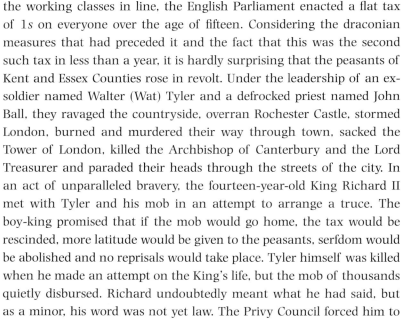

Detail of a Dutch engraving of about 1590, one in a series of 53 showing the massacre of the protestant citizens of Antwerp by the Spanish on 5 November 1576. Here we see three victims being tortured by suspension. The male is being suspended by his genitalia, the female by her breasts and the man in the background by his wrists. We do not think anything further needs to be said here to convey the agony of the victims which is not otherwise clear in the image.

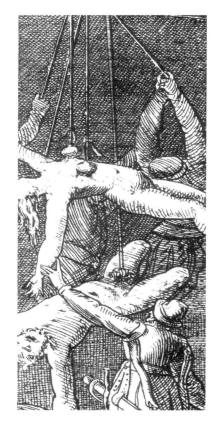

the working classes in line, the English Parliament enacted a flat tax of 1s on everyone over the age of fifteen. Considering the draconian measures that had preceded it and the fact that this was the second such tax in less than a year, it is hardly surprising that the peasants of Kent and Essex Counties rose in revolt. Under the leadership of an ex-soldier named Walter (Wat) Tyler and a defrocked priest named John Ball, they ravaged the countryside, overran Rochester Castle, stormed London, burned and murdered their way through town, sacked the Tower of London, killed the Archbishop of Canterbury and the Lord Treasurer and paraded their heads through the streets of the city. In an act of unparalleled bravery, the fourteen-year-old King Richard II met with Tyler and his mob in an attempt to arrange a truce. The boy-king promised that if the mob would go home, the tax would be rescinded, more latitude would be given to the peasants, serfdom would be abolished and no reprisals would take place. Tyler himself was killed when he made an attempt on the King's life, but the mob of thousands quietly disbursed. Richard undoubtedly meant what he had said, but as a minor, his word was not yet law. The Privy Council forced him to renege on his agreement. Later, addressing the representatives of the peasants, Richard is recorded to have said: 'serfs and peasants you are and serfs and peasants ye shall remain'. Hardly a statement likely to engender good behaviour among the masses.

As enlightened as he had been as a teenager, the harsh realities of politics and life in the Middle Ages eventually made King Richard as hard as his ministers. In 1383, an Irish monk gained an audience with the king and openly accused the Duke of Lancaster of treason. Whether or not Richard looked into the matter is unknown, but his reaction toward the monk's effrontery was recorded by a court chronicler. 'Lord Holland and Sir Henry Greene, Knight, came to this friar and, putting a cord about his neck, tied the other end about his privy members and after hanging him up from the ground [by this rope], laid a stone upon his belly, with the weight thereof . . . he was strangled and tormented, so his very backbone burst asunder herewith, besides the straining of his privy members; thus with three kinds of torments he ended his wretched life.'

By the end of Richard's reign (1399) it was obvious that petty crime was completely out of control. To punish those who insisted on breaking the law, stocks were ordered to

This device, once locked about a victim's neck, would tether them to a wall, post or similar fixed object. Whether publicly (such as within a church or town square) or privately (such as within a prison or dungeon) it was a cruel and merciless form of restraint which would frequently be used in conjunction with additional tortures or torments.

be constructed in nearly every town and village across England. As they had done in the past, the stocks provided both a means of non-damaging punishment and a satisfying form of public sport. Slightly less public, but equally effective, were the Jaggs; an iron collar attached to a length of chain fastened to the wall of the local church. Wrongdoers, particularly those who had broken church law, were locked in the Jaggs for a specified period of time so they might contemplate their sin in the shadow of God's house. Similar iron collars and shackles were common in castle dungeons everywhere. In Carlisle Castle the iron collar was provided with such a short chain that if a prisoner happened to fall off the stone sleeping shelf they would almost inevitably strangle themselves. In some places such tragic accidents were avoided by fastening prisoners safely to the wall not only with an iron collar, but also with a waist band and shackles for the wrists and/or ankles – no chance then of tumbling out of bed and hurting yourself.

In addition to stocks and chains there were specific forms of minor punishment devised for women. For common shrews and scolding housewives there was the 'chucking stool' – a chair to which these nagging women were tied before being processed through the town or village to the delight, taunts and hurled objects of passers-by. To make the humiliation as complete as possible, the chair had an open bottom and the woman's skirts were hiked up before she was seated, leaving her rump exposed for the abuse and amusement of all and sundry.

For such mouthy women there was also a device known as the 'scold's bridle', a nasty little cage of iron straps that could be locked over the condemned's head. When the face plate was closed an iron

This image shows the punishment of women in a poorhouse found to be too lazy. It is similar to the punishment of the chucking stool in that the only real tortures endured by these women are a result of their isolation and exposure to public ridicule. In the case of a chucking stool, this might be in the public market square, whereas here it is in the communal dining hall of the workhouse.

tongue, fastened to the inner face of the bridle, was shoved into the woman's mouth, preventing her from hurling curses at her tormentors and often causing severe lacerations to the tongue, cheeks and gums. Once locked firmly inside the bridle, the woman was then paraded through the streets of town.

For slightly more serious offences there was the 'ducking stool'. Intended specifically for women of loose virtue and those

for whom a turn on the aforementioned chucking stool had not proven a sufficient deterrent to their nagging ways, the ducking stool was suspended over the local pond and its occupant given a free swimming lesson. The amount of time she was likely to spend in the water was substantially increased if she were suspected of being a witch. If an accused witch floated, the assumption was that God's good, clean water – used, as it was, in baptism – had rejected her evil person; if she sank, she had been accepted by the water and was therefore not a witch. She may have drowned by the time the determination was made, but at least she had died free of guilt. The pillory was also in constant use during the 1400s. Those found guilty of brawling, habitual drunkenness, rumour mongering (especially if it was against a public official or a noble family), slander and blatant infractions of fair-trade rules were all subject to having their head and hands locked into the pillory's wooden frame and exposed to the contempt of the public for a period ranging from a few hours to several days. For those who continued to insist on the life of a vagrant when they were physically capable of holding down a job, the standard punishment was to be stripped naked, tied to the back end of a cart and hauled through the public streets while being whipped until the blood dripped to the ground.

Throughout the fifteenth century the most common form of punishment for capital crimes was hanging. This is not the form of hanging familiar to us from nineteenth-century photographs and cowboy movies, however. The condemned was not dropped through a trap-door where the sudden jerk would break their neck and end their life in a split second. All hangings, up until the mid-nineteenth century, were slow, painful, macabre affairs. Rather than being dropped through a trap, the convict was simply hauled into the air and left to dangle in the noose until they choked to death. In the case of the physically fit, or those with a heavily muscled neck, this could mean as much as twenty minutes of kicking and choking their life away. Unlike earlier periods, by the 1400s the right to hang someone found guilty of a capital crime was not limited to royal courts; every town and village worth its name had its own gallows and regularly dispatched those found guilty of murder, grand theft, desertion from the local militia, forgery, arson and any other crime which seemed to warrant it at the moment. Even when the gallows were kept busy it did not always satisfy the public demand for justice. In 1429 a woman accused of murder was seized and lynched by an entirely female mob – this was England's first recorded case of an individual having been hanged without the benefit of at least some form of trial. Even in the face of such rude justice the social structure in England was about to break down even further.

For the three decades between 1455 and 1485 the English nobility went to war with itself. What has become known as the Wars of the Roses was actually a dynastic struggle between the noble houses of Lancaster and York for control of the throne. For a generation and a half the Lancastrians, the Yorkists and their hired armies of mercenary thugs slogged it out across the English countryside; the balance of power shifting one way and then the other until the nation, and the families involved, were nearly decimated. In August 1485, an army led by Henry Tudor – last surviving claimant to the Lancastrian line – met and defeated the forces of King Richard II at Bosworth Field. In claiming Richard's crown, Henry Tudor (now Henry VII) inherited a kingdom where order existed only in theory. A few months after Henry's ascension to the throne, the Venetian envoy to England wrote: 'There is no country in the world where there are so many thieves and robbers as in England. Few venture to go alone in the country excepting in the middle of the day, and fewer still in the towns at night, and least of all in London'.

During the decades of turbulence the local courts had become corrupt beyond imagining, blithely condemning the innocent if there were a profit to be made in it, and for the same reason frequently turned dangerous criminals loose on society. Even where there was no corruption, there was massive incompetence. In an attempt to prevent wholesale injustice from consuming society, the Church routinely granted sanctuary to all who requested it and even those who did not seek sanctuary often escaped punishment by pleading 'benefit of clergy' – that is to say, ordained or not, the person in question claimed to be in the service of God. In a world where almost no-one except the clergy could read, the only proof required to qualify for benefit of clergy was to read the first verse of the fifty-first psalm: 'Have mercy on me, O God, according to Thy loving kindness; According to the multitude of Thy tender mercies, blot out my transgressions'. How clever did a criminal have to be to memorise these few lines and simply pretend to read them when handed a Bible? The benefit of all this was that civil courts had virtually no control over clerics and clerical courts had no power to execute and seldom even imprisoned. Contrition and penance were considered the only earthly punishments needed by those in the Church – any additional punishment would be dealt with by God, in the hereafter. It may have been sufficient for legitimate clergymen and it may have provided a grand loophole for criminals, but it was not at all good enough for Henry VII and his Chief Justice, who is quoted as having said: 'The devil alone knoweth the thought of man'.

Henry's first step in redressing the shortcomings in his legal system was to limit the number of times someone could claim benefit of clergy to a single incidence; after that they would be tried in lay courts. To make certain that no one could hide their past conviction in an ecclesiastic court, Henry decreed that those being granted benefit of clergy be branded on the thumb. Upon conviction, the prisoner's thumbs were tightly bound together with cord while a hot iron was pressed against the flesh. As the skin seared and smoked, the torture master declared to the judge: 'A fair mark, my Lord'.

When Henry VII died in 1509 he was succeeded by his son, the much-married Henry VIII. Following in his father's reforming footsteps, the new Henry declared that anyone accused of murder on a public highway or in church could not claim benefit of clergy, thereby making them liable to receive the death penalty. He soon extended these crimes to include all murder, piracy, rape, abduction and sacrilegious acts of all kinds. As Henry aged, his once sunny disposition soured. His protracted war with the Pope, brought about by the Vatican's refusal to grant him a divorce, did nothing to improve his mood and he soon took out his frustrations on his subjects. Punishments of all types became ever more creatively brutal. When a sailor and his common-law wife were accused of stealing a chest of Henry's gold from the hold of a ship, he ordered them to be wrapped in chains and suspended from the Thames embankment; when the tide came in they were slowly engulfed by the rising water.

Three cages hanging ever since the early 1500s from the apse of the cathedral of Munster Germany. It was within these cages that wrongdoers would be left to die of starvation, dehydration and exposure for their perceived crimes. Their public display would have served as a warning to other members of the populace and would also serve to underline the authority, control, and power of the church and city government over the citizens of the city.

The Roman Inquisition burning off the tongue and lips of a dissenter with a red-hot iron.

A guard at the Tower of London who was suspected of complicity in their crime was similarly bundled in chains and hung from the walls of the Tower where he was left to die of exposure.

Vagabonds, hobos and the homeless always bothered Henry. People with too much time on their hands were probably trouble-makers and likely to foment rebellion. The old law prescribing a good whipping for layabouts was amended to include being burned through their right ear with a hot iron, marking them, as well as their crime, for life. A second offence brought them to the hangman's noose. Worse crimes brought such creative sentences as having the tongue ripped out, hands chopped off and – in a move reminiscent of the worst of Roman atrocities – boiling in oil. When the Bishop of Rochester died of food poisoning in 1531, his cook was accused of the crime and boiled alive at London's Smithfield Horse Market without even being allowed to make his last confession. This was one of two such instances that same year.

Not everyone in Henry's government agreed with such harsh measures. Henry's Chief Minister of State, Sir Thomas More, pleaded for less severe laws, but when he openly opposed Henry's separation with the Catholic Church and establishment of the new Church of England, More went to the headsman's block and his proposed reforms died with him. Henry formally established his own religion in 1534 and by 1539 made his power absolute over both Church and State with the Act of Six Articles. Crimes against the Church were now considered crimes against the king; crimes against the king were crimes against God. Henceforth, a person's failure to attend Henry's Church regularly brought a sentence of having their ears cut off. Anyone denying the king's right to decree the word of God could be hanged. Anyone adhering to either traditional Roman Catholicism, or taking up the new Protestant religion would be burned as a heretic. Anyone caught eating meat on Friday, or denying the doctrine of transubstantiation (the belief that the wine and bread used in Holy Communion literally transformed themselves into the body and blood of Christ during the service) would be burned as a heretic. When a merchant named Thomas Sommers was caught in possession of the writings of the German Protestant Martin Luther he was condemned to be stoned to death. Heresy and treason were now the same crime and even being heard to utter a word against King Henry was liable to lead to the torture chamber and the burning stake.

To forestall any possible, organised opposition, Henry spent the years between 1535 and 1539 disassembling the English monastic system and tearing down monasteries. The fact that these religious houses provided the entirety of the kingdom's charity to the poor, all of its hospitals and nearly all of its educational facilities, mattered not to the king. When an army of somewhere between 50,000 and 75,000 common people rose in revolt against the dissolution of the monasteries, Henry became convinced that the Roman Church was out to destroy him. Hundreds were sent to the burning stake, hundreds more were hanged in towns, villages and crossroads across the kingdom, but Henry remained certain that a rebellion was fomenting and the only way to get to the bottom of it was to torture the truth out of everyone who even looked like they might be a closet Catholic or a private Protestant.

The problem with this idea, despite what you have read over the past eight or nine pages, is that torture still remained illegal in England. No

This scene from Johan Coppenburg's *Le Miroir del la tyrannie espagnole perpetree aux Indes Occidentales* (The mirror of Spanish tyranny perpetrated against the Indians in an effort to Christianize them) shows a collection of 'heretics' being burned together in a great conflagration. Remember that this was believed by the executors to be a charitable act of redemption and salvation imposed upon the perceived heathens.

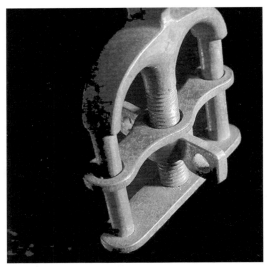

This simple but devilish device shows the functional mechanics of how thumbscrews (and later thumbcuffs) would function. Of course there were many different types and styles and designs, but they all (for the most part) functioned the same … they could be tightened, more and more increasing pressure on the thumbs until such time as the thumbs were completely severed. To get a sense of what this may have been like, we suggest that you use one hand to squeeze the knuckle of your other thumb. … Now imagine that sensation times about a billion … and only ceasing when someone else decides to release you. This sort of empathy for the victims of torture should perhaps not be attempted in every description of this book.

This device (aptly named 'the boot') would slowly crush the bones of the foot. Some devices ground the bones together laterally – others were designed for breaking each bone in turn vertically – this contraption applied increasing amounts of pressure linearly from the heel, crushing first the bones in the toes and then further application would shatter the metatarsals in the feet. Achbishop Gandier was famously subjected to the boot in order to confess his heresies to the Inquisition only to then be forced to 'walk' to his own execution where he would be consigned to the fires of faith. Of course walking after having endured such devastating torture was wholly impossible.

This image (taken by the authors at the museum of medieval torture in Prague, Czech Republic) shows an example of the rack. The victims would be laid on their back on the 'bed' and their ankles would be locked into the restraints while their hands would be stretched up over their head and attached to the rope on the windlass. Spiked rollers would penetrate along the length of the spine and lower back augmenting the agony of having the wrists, elbows, shoulders, hips, knees and ankles systematically dislocated before the separation of the vertebrae of the spine. However, few victims held out long enough for it to reach that stage.

This image shows a synthesis of breaking with and braiding into the wheel. Whether the official on the left is holding a staff of office or a club to be used on the victims is uncertain. If the torturer did his job correctly, the victims would have every major bone in their bodies broken but with no fatal injuries and would then be left in their excruciating condition to slowly die of exposure.

matter how much pain and mutilation was inflicted on an individual, if it was a part of a punishment or death sentence it was not considered torture. Extracting information by means of applied pain, however, was. To circumvent this little glitch in the system, Henry created the Star Chamber, a court which answered to no-one and was not subject to the laws of Parliament nor to the dictates of Common Law. As a result, the thumb screws (which could crush a victim's thumb knuckle), the boot (an iron boot that could crush the ankle bone and was sometimes applied red-hot), the scavenger's daughter (which crushed the body until blood squirted from the nose, mouth, ears and finger tips), and the rack (which pulled a person's limbs until the joints were dislocated) all became common methods of extracting information. Reserved for special prisoners were hell-holes in the Tower known as Little Ease (a cell so small that a man could neither lie down, nor stand up but was forced to remain in a crouched position) and the Dungeon Among the Rats (a cell so filled with rodents and insects that occupants frequently had the flesh eaten from their arms and legs while they slept).

Everywhere, victims of Henry's paranoia were tortured, hanged and burned. Monks, priests and nuns were burnt for their faith as were

Here we see an impaling. The spike has been passed up through the victim's rectum and in this case has emerged out of his chest. If the spike managed to miss the heart, lungs and brain, then the victim could be alive for a considerable amount of time before finally succumbing to their wounds. Some executioners who favoured this method took great pride in their ability to achieve this.

protestant ministers and deacons. Noblemen went to the block or were hanged, drawn and quartered for defying the king's orders to slaughter the common people in ever greater numbers. In one tragic case a boy of fifteen was burnt for repeating snatches of banned liturgy that it would have been nearly impossible for him to understand because they were in Latin. Over the course of Henry VIII's thirty-eight-year reign it is estimated that 72,000 men, women and children were executed. How many more were tortured is impossible to guess.

It would be heartening to say that the England of Henry VIII represented a tragic but isolated instance in the increased use of torture, but such was not the case. Throughout Europe, as religion factionalised and intolerance and fear increased, torture became more prevalent than it had been since the Roman persecution of the Christians more than 1,000 years earlier. Breaking on the wheel was becoming one of the most common means of execution in both France and Germany and for lesser crimes the French now sent men on extended sea cruises

as galley slaves – a practice not employed since the Roman Empire. Half a century earlier, in the Eastern European principality of Walachia (now part of Romania), Prince Vlad III, known alternatively as Dracula (son of the dragon) or Tepes (the impaler) executed local miscreants, recalcitrant noblemen and captured enemy soldiers by impaling them on sharpened poles and using their carcasses as a warning along the border he held against the Turks.

When Henry VIII finally had the good grace to die, his throne was assumed by his son, Edward VI. In addition to ending the religious terror and firmly establishing the Church of England as a Protestant institution, Edward outlawed many of his father's more barbaric punishments, including boiling alive. Would that this reform could have lasted. Sadly, Edward died at the age of fifteen after ruling for slightly less than six years and his place was taken by his eldest sister, Mary, whose enforced reversion of England to the Catholic faith earned her the undying sobriquet 'Bloody Mary'.

Mary's particular brand of faith did credit neither to herself nor the Catholic Church which

she claimed to represent. Everyone who had converted to her father's Church was ordered to re-convert to the Church of Rome or suffer penalties even her monstrous father had never dreamed of. To enforce her draconian laws she selected Edmund Bonner, Bishop of London. Known as 'The Devil's Dancing Bear', Bonner was the sort of man who enjoyed taking his work home with him. In his house he installed a private torture chamber where he could discuss matters with his more reluctant victims. Even in public court, Bonner delighted in torturing witnesses and defendants alike. In one instance, a witness who did not give the answers Bonner wanted to hear had a candle flame held beneath the palm of his hand until the flesh burnt. On another occasion, a witness had his thumbs tied together and a barbed arrow pulled backward between them. The rack was in such constant usage that seldom a day went by when some poor soul was not being disjointed in the basement of the Tower of London. Single punishments were seldom enough to satisfy Bonner. When a Protestant Minister was accused of possessing 'scandalous books [which spoke] against kings, peers and prelates', Bonner had him severely whipped before being locked into the pillory where one ear was cut off and one side of his nose was split with a knife. He was then branded on one cheek

This image depicts a Swiss version of the pillory. The result is the same. Note how the figures on the right-hand side of the image are selecting stones to throw at the culprit. And while the image does not show his wrists bound and thereby incapable of self-defense, it appears as though the entire pillory is designed to spin which may make for additional sport for the outraged public.

with a red-hot iron. A week later he was returned to the pillory to be whipped until his back looked like half-digested meat, the remaining ear was hacked off, the other side of his nose split and the other cheek branded. Obviously the man had said something to offend the Devil's Dancing Bear. In most cases, a turn at Bonner's pillory consisted of little more than the usual public humiliation – with the exception that the victim's ears tended to be nailed to the wooden back-board. When their stretch in the pillory was over, their ears were either ripped free or cut loose with a knife.

Precisely how many people died for the sin of holding fast to their faith during Bloody Mary's five years on the throne is unknown. What is known is that in London alone, between 1553 and 1558, 113 men, women and children were consigned to the flames; eighty-nine of them sent there by Bishop Edmund Bonner. For his part in this crime spree, when Mary's sister Elizabeth assumed the throne in 1558, she sent the former bishop to the Tower where he spent the ten years until his death contemplating his sins.

When compared with the rest of her family, Elizabeth I had an amazingly enlightened outlook on how she intended to govern her kingdom. In a land exhausted by three decades of religious turmoil her first task was, obviously, to heal the festering wounds of fanaticism. In her maiden speech to Parliament, Elizabeth said: 'There is one God and one Christ Jesus, and all the rest is a dispute over petty trifles'. Although she reverted England to the Protestant religion established by her brother, Edward, and imposed a tax on Catholics, she would not allow them to be persecuted. In an honest, and startlingly progressive, move to deal with the poverty brought on by her father's decimation of the country and the Wars of the Roses of the previous century, she established work houses for the poor, hospitals for the ill and extended and improved the prison system. None of this is to imply that she did away with either torture or plentiful executions. Indeed, torture to collect information probably reached its height during her reign and the annual number of executions hovered around 800 per year when Elizabeth assumed the throne and climbed steadily throughout her reign. Elizabeth might well have reversed this trend despite the fact that her Privy Council, and particularly her spy master, Sir Francis Walsingham, used torture as a routine method of discovering desirable information. She might have reversed the trend, that is, had it not been for one thing: her meddlesome cousin, Mary Stuart, Queen of Scotland.

Mary, herself, was more French than Scot. Her mother was French and Mary was the widow of a French king and only returned to

Here we witness a victim who has been staked out and is about to be broken on the wheel. Further torments undoubtedly await this unfortunate wretch.

Scotland following her husband's death. After the glories and grandeur of the French court, Scotland must have come as something of a shock. Hard, cold and unforgiving, Scotland bred people as tough as its climate. Brutal tortures were routine in Scotland. Thieves and forgers had their hands struck off, branding on the hands, face and body were common and whippings and scourgings were carried out for the smallest offences.

One of the more decorative forms of execution popular in Scotland (as it was in France and Germany) was being 'broken on the wheel'. The wheel in question was not the elaborate drum used by the Romans, but a simple cart wheel. The condemned was tied, spread eagle, to the wheel and his limbs and joints were then smashed with a mallet or an iron bar. Next, great pieces of flesh were torn from his body with red-hot pliers and only then was his head struck off with an ax. All of this, combined with the religious fanaticism of John Knox, head of the Scottish Presbyterian Church who openly referred to the new queen as a 'bloody Catholic whore', made Mary feel a little uncomfortable. All she wanted was a nice, relatively civilised country to rule – preferably one that was Catholic, or one that she could convert to Catholicism. England seemed an ideal choice. Escaping across the Scots/English border, Mary demanded that her cousin Elizabeth provide her with political refuge. Being no fool, Elizabeth complied, but the sanctuary came with a price – perpetual imprisonment. Both Elizabeth and her Privy Council knew that Mary, like her mother, Marie de Guise, was an inveterate plotter and England was full of ardent

Catholics who would have loved to see the kingdom revert to the Church of Rome.

Elizabeth's advisors and Spy Master, Sir Francis Walsingham, begged the Queen to have Mary executed. For seventeen years they begged her, but Elizabeth had no intention of being the first monarch in modern history to order the death of another. At least not until the late summer of 1586 when Walsingham informed his queen that he had uncovered a plot by Sir Anthony Babington, a high-born English Catholic, wherein Mary had agreed to Babington's suggestion that he and his friends kidnap and murder Elizabeth and put Mary on the throne. There is little doubt that Walsingham had carefully amended Mary's letter to make her seem more complicit than she actually was, but in the world of political manoeuvring it is results that count. Elizabeth went into the kind of rage that seems to characterise a Tudor monarch. In a letter to Walsingham, she wrote: 'In such cases there is no middle course, we must lay aside clemency and adopt extreme measures. If they shall not seem to you to confess plainly their knowledge, then we warrant you cause them to be brought to the rack and first to move them with fear thereof ... Then, should the sight of the instrument not induce them to confess, you shall cause them to be put to the rack and to find the taste thereof ... until you shall see fit'. Mary was hustled into seclusion and

Before being put to 'the question' the victim would be shown the various tools of their destruction. This was known as questioning in the first degree. The sight of these horrific implements and the ability of the victim's imagination to picture their use would often be enough to elicit any cooperation that the torturers required.

's-Gravenhage
Gevangenpoort. Gruwelkamer
(Instruments of torture)

Babington and fifteen co-conspirators were hauled to the Tower. Two were released because they were actually Walsingham's spies but the remaining fourteen were found guilty of high treason and sentenced to be hanged, drawn and quartered.

It may be an indication of the changing times that these were the first such gruesome judicial killings to be ordered during the twenty-eight years Elizabeth had so-far spent on the throne. On 20 September 1586, Babington and six of his companions were publicly executed in the manner proscribed, each one watching the others being hacked open, gutted and chopped to pieces before their own turn came. The public reaction to this grim spectacle is marginally reassuring: the crowd was appalled at the brutality of the entire affair. So was Elizabeth. The following day the remaining seven traitors were simply hanged in public. It was the last time anyone would be hanged, drawn and quartered in Great Britain. The following February Mary Queen of Scots was beheaded inside the walls of Fotheringay Castle. No members of the public were permitted entrance.

The Babington plotters and the Scottish Queen were not the only ones to suffer under Queen Elizabeth I. Throughout her reign, the rack, the gibbet and the noose seldom stood idle and petty offenders of every type were persecuted mercilessly. Cutpurses or pick-pockets lost an ear for a first conviction, the other ear for the second, and when they ran out of ears they were hanged. Prostitutes, too, lost one ear at a time and a third offence meant the loss of their nose.

In 1584, only two years prior to the discovery of the Babington plot to assassinate Queen Elizabeth, a more successful attempt was made on the life of Prince William of Orange, ruler of the Netherlands. William had just successfully ousted the Spanish who had held the Dutch as virtual political and religious vassals since the beginning of the century and, in the process, made himself one of the most popular rulers in Europe. Woe-betide then, Balthazar Gerard, a fanatical Catholic, who murdered Prince William in 1584. Seized by an enraged mob even before the local guard could arrive, Gerard was beaten half to death, had salt rubbed into his cuts and wounds and wrapped in a cloak soaked in vinegar and brandy before he could be rescued and hustled off to a prison. Over the ensuing eighteen days Gerard was tortured and racked mercilessly, this punishment commencing when he was hauled onto a public scaffold only to have the hand which had struck the fatal blow thrust into a cauldron of boiling oil. Amazingly, Gerard never showed any sign of experiencing pain. The following day he was returned to the scaffold only to have the hand chopped off. Again,

Gerard remained so calm that his only reaction was to kick his severed limb off the platform. For the next eleven days Gerard was publicly mutilated, the skin ripped, piece by piece from his body, with red-hot pliers. On the eighteenth day he was tied to a burning stake but instead of letting the flames do their work, after a few minutes the fire was doused and Gerard was cut down – his flesh charred and blackened – only to be broken on the wheel, slowly, over the next six hours. Finally he was strangled to death.

It would be nice to say that this episode ended both judicial brutality and religious conflict in Europe. The fact is, however, that at this time, and for centuries both earlier and later, religious intolerance was one of the biggest businesses in Europe; particularly in Spain, where the Holy Office of the Inquisition did its mighty best to purge the world of anyone who would not submit to its authority.

What has become known as The Inquisition did not begin in Spain, nor was it intended as an instrument of religious and social terror. The word 'inquisition' simply means an official, judiciary inquiry; in this instance, an inquiry by the Roman Catholic Church into possible instances of heretical activity. As late as 1139 the only punishment sanctioned by the Church for such activities was excommunication, and it is unlikely that excommunication would have held much weight for die-hard heretics. There were instances where secular authorities, or mobs of angry Christians, killed suspected heretics but such activities were as likely to be as roundly condemned by the Church as was heresy itself. In fact, even as respected an authority as St Bernard of Clairvaux (1090–1153) said: 'Faith is to be produced by persuasion, not imposed by force'. Somehow, this tolerant attitude began to disappear shortly after St Bernard's death.

In 1198, Pope Innocent III began exhorting his flock to seek out and destroy heretics on the grounds that heresy was as much a crime against God as treason was against the State. He did not, however, suggest that the Church should become involved in such activities; that did not take place until 1229 when Pope Gregory IX proposed the formation of a body of monks, learned in heretical matters, which he called the *Inquisitores haereticae pravitatis*, or Private Investigators of Heresy. Four years later, Gregory sent out letters to bishops in France informing them of the inquisition's existence and urging them to cooperate with its work. Even at

This is the sort of 'rosary' as worn by penitents and recalcitrant sinners. Whether voluntarily adorned as a demonstration of faith or prescribed as penance for some perceived sin, this would have been worn while on pilgrimage or in a religious procession. Note the spiked chain which would have supported its weight about the neck of the devotee.

this point, however, the inquisitors had no intention – and indeed, no authority – to inflict physical damage on convicted heretics.

Standard punishments included such humiliating penances as being forced to go on pilgrimage to a holy site or having the image of a cross sewn onto one's gown. As soon as the condemned had recanted their sins and done appropriate penance, the stigma was rescinded and they were reunited with the Church. Only in those rare cases when the heretic refused to acknowledge the error of their ways, or when they insisted on repeating their heresies (estimated as something less than 10 per cent of those convicted on such charges) were they handed over to secular authorities for judicial trial and punishment. Even among the educated Franciscans and Dominicans who formed the new inquisitional tribunals, the question of just what constituted a punishable heresy and how severe the penance, or the recommended secular punishment, should be was a matter of great debate. Enter Bernardo Gui.

Gui (chillingly portrayed in the film *Name of the Rose* by F. Murray Abraham) was a Dominican monk and inquisitor who, between 1307 and 1324, passed sentence on upward of 1,000 accused heretics and detailed his methods of examination in a 394-page tome entitled 'The Conduct of Inquiry Concerning Heretical Depravity'. The book is divided into five chapters, the first three of which deal with procedural matters such as interrogation of prisoners and how the tribunal should be organised. The fourth is a recapping of relevant papal proclamations defining the inquisitor's powers and the final chapter deals with what, precisely, constituted heresy at that time – at least according to Bernardo Gui. The most interesting thing about this early ecclesiastical bestseller is the way in which the inquisitorial panel is taught how to phrase the questions they put to suspected heretics. As any good trial lawyer today knows, a witness should never be allowed to get the upper hand. Questions should be designed so even one false word can make the innocent look guilty and confusion is paramount in keeping the witness off balance. This one book, as much as any other single factor, set the tone for inquisitions to come.

While Gui was just beginning to toil away on his book, Pope Clement V was ordering the arrest and trial of the Knights Templars on charges of heresy – mostly because they were too rich and too powerful for the comfort of either the Church or the King of France. While King Philip IV of France (known as Philip the Fair), who owed a lot of money to the Templars, was arresting, torturing and burning Templars in an orgy of destruction, King Edward II of England took a more reasonable approach – he refused to cooperate. The Pope was having none of it and sent a letter to Edward in which he said: 'We hear that you forbid torture as contrary to the laws of your land; but no state can override Canon Law, Our Law; therefore I command you at once to submit these men to torture.' Ominously, the Holy Father added: 'You have already imperiled your soul as a favourer of heretics.' Reluctantly, Edward caved in and ordered the arrest of English Templars, but managed to give most of them ample warning and time to escape to the safety of Scotland.

By 1401, three-quarters of a century after the destruction of the Templars, the burning of heretics had become legalised in England and an international pattern for inquisitional justice had taken shape. Suspected heretics were arrested by Church authorities and subjected to questioning by secular authorities: the Church still wanted to keep its hands clean of causing physical harm to anyone. The procedure was eminently simple. When found guilty of heresy, the head of the ecclesiastic court sentenced the condemned by saying: 'Since the church can do nothing with a heretic of your stamp, we do hereby abandon you to the secular courts; recommending them nevertheless, as strongly as we may, according to the prescription of Canon Law, to preserve your life and limbs from the perils of death ...' Then came the clincher: 'so long as you fully admit the charge of heresy laid against you.' There could be no doubt that the accused would eventually confess; if they did not, they would be tortured until they did.

When the suspect had 'freely' confessed their sin, they were sent back to the Church for an ecclesiastical trial, but the Church still had no power to inflict any punishment greater than excommunication. Once convicted of heresy, however, the condemned was again passed back to secular authorities where they would be tried again and (unless the court wanted to risk the wrath of Rome) end their lives tied to a stake with a pile of brushwood heaped around their feet.

The institution of the burning post as the most popular means of dispatching unwanted heretics came about as the

Here we see heretics being executed at an auto da fe by the Spanish inquisition. Two naked men supported on iron spikes have been or are about to be garroted, while two other heretics wearing robes and hats which indicate their offences are led away for their own executions or punishments.

result of a legal opinion written by an Italian jurist named Bartolus of Sassoferrato (1313–57). According to Sassoferrato, this unspeakable death was sanctioned by Christ, Himself, in the Gospel of John. In John 15:16 are the words: 'If a man abide not in me he is cast forth as a branch, and is withered; and men gather them and cast them into the fires and they are burned'. The mind-set that allows Jesus' parable of comparing non-believers to brushwood to be taken so literally is beyond modern comprehension, but the Holy Office of the Inquisition seemed all too pleased to adopt it. If nothing else, it certainly drove home the point that failure to submit to official dogma would not be tolerated under any circumstances. Whether it increased church attendance is unknown, but there is no question that it put people everywhere in fear of their lives and their immortal souls. As the penalties for (and fear of) opposing the Inquisition spread across Europe, an ever greater variety of applications were found for the heresy laws – particularly in multicultural Spain.

During the High Middle ages, Spain was a fractured, polyglot society peppered with numerous small states, competing monarchs and peoples of many races and religions. Beginning in the early eighth century, much of Spain had come under the control of the Moors – Moroccans who followed the Islamic faith. Immediately, the Christian Spanish began to fight back, but it was not until 1492, when the city of Granada was reclaimed, that the Moors were finally defeated. During their more than seven centuries of occupation, the Moors had welcomed a large influx of Jews into their Spanish territories, adding to the complex cultural mix of the country. As the Moors were slowly driven from power they and the Jewish population were either expelled or forced to convert to Christianity. Naturally there was always the sneaking fear that they only pretended to convert and were really practicing their various religions in secret. Anxious to complete the process of cleansing their country of all those 'foreigners', as early as 1478 dual-monarchs Ferdinand and Isabella (the same ones who funded Christopher Columbus) asked Pope Sixtus IV to allow them to establish their own, home-grown, version of the Inquisition. The suggestion was probably Isabella's and had most likely originated with her personal confessor, a fanatically xenophobic Dominican monk named Thomas de Torquemada. Bowing to the pious monarchs' request, and the recommendations of Torquemada and the Archbishop of Seville, the Pope issued the necessary Papal Bull. The Spanish Inquisition had commenced and Thomas de Torquemada was placed at its head.

Although the primary targets for this long-lasting reign of terror were the *Conversos* and *Moriscos* (Jews and Islamic Moors respectively) who had converted to Christianity, included on the 'enemies list' were unconverted Jews and Moors, Freemasons, Catholic heretics and members of emerging non-Catholic Christian sects grouped together under the catch-all title 'Protestants'. To increase the efficiency of the persecution, the populace was encouraged to cooperate with the authorities by denouncing suspects, be they neighbours, friends or family members. Once a person had been denounced the procedure never varied. The evidence, no matter how slim, was examined by an inquisitorial panel who would decide if there was sufficient evidence for an arrest ... there almost invariably was. To keep the accusers conveniently free from public condemnation or having to explain their accusations, their names, like every other step in the inquisitorial process, were kept secret.

When an arrest order had been issued, a group of Inquisitors, priests, commissioners and heavily armed soldiers went to the suspect's house – always in the middle of the night. If the suspect resisted arrest in any way they were bound and gagged by having a metal, pear-shaped object inserted into their mouth. A small crank on the small end of the 'pear' was turned, expanding the device until it wrenched open the jaw, often breaking teeth and sometimes dislocating the jawbone. Once the suspect was safely locked in an inquisitorial dungeon, their

Without going in to too much graphic detail, these devices were inserted into the mouth, vagina or anus and then opened wider and wider to stretch and tear the tissues (or in the case of the mouth, breaking the teeth and jaw). We have inspected several examples of this type and all have invariably been extremely well made and almost artistic in their construction. These are not mere implements of pain from some dark age torture chamber. The individuals who had these constructed were men who took pride and pleasure in inflicting torture upon their victims.

property was confiscated on the grounds that it would be used to pay for their upkeep in prison and the cost of their questioning and trial.

The accused were, of course, free to confess their guilt prior to being tortured but since they often had no idea what they had been accused of, it was nearly impossible either to confess or deny the charges and attempt to defend themselves. Following the initial questioning, the victim was hauled to an underground room, often draped in black, where an official inquisitor, along with an 'inspector' and a secretary were seated at a table at one end of the room. Also present was a torture master dressed all in black, with only his eyes exposed. Nearby lay an array of the diabolical tools of his trade. What all those present knew that the prisoner did not, was that there were five distinct phases of torture. First, the prisoner was threatened with torture; second, he was shown the implements of torture; third, he was stripped and blindfolded; fourth, he was tortured and, finally, given another chance to confess. If they still insisted on their innocence the fourth and fifth steps would be repeated indefinitely, until he or she either talked or died. This process was administered without distinction to age, sex or social condition and the methods of torture used were completely random, being limited only by the whim of the inquisitor, the inspector and the type of equipment available.

Even when elaborate torture equipment was lacking, the inquisitor was happy to make do with those old standbys, the whip and a length of rope. Just how common inquisitional floggings were is revealed in the writings of a Portuguese chronicler:

> Should anyone commit a fault he is flogged in a most cruel manner. They strip him naked and lay him on the ground with his face downward, and in this position he is held by several men while others flog him most unmercifully with cords stiffened by being dipped in melted pitch, which brings away flesh at every stroke, until the back is one large ulcer.

In one such case, a fourteen-year-old boy was simply whipped to death for indeterminate reasons. In another instance, a woman was savagely whipped for having been heard to say: 'I do not know whether the pope is a man or a woman, but I hear wonderful things of him every day ...' Six days later she died from her wounds. When a Portuguese jeweller was arrested on suspicion of being a Freemason, he was subjected to an amazing array of tortures. The following is his own account of the experience:

> [After] strip[ing] me naked ... they put round my neck an iron collar ... then they fixed a ring to each foot, and ... they stretched my limbs with all their might. They next tied two ropes ... which were the size of one's little finger ... round each arm and two round each thigh, which ropes passed through holes in a scaffold; and were all drawn tight at the same time by four men. [The

These interrogation chairs are basic to the art of the inquisitor. In the modern world updated versions are used, and have been made even more effective through the use of electricity.

The effect of the spikes – even non-electrified ones – on the victim, who is always naked, is obvious and requires no detailed explanation. He or she suffers horribly from the first instant of the questioning, a procedure that can be heightened by rocking them or striking the limbs or through the application of weight or pressure.

The image here on the right and the one on the preceding page depict acts of evisceration (disembowlment). The victim is staked out on his back alive and fully conscious. A small cut is then made in the lower abdomen or stomach and his entrails are wound up onto the windlass. This horrifying process would be done slowly and carefully so as to prolong the execution as long as possible before the victim eventually died. It is a type of punishment which seems to have been common to several early Christian Martyrs.

There are two basic types of the legendary garrotte. The first type is the Spanish garrotte, in which the screw draws back the iron collar, strangling the victim and killing him through the process of asphyxiation. The second type is the Catalonian garrotte which differs in that it has an iron point which penetrates and crushes the cervical vertebrae whilst at the same time forcing the entire neck forward and crushing the trachea against the fixed collar, thus killing by both asphyxiation and slow destruction of the spinal cord. The agony could, therefore be prolonged according to the executioner's whims. It must be remembered that the garrotte was a public spectacle and crowds could be unsatisfied by quick executions.

It is worth noting that there were variations in the functional mechanism at work in these devices. In some cases, the iron band around the throat was drawn back with the screw. In other cases, the iron spike at the back of the neck would be screwed forward. And in still other cases, the band would contract while the spike simultaneously bored forward.

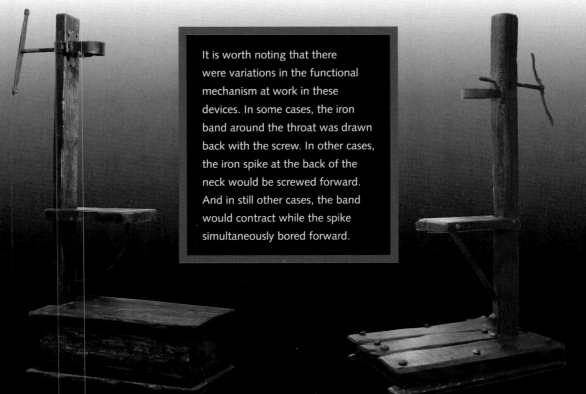

The history of torture records many devices that worked on the principle of anthropomorphic containers with double doors, fitted with spikes on the inside that pierced the victim contained within. The most famous example has always been the so-called 'Iron Maiden of Nuremberg', which was reportedly destroyed in the air raids of 1944.

It is difficult to separate legend from fact concerning this contraption because most published material is based on nineteenth century research distorted by romanticism and fanciful popular tradition. The first reference to an execution with the Iron Maiden is on 14 August 1515, although the device had supposedly been in use for decades by then. On that day a coin forger was put inside the Maiden and the doors shut 'slowly, so that the very sharp points pierced his arms, and his legs in several places, and his belly and his chest, and his bladder and the root of his member, and his eyes and his shoulders, and his buttocks, but not enough to kill him; and so he remained making great cry and lament *(gross Geschrey and Wehklag)* for two days, after which he died'. It is likely that the spikes were moveable among various sockets so as to be more or less lethal or mutilating according to the stature of the victim and the requirements of the sentence.

Investigative torture fell slowly into disuse in Germany with the passing of the eighteenth century, so that a tourist guide of 1784 speaks of 'the Iron Maiden, that abominable work, of horror that goes back to the times of Frederick Barbarossa', (an error of nearly four centuries, but one that showed the Maiden had already been relegated to the museum). Nevertheless, in 1788 sentences of drawing-and-quartering, breaking on the wheel and cutting off of tongues and hands were still being carried out in Nuremberg.

Appearing disturbingly like an over-sized baby's cradle or bassinet, the Pass was a large, rectangular wooden box with rockers affixed to the bottom. The interior surfaces of the 'cradle' were set with sharpened iron spikes; when the victim had been stripped naked and lowered into the Pass, it would be 'rocked' violently back and forth. The results of which seem too self-evident to require further detailed description.

It is worth noting, however, the presence of the 'spiked pillow' within this device. Obviously this would not have afforded the victim any comfort whatsoever and may even be the product of a vicious and twisted sense of humour.

The Pillory is a form of torture similar to stocks. The victim's head and/or limbs were locked in place, leaving them both helpless and defenceless. This device could be fixed solidly to any immovable object, or could be worn freely (as in the case of the Chinese Cangue), or perhaps tethered to a stationary point. In addition to the public humiliation the victim had to endure, they were commonly assaulted, molested and abused by members of the passing populace. Anyone sentenced to be pilloried was fair game as an open target to one and all unless loyal friends or family stepped forward to protect them.

After hanging, 'breaking with the wheel' was the most common means of execution throughout Germanic Europe from the early Middle Ages to the beginning of the eighteenth century. The victim, naked, was stretched out supine on the ground with his or her limbs spread and tied. Crosspieces were placed under the wrists, elbows, ankles, knees and hips. The executioner then smashed limb after limb and joint after joint, including the shoulders and the hips, using the iron edged wheel, being careful to avoid fatal blows. The victim was transformed, according to the observations of a seventeenth-century chronicler, 'into a sort of huge screaming puppet with four tentacles, like a sea monster, of raw, slimy and shapeless flesh mixed up with splinters of smashed bones'. Then the shattered limbs were 'braided' into the spokes of the wheel, and the victim hoisted up horizontally to the top of a pole, where they were left for the birds and exposure to the elements to slowly perish. Death came after a long and atrocious agony. This method of execution seems to have been a popular spectacle in medieval Europe.

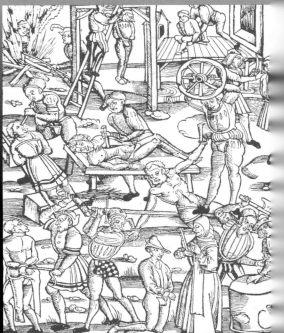

Although forever associated in the cultural imagination with the French Revolution, devices which mechanically decapitate by means of a falling blade existed long before the birth of Dr Joseph Guillotin. Primitive ancestors of the guillotine were used in Ireland, England and Italy in the fourteenth and fifteenth centuries. Several known decapitation devices, such as the Italian Mannaia, the Scottish Maiden and the Halifax Gibbet are well documented and pre-date the use of the French guillotine by as much as 500 years.

At the bottom of the page is an image depicting one of these early ancestors of the guillotine, known as a Fallbrett (literally, a 'falling board'). In this instance, there is no sharpened (or even metal) blade to sever the head from the body in one swift stroke, but rather this device is simply constructed of planks of solid oak. Here it is the blunt edge of the wood alone which rips and chews the flesh and vertebrae under the impact of the sledge blows. Presumably by breaking the neck on the first blow the victim would be spared a prolonged and tortuous death, though that would be rather uncertain. It is of course possible, that a broken neck may simply result in paralysis rather than death and so the victim woud have to suffer through the entire ordeal as the executioner wielded sledge blow after sledge blow.

When one thinks of torture by stretching, this device – known by many names, but most commonly referred to as the rack – springs immediately to mind.

When 'racked' the victim is literally 'prolonged' by force of the winch, and various sources testify to cases of thirty ems or twelve inches! This inconceivable length comes of the dislocation and extrusion of every joint in the arms and legs, of the dismemberment of the spinal column, and of course of the ripping and detachment of the muscles of the limbs, thorax and abdomen – effects that are, needless to say, somewhat fatal.

But long before the victim is brought to the final undoing, he or she, often in the 'Question of the first degree' suffers dislocation of the shoulders because his arms are pulled up behind his back, as well as the agony of muscles ripping like any fibre subjected to excessive stress. In the 'Question of the second degree', the knee, hip and elbow joints begin to be forced out of their sockets; with the 'third degree' they separate, very audibly. After only the second degree, the victim is maimed for life; after the third he is dismembered and paralysed and gradually, over hours and days, the life functions cease one by one.

This example has spiked rollers, which is a refinement that is more of an exception than a rule.

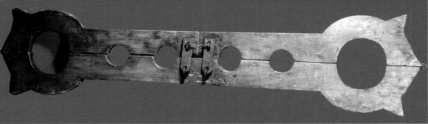

The Shrew's Fiddle, or *Halsgiege* (neck-violin) is akin to other devices meant to humiliate and torture a person. The head went through the larger hole with the wrists clamped within the two smaller holes. In this way the victim could be easily directed and pulled along. Some examples were chained together near the 'neck' of the violin, still others consisted of one long 'standing pillory' of two fiddles joined neck to neck by a solid piece of wood.

An iron version was widely used during the years of slavery in the United States until its abolition in 1865.

(See also: stocks; pillory; drunkard's cloak; brank; noisemaker's fife, masks of shame or infamy; and the Chinese Cangue)

This device is known as the noise-maker's fife or flute. A variety of instruments of this form (trumpet, trombone, oboe and recorder made of wood or brass or iron) are known to have existed in the sixteenth–seventeenth centuries – though earlier and later representations can be found. The iron collar was locked around the victim's neck, and his or her fingers, posed like those of a playing musician's under notches in the long vice, were squeezed with a force varying from uncomfortable to unbearable.

This was essentially a form of pillory *(see also pilliwinkes)*, of exposure to public ridicule, with all the customary painful and sometimes fatal consequences that marked the fate of all those treated in this manner. It was inflicted for relatively minor crimes and sins such as disturbing the peace. In Italy, it was often meted out to those guilty of *baldoria e baccano* – 'revelry and din' – in front of a church during holy functions. The term *'piffero del baccanaro'* or 'noise-maker's fife', appears in several eighteenth-century Bolognese documents.

The horrific procedure of torture by means of the Judas Cradle has remained essentially unchanged from the Middle Ages to the present day. The victim is hoisted up in the manner shown in the illustration (opposite below), and lowered onto the point of the pyramid in such a way that his or her weight rests on the sharpened point. This point would be positioned at the anus, in the vagina, beneath the scrotum or under the coccyx.

The torturer could then, according to the pleasure of the interrogators, vary the pressure from zero or that of total body weight (or even greater through the addition of weights). The victim could furthermore be rocked or made to fall repeatedly onto the point. And, of course, they could be left in this 'perched' position for indefinite periods of time.

The Judas cradle was also known as *culla di Giuda* in Italian and *Judaswiege* in German, but in French it was referred to as *la veille*, 'the wake' or 'nightwatch' (this presumably because victims would be left in this precarious suspended anguish overnight). In the modern world, this method of torture and interrogation has been known to be used in Latin America (and elsewhere) both with and without 'improvements' such as electrified waist rings and bladed 'points' to the apex of the pyramid.

A staple, in one variation or another, of any respectable torture chamber. A deviously simple design which delivered the requisite amount of pain to any victim unlucky enough to be seated within, the chair was of a sturdy wooden construction strategically embedded with up to 2,000 metal spikes.

The victim, always naked, was strapped within the chair using tight leather straps, wooden braces, and/or metal cuffs. The initial pain of hundreds of sharp rusty spikes penetrating the flesh could always be increased by the torturer forcibly pressing the prisoner down and back against the spikes. Variations (without spikes) were used to bind the victim so that the torturer could easily baste his or her feet with lard or oil heated by nearby braziers.

Often, the 'seat' would be made of metal so that a fire could be lit beneath with obvious painful consequence. Note also in the image above left, the presence of the spiked plank designed to be tightened against the shins forcing the calves tight against the spikes of the frame. And of the second plank designed to rest beneath the soles of the victim's bare feet.

A modern 'improvement' features systematically sending an electric current through the chair.

These images depict various military punishments inflicted on soldiers for various transgressions as a means of maintaining discipline.

In the field, summary punishments were unusually preferred to more formal legal proceedings. Facilities for imprisonment were limited, and every convicted soldier removed from active service placed an added burden on the rest of the troops in the company.

Field Punishment Number 1 consisted of the convicted man being shackled in irons and secured to a fixed object, often a gun wheel or similar. He could only be thus fixed for up to two hours in twenty-four, and not for more than three days in four, or for more than twenty-one days in his sentence. This punishment was often known as 'crucifixion' and due to its humiliating nature was viewed by many soldiers as unfair.

Field Punishment Number 2 was similar except the man was shackled but not fixed to anything. Both forms were carried out by the office of the Provost-Marshal, unless his unit was officially on the move when it would be carried out regimentally i.e. by his own unit.

ESCLAVES CHRETIENS

Enterrés

Empalés

Brûlés

Sié's

Ecorché's

Falaca ou Bastonnade

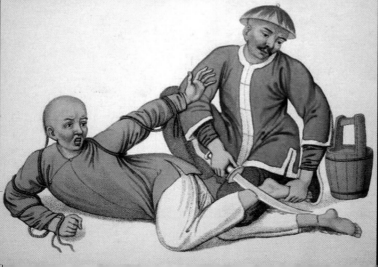

In the left-hand image we see an illustration depicting savage tortures used by 'primitive peoples'. This illustration is typical of the sorts of propaganda which underlined and supported the expansive policies of colonisation espoused by Europeans from the sixteenth–nineteenth centuries. Ironically, the tortures depicted as evidence of 'savagery' were each readily identifiable in Europe as well. We see the torture of the saw, of impalement, of burning at the stake, or burying alive, of cutting off ears or tongues and of bastinado (caning of the feet).

Below we see one of the many forms of torture and punishment which were commonplace in the Orient. In this case we see an instance of 'hobbling' whereby the achilles tendons of a victim are severed so he cannot walk or even stand. This sort of punishment was probably imposed on slaves who attempted to run away (though of what use a recaptured slave who is incapable of standing would be is uncertain).

Here we see the 'inquisition chair' (sometimes referred to as the 'witches chair' or the 'interrogation chair' or even simply as 'the throne'). Its function should be clear from the image. Consider first, however, that it is made to appear frightening – as the first stage of torture was to show the victim the instruments of their destruction in the hope that the sight alone might persuade them to confess. While it would have undoubtedly been a painful place to sit, the real agony of the device lies in the spiked board which would be tightened down on the victims thighs (above the seat) and across their shins (on the front). Note also the sockets on the side of the chair through which bars could be threaded so that the entire piece could be transported like a sedan chair – perhaps even displayed to the populace. Naturally once the victim was strapped and clamped into the seat other even more diabolical tortures could (and probably would) be applied to them.

ropes] pierced through my flesh quite to the bone, making the blood gush ... Finding that the tortures ... could not extort any discovery from me ... six weeks after [they] expos[ed] me to another kind of torture. They made me stretch my arms in such a manner that the palms of my hands were turned outward; when by the help of a rope that fastened them together at the wrists, which they turned by an engine, they drew them nearer to one another behind [me] in such a manner that the back of each

Here we see two men being racked. One of them is being racked by the ladder (which we shall discuss later in the book) and the other is being racked on a table while being subjected to the torture of the funnel. A thorough description of the use of this commonplace, yet devious, device can be found in the main body of the text. The torturer operating the rack pulley seems poised to burn the victim's stomach with a flaming torch. Also note the pulley in the centre of the room which awaits these two unfortunate souls should their current torments not elicit the desired results.

hand touched ... whereby my shoulders were dislocated and blood issued from my mouth.

When Jewish physician, Isaac Orobio was arrested, he lingered for three years in an inquisitional dungeon before they got around to questioning him. When they did, Orobio first had his thumbs tied together with fine cord which was pulled so tight that blood spurted from beneath his thumbnails. Having thus gotten the poor man's attention, the torturers next slammed him against a wall and sat him on a narrow bench. Attached to the wall were several pulleys with ropes hanging from them. His arms, hands, legs and feet were thrust through the ropes, which were then pulled as tight as possible; the bench was then pulled from beneath him, leaving the weight of Orobio's body suspended by the ropes alone.

When an Englishman named William Lithgow was arrested on suspicion of being a spy, he was subjected to one of the Spanish Inquisition's most popular tortures in which the victim had their mouth forced open and a funnel pushed down their throat. Water was then poured into the funnel until the stomach nearly burst, the throat filled and water gushed from their mouth and nose. In this condition Lithgow was prevented from vomiting by having a noose tied around his throat; then he was rolled back and forth across the floor of the dungeon. When he was nearly unconscious, ropes were tied around

his big toes and he was hoisted, feet first, into the air. At his point the rope was removed from his throat and he was allowed to vomit out the water while hanging upside down. He was then manacled and returned to his cell.

Inevitably, word of such horrific goings-on filtered back to Rome and the Pope. Sixtus was outraged, and sent a letter to King Ferdinand.

> Many true and faithful Christians, because of the testimony of enemies, rivals, slaves and other low people – and still less appropriate – without tests of any kind, have been locked up in secular prisons, tortured and condemned like relapsed heretics, deprived of their goods and properties, and given over to the secular arm to be executed, at great danger to their souls, giving a pernicious example and causing scandal to many.

Ferdinand applied political pressure on His Holiness, the Pope relented, and the inquisition continued its deranged crusade against evil-doers.

One of the inquisition's favourite forms of torture was known as the *garrucha* – the torture of the pulley. In this exercise in pain, the victim's hands were tied behind their back and a rope run from their wrists through a pulley suspended from the ceiling. When the rope was hauled in the prisoner was lifted into the air as their shoulder joints were slowly dislocated. After being left to swing for an appropriate spell, the rope could either be released all at once, sending the prisoner crashing to the ground, or only a few feet at a time, jerking again and again at the arm sockets. If this failed to elicit the desired response, the entire exercise would be repeated with a heavy stone tied to the prisoner's feet.

Occasionally, the outside world got an inadvertent peek into the inner workings of the Inquisition. When a goldsmith named Lawrence Castro went to the house of inquisitor Don Pedro Guerrero, he was invited on a tour of the good Don's house, a part of which included the inquisitorial chambers. In the cellars, Castro passed one iron-bound door after another, hearing the muffled screams and moans of the prisoners beyond. When he was about to leave, Don Pedro asked him how he had liked the house; Castro replied that from what he had seen and heard it seemed like the mouth of hell. That was offence enough. For insulting the Holy Inquisition, Castro lost all his property, was whipped through the streets, branded on the shoulders and condemned to be worked to death as a galley slave.

The victim's wrists are tied behind his back, a rope is attached to the wrist restraints and the sufferer is hoisted up high. At once each humerus is pried out of its joint with the scapula and clavicle, an injury that results in horrendous and permanent deformations of the breast and back. The agony can be heightened by means of weights (such as the one shown here) progressively attached to the feet, until at last the skeleton is pulled apart as it is by the bench and ladder racks. The victim is finally paralysed, and dies.

Although most of the inquisitional tortures we have examined so far were unimaginably painful, the instruments of torture were fairly mundane. On occasion, as time and money allowed, the inquisition came up with some of the most complex and grotesque torture devices imaginable. There is an account of a device much like a giant drum into which a prisoner could be shoved. The inside of the drum was fixed with chunks of razor-sharp iron which would, when the drum was rotated, flay the hide from the victim.

There are reports of giant roasting pans into which hapless victims would be thrown before being slid into an oven and roasted like a side of beef. Such roasting might also be limited to certain parts of the body. In a torture known as the 'Spanish Chair', the victim was strapped to a chair while their feet were locked in a pair of stocks, next to which stood a red-hot brazier. To keep the poor wretch's feet from burning too fast, they were constantly basted with grease. There was, of course, always the old reliable rack for separating a person from both their information and limbs, but next to these more creative punishments the rack seems mundane.

Eventually, if they had not died under interrogation, the prisoner would confess to any charge the inquisitor cared to levy against them. At this point they were bound over for trial. Trials, like hearings and questionings, were carried out in private. The court, like the torture chamber, was likely to be hung with black drapes and buntings; the only ornament in the room being a large crucifix – whether this was to remind the condemned that this was an official church proceeding or to show them how they were likely to end up may be open to question. When a bailiff appeared and shouted: 'Silence, silence, silence; the Holy Fathers are coming!', the robed inquisitorial tribunal entered and took their seats, the head inquisitor ringing a small, silver bell to indicate that the proceedings had begun. The defendant had no advocate to speak for them and while the prosecution could call women, children, other condemned heretics, Jews, Moors, slaves and criminals to testify against the accused, the defendant could only call adult, Christian males – not that many people were willing to risk joining the condemned in the docks. Anyone who refused to give evidence when called, gave evidence contradictory to the prosecution's predetermined game-plan, or reversed their testimony was subject to being sent to the torture chambers to have their memory refreshed.

Chillingly, if a condemned person denounced a sufficient number of their friends to the inquisitors, they might well find themselves absolved of all charges and accepted back into the bosom of the Church. Lesser degrees of cooperation might bring a sentence of a few years to a few months in the dungeons; not many survived such a stretch, but it was better than being burned at the stake. But all it took to avoid one unspeakable fate or another was to admit guilt. The guilty were still burned, but they were given the consolation of knowing that they would be strangled to death before being consigned to the flames. Strangulation by means of a leather strap threaded through small slots cut into the back of a chair was a conventional means of execution in Spain, and was simply adopted by the inquisition as a matter of convenience. From beginning to end Spanish Inquisitional trials were nothing short of a grotesque mockery of both justice and religion.

Following their trials, the condemned would take part in what is known as the *auto-de-fe*, a public celebration of the power of the Inquisition over the malign forces which Satan had loosed on God's world. Most *auto de fe*s were held on some public holiday to ensure that they would draw the largest possible crowd – thousands of spectators watching thousands of victims being publicly humiliated before being horribly murdered. In the great parade that opened the official ceremonies the inquisitional monks would parade through the crowd. Following them were the penitents (those found innocent), dressed in black and carrying huge candles as a sign of their renewed faith. Next came the reformed who had, by whatever means, escaped the flames; on the back of their black gowns were sewn inverted flames. Then came those about to die – the flames on their backs were shown pointing upward. This last group is closely guarded by soldiers and members of the Jesuit order who extolled them to last-minute repentance. Finally came the inquisitors mounted on mules and the Inquisitor General riding a white horse. It was not uncommon for the condemned alone to number in the thousands.

After the prescribed chants had been sung, a priest mounted a scaffold, read out the sentence and symbolically handed the condemned over to the secular authorities, hypocritically pleading with them not to harm these poor lost souls in any way. The victims were then led away for as long as it took for the civil authorities to review their individual cases. An hour or two was usually sufficient for several thousand judicial reviews. They were then paraded back into the courtyard and asked in what religion they wished to die. Those who professed that even after being tortured beyond human endurance, they remained good Catholics were strangled before being tied to the burning stake. The remainder were burnt alive. When the victims had been tied to the stakes, the crowd screamed: 'Let the dog's beards be made!' and anyone wearing a beard (mostly the Jews) had a flaming torch shoved in their face, burning away their beard and charring their face black. Finally, the pyres were lit and over the next hour the condemned died, shrieking and screaming, the fat oozing through their charred and cracking skin, their hands and feet reduced to blackened stumps while they still lived.

As though it were not enough that Spain inflicted this disease on its own people, throughout most of the sixteenth century the Low

Countries (Belgium, Holland and the Netherlands) were under the fanatical control of the Spanish crown and they, too, were subject to the Spanish Inquisition. Between 1568 and 1573 roughly 18,000 Dutch men and women were executed by the Inquisition, mostly for adhering to the Protestant faith. Many were burnt, some were drowned and some buried alive. Impossible as it is to believe, the Spanish Inquisition did not cease in Spain until 1808 when Spain was invaded by the armies of Napoleon Bonaparte and, despite the fact that in 1816 the Pope flatly forbade inquisitors from forcibly extracting confessions, torture was not formally abolished until 1821. Between 1481 and 1808 more than 33,000 Spanish men, women and children were burnt alive and more than 290,000 were tortured and imprisoned with the loss of all their property. How many thousands may have died under torture remains unknown. During the seventeen years he spent as Grand Inquisitor,

In this image of an *auto-de-fe* courtesy of the Spanish Inquisition, we see an entire row of heretics being burned in the background, while the foreground shows us (from left to right): a man being slowly roasted over a fire (for what purpose we can only guess); an impaling (presumably the variation in sentence being linked to the variation in 'crime') and a comparatively merciful beheading by the sword.

Here we see another mass burning. This woodcut depicts the burning of twenty-three Jews convicted of the murder of Christian children for the Passover rites – a charge trumped up against Jewish communities all over Europe and always "proved" with the methods that were applied to witchcraft and heresy trials. Once the Torturers elicited the confession they required, that confession was used as 'proof' for the condemnation of others.

Thomas de Torquemada, alone, sentenced upwards of 10,000 to the burning stake and 100,000 to imprisonment. One can hope that during the more than three centuries of the Spanish Inquisition's existence the rest of the world managed to drag itself out of the mire. How well they achieved this goal will be examined in the following chapter.

3

TORTURE IN THE AGE OF REASON

T he period between 1600 and 1700 is often called the Age of Reason. This may be an appropriate enough term when referring to the scientific advancements of the period, but in the field of juris prudence and corporal punishment things remained pretty much business as usual. When Queen Elizabeth I died in 1603 she was succeeded on the throne of England by her second cousin, King James VI of Scotland. Having already spent eighteen years on the Scottish throne, the thirty-nine-year-old monarch had no intention of changing the way he did things, and the accepted ways of doing things in Scotland were even harsher than they had been in England under the Tudors.

Of all the things James was afraid of, and there seem to have been an over-abundance of them, one of his most deep-seated fears was of witchcraft. In 1590, while still on the throne of Scotland, he had ordered the arrest of one Dr Fian (alias John Cunningham), along with forty accomplices, on charges of sorcery and trying to kill King James by bewitching him to death. There is no doubt that Cunningham was a dangerous and foolish man; he openly styled himself as a magician and was long suspected of dealing in poisons, so James' subordinates had ample reason to believe that if, indeed, there was a plot against the king, Cunningham was probably involved. In an effort to extract details of Cunningham's evil doings the royal torturers ripped off his fingernails and drove needles into the bleeding flesh of his finger tips.

When that failed to elicit a confession, the good doctor was subjected to the 'boots', a device in which his lower legs were so horribly crushed that blood and bone marrow oozed from the edges of the iron shoe.

Here we have an illustration of the inquisitorial process at work. The victim is enduring the torture of the brodequin. A wooden framework encases his legs from the knees to the ankles while wedges are hammered in with a large mallet until all of the bones in his knees, lower leg and ankles have been broken. This would be deliberately slow and painful, but also intentionally non-lethal and not too shocking, sudden or overwhelming to cause the victim to faint. He is being continually questioned about his supposed 'crimes' and the scribe is dutifully recording his responses.

Still, the stalwart Cunningham refused to confess but his denial failed to save him. He was strangled and his body burnt at the stake. The following year, 1591, another Scottish 'witch' had her fingers locked in a clamp-like device called the 'pilliwinckes' while her head was lashed with ropes and jerked violently back and forth. Finally being identified as a witch by a 'witch's mark' on her throat (probably a mole, wart or birth-mark, commonly known to witch hunters everywhere as a *stigmata sagarum*), she confessed and was executed.

Obviously these tortures were not only in accordance with accepted practices of witch hunting, but also in line with King James' own thoughts on the subject, all duly recorded and expounded upon in a book entitled *Daemonology*. Just how hell-bent on rooting out witches in Scotland James was, was best expressed by a contemporary Edinburgh jurist when he said: 'An old wife circumstantially accused of witchcraft at a Galloway kirk-session [church service] has as little chance of mercy as a Jew before the Spanish Inquisition'.

Naturally, when James came to the throne of England, neatly tucked away among his baggage were all his fears and superstitions against those who made pacts with the Devil, and he quickly enacted laws making it a capital offence to 'feed or reward any [evil] spirit, or any part of it, skin or bone'. At James' behest a special act was passed against 'Conjuration, Witchcraft and dealing with evil and wicked spirits'.

There were other high crimes and misdemeanours rampant in England as well as witchcraft and James had to deal with these as well; some of the punishments he decreed were bizarrely tailored to suit the particular crime. A first-time arrest for drunkenness was met with a simple fine of 5s, but subsequent arrests on the same charge would condemn the inebriate to wear a 'Drunkard's Cloak' – a beer keg with one end knocked out and a hole cut in the other large enough for the miscreant's head to fit through. The man was then condemned to wear this humiliating costume in public for a proscribed period of time. Considering that a cask large enough to fit over a man would weigh as much as the man himself, it would have been a terrible experience. The Drunkard's Cloak must have become a standard punishment because there are records of it still in use as late as 1690.

An example of the pilliwinckes or finger pillory in the church of Ashby-de-la-Zouche in Leicestershire, England. Such devices were instilled in great estates everywhere probably as a punishment for thieving servants, but those which were in churches might also be employed to publicly shame penitents before the congregation.

In other instances of making the punishment fit the crime, a Jew convicted of being a heretic was sentenced to prison where he was kept on a diet of pork; and false witnesses and perjurers were forced to wear a tongue-shaped piece of red cloth sewn to their clothes.

More serious were the punishments and tortures meted out to those suspected of treason. In 1604, during King James' second year on the throne, Guy Fawkes and a gang of Catholic plotters were discovered to have buried more than two dozen kegs of gunpowder under the houses of Parliament. James ordered that Fawkes was to be questioned rigorously and: 'If he will not otherwise confess, the gentlest tortures are to be first used on him, and so on, step by step, to the most severe, and so God speed the good work'. What 'gentle' tortures were applied to Fawkes is unknown, but before being tried and executed

A species of pillory inflicted for the most part on chronic drunkards, who were exposed to public ridicule in this fashion. The 'drunkard's cloak' could take one of two primary forms: those closed on the bottom, with the victim immersed in faeces and urine, or merely putrid water; or else open, so that the victim could walk and be led about the town with the enormous and very painful weight on his shoulders.

The victim of this device would be "prolonged" by force of the winch, and various sources testify to cases of thirty centimeters or twelve inches, an inconceivable length that comes of the dislocation and extrusion of every joint in the arms and legs, of the dismemberment of the spinal column, and of course of the ripping and detachment of the muscles of the limbs, thorax and abdomen – effects that are, needless to say, fatal.

along with his companions he was racked mercilessly. While hanging, drawing and quartering had gone out after the Babington plot during Elizabeth's reign, Fawkes and his companions' carcasses were publicly hacked to pieces after they had been hanged.

Hanging, that long-established and wildly popular form of public entertainment, was given greater standardisation under King James. No longer would hangings in London take place wherever seemed convenient at the moment. Henceforth they would all take place at Tyburn – located near the spot where London's Marble Arch now stands. If you are going to host a public spectacle it is nice if people know where to find the show; and hangings at Tyburn were nothing less. Bleachers were built to accommodate the crowds and seat prices varied according to how close to the victim you wanted to sit and how important a personage the condemned happened to be. Along the route from the prison to Tyburn, the cart bearing the condemned first stopped at a church where a priest begged the condemned to repent. Next stop was the Hospital of St Giles-in-the-fields where a last mug of ale was offered to the soon-to-be departed. Sometimes, if a simple hanging was deemed to be too good for the villain, he was wrapped in chains, or locked in the human-shaped, iron cage known as a gibbet, and allowed to swing in the breeze until he died of exposure and thirst.

Until the end of the eighteenth century, European urban and suburban panoramas abounded in iron and wooden cages attached to the outsides of town halls and ducal palaces, to halls of justice, to cathedrals and to city walls. The naked or nearly naked victims were locked into the cages and hung up. They perished of hunger and thirst, a fate seconded in winter by storm and cold, in summer by heatstroke and sunburn; often they had been tortured and mutilated, to make more edifying examples. The putrefying cadavers were generally left in place until the bones fell apart.

This two-legged iron cage comes from Florence in the late seventeenth or early eighteenth century. It is in the possession of a Florentine patrician family descendent from an early eighteenth-century.

Occasionally a sympathetic passer-by would put a bullet through his head and end his suffering but just as often they were used for target practice.

Charles I succeeded his father, James, in 1625, bringing with him new ideas. Some of these, like the king's insistence on ruling without having to consult Parliament, were annoyingly old-fashioned, but his

An instrument of public ridicule, the gambler's rosary was reserved in some places for smokers and gamblers who, thus ornamented, were exposed in the market square, subject to the usual consequences – at the very least embarrassing – but frequently painful, sometimes serious, and even fatal. Similar "necklaces" made of heavy wooden or stone "bottles", or equally onerous "balance weights" or huge "coins" were hung around the necks of, respectively, drunkards and dishonest shopkeepers. Poachers were known to be decked out with chains to which the cadavers of their ill-got prey were strung and left until they putrefied and fell apart (particularly effective in the summertime) – but only after having the first and second finger of their right hand cut off so that they could no longer draw an arrow (or later pull a trigger on a musket).

thoughts on crime and punishment were both enlightened and liberal. Branding was greatly diminished, as were a number of other forms of corporal mutilation. Torturing a prisoner to obtain a confession was outlawed – although it was never legal under the terms of Magna Charta – and almost immediately hangings at Tyburn dropped from 150 or so per year to around ninety. Unfortunately for Charles, Parliament was no more impressed with liberal laws than they were with the king ruling behind their collective back. Both the judiciary and Parliament were now packed with reactionary, fundamentalist Puritans who had no intention of liberalising anything. In 1634, a Quaker Member of Parliament, William Prynne (Quakers being far too liberal to suit the Puritans) was sentenced to life in prison for his faith. A part of his sentence was to be pilloried, to have both ears cut off and branded with the letters S.L., for 'seditious libeler'. Another Quaker, Anne Auckland, was sentenced to eight months' imprisonment in an underground sewer and James Parnell was imprisoned in a hole in a wall 12ft above the ground. Torture to obtain a confession may have been outlawed by King Charles, but torture as punishment remained standard operating procedure under the Puritans.

In the early 1640s, Parliamentary forces seized control of the government and declared open war on the king. Even while Civil War raged across England, Parliament took time to enact draconian laws against anything that seemed to contravene the strict Puritan moral

Der Falschspieler?

code. Sex outside the marriage bed became a crime, and adultery was declared a felony. By 1648 anyone convicted of being a theatrical actor could be publicly flogged and anyone caught attending a play could be fined. Cock-fighting was also outlawed; not because it was cruel, but because it was 'commonly accompanied by [betting], drinking and swearing'. Soon, anyone caught having fun of any kind could expect to be stocked, pilloried and/or whipped to within an inch of their lives.

Swearing, blaspheming, playing cards or dice, doing business on Sunday, failure to attend church or even 'vainly or profanely walking on the Lord's Day' were all liable to a heavy fine and public punishment. When a non-Puritan fanatic named James Naylor insisted he was God and that it was permissible for an unmarried couple to have sex so long as they went to the same church, he was sentenced to the following punishment: first he was pilloried in Palace Yard, then whipped through the streets of London all the way to the Old Corn Exchange. Two days later he was again pilloried at the Corn Exchange before having a hole bored through his tongue and being branded with a 'B' for blasphemer. He was then carted to the town of Bristol where he was again flogged and placed in solitary confinement, at Bridewell Prison, for an unspecified period of time.

Parliament began the next year of judicial progress – 1649 – by beheading King Charles and setting up a new government under Oliver Cromwell who, in order to better torture everyone in England, promptly closed the taverns. Like all dictators before and since, Cromwell and the Puritans needed a bogeyman to keep the people frightened into obedience. They already had Catholics and closet-monarchists, but they needed something more general – a blanket fear that would keep every man and woman in England shaking in their boots. The perceived threat of witches serving as agents of the devil seemed to fit the demand admirably.

Witchcraft had always been feared as an enemy of Christianity but it had not been until 1484 that Pope Innocent VIII had made the persecution of witches a doctrine of the faith. The same year that he allowed Spain to set up its own Office of the Inquisition he issued a Papal Bull on witchcraft. In it, he said:

> It has indeed lately come to our ears, not without afflicting us with bitter sorrow, that ... many persons of both sexes, unmindful of their own salvation and straying from the Catholic faith, have abandoned themselves to devils, incubi and succubi [male and female demon spirits] ... and at the instigation of the enemy of mankind they do stink from committing and perpetrating the foulest abominations and filthiest excesses to the deadly peril of their own souls, whereby they outrage the Divine Majesty and are cause of scandal and danger to very many. ... In virtue of Our Apostolic authority We decree and enjoin

that ... Inquisitors be empowered to proceed to the just correction, imprisonment and punishment of any persons ... designated in Our letters.

Frightening as this Papal Bull is, there was ample religious authority to back it up. In Exodus 22:18 it says: 'Thou shalt not suffer a witch to live' and no less a respected figure than St Thomas Aquinas had preached against the evils and dangers of witchcraft.

To help win the fight against the satanic legions, Pope Innocent appointed two German Dominican monks, Heinrich Kraemer and Johann Sprenger, to carry out enquiries in northern Germany where witchcraft seemed to be particularly rampant. Kraemer and Sprenger were uniquely qualified to fulfil their new assignment; they were cunning enough to twist both secular and Canon Law to whatever end they desired, they were dyed-in-the-wool fanatics and they hated women vehemently. During the course of their investigations, Kraemer and Sprenger compiled a book that would serve as the guide for all witch hunters to follow – the *Malleus Maleficarum*, or 'Hammer of Witches'. Actually its full title reads: '*MALLEUS MALEFICARUM, Maleficas, & earum hæresim, ut phramea potentissima conterens.*' This translates as: 'The Hammer of Witches which destroyeth Witches and their heresy like a most powerful spear.'

This woodcut depicts three women convicted of witchcraft being burned alive while the devil flies into or out of one of their mouths. As horrific as this scene would have been to witness, we must remember that this method of execution was seen by contemporaries as merciful in the sense that the torments of the flames endured here on earth were thought to help with the victim's chances of eternal salvation. Note also the 'witches sabbath' on the right and the comparatively merciful beheading in the background.

In addition to guiding witch hunters through the process of enquiry and torture, the *Malleus* identified precisely how witchcraft worked. 'All witchcraft comes through carnal lust which is insatiable in women, wherefore for the sake of fulfilling their lusts they consort with devils'. According to Kraemer and Sprenger, the Devil appeared to women in any form they might find sexually pleasing and thereby seduced them into becoming his servants.

The authors of the *Malleus*, as well as other writers, quickly expanded on their concept of just how dangerous witches could be:

> they raise hailstorms and hurtful tempests and lightning; cause sterility in men and animals; offer to devils, or otherwise kill, those children whom they do not devour. [They] make horses go mad under their riders; they can transport themselves from place to place through the air ... they can affect Judges and magistrates so that they cannot hurt them; they cause themselves and others to keep silent under torture ...

Naturally, to be capable of so much evil the witches had to be organised and thus the concept of the witches' Sabbat – or unholy conclave – developed. According to a tract dating from forty years prior to Pope Innocent's Bull, witches gathered together at the Sabbats, swearing before Satan that they would kill as many children under the age of three as possible. After sealing the deal by kissing the Devil's ass, they engaged in the ultimate outrage – a feast of succulent roast baby.

As outrageous as this may seem, thanks to the newly invented printing press, the *Malleus* was widely circulated among ecclesiastical and lay authorities – both of whom Pope Innocent had enjoined to ferret out witches. Initially non-ecclesiastic lawyers balked at the concept of arresting, questioning and torturing people on the strength of unfounded and un-provable accusations, but since anyone who denied the reality of witches was likely to be accused of witchcraft themselves, the lawyers finally knuckled under and began persecuting, and prosecuting, anyone unlucky enough to be accused of witchcraft. Thus was the full force of the legal system brought into play in what was technically a matter for ecclesiastical courts. But Church courts were not authorised to torture, nor execute, people; lay courts were. When a woman in Lausanne was charged with poisoning and attempted kidnap, the inquisitors were called in. Within two days she had confessed not only to the original charges, but to attending Sabbats, having sex with the Devil, creating storms and murdering children.

It seems obvious that the woman mentioned above was condemned on the strength of her forced admission, but when torture failed to extract a confession there were ample alternative methods to confirm guilt. A great enough number of accusations, no matter how outrageous they might be, could easily serve the purpose. If there were not sufficient accusers, physical proof of guilt could be found in the form of 'Devil's marks', the *stigmata sagarum* mentioned earlier. The Devil's mark might be no more than a mole, wart or birthmark but it might also be something as blatant as a third nipple; a rarity to be sure, but not unheard of. To search for these signs of a pact with the devil, the accused was stripped naked and had their head shaved before being searched for evidence of their sin. If this failed it was assumed that the Devil's mark was simply invisible. Invisible marks were believed to be either insensitive to pain or unable to bleed when pierced. To determine whether or not the accused had such a mark, they were 'pricked' – that is, jabbed repeatedly with a sharp, heavy needle – until a spot without a nerve-end was found or until shock caused their nervous system to shut down, making them insensitive to continued punctures.

The point of all this torture was not just to elicit a confession of personal guilt. Integral to ferreting-out witches was making them reveal the names of their accomplices – the other members of their coven. In exchange for naming other witches, victims might be promised that their lives would be spared; spared, that is, to spend the rest of their lives in a dungeon or being handed over to a judge who had not been a party to the plea-bargain, leaving them free to condemn the prisoner to the noose or burning post. By getting suspected witches to confess that they were members of an organised coven and to get them to name other supposed satanic conspirators, it gave credence to the Church and State in their claims of the threat to society. These confessions were paramount to the ability of both the Church and State to wield unchallenged power.

Witch hunting may have originated with the Roman Catholic Church but the Protestant Reformation, which began in 1517, did not list witch burning among its list of grudges against Rome and the Papacy. Even Martin Luther, who instigated the Reformation in Germany, was convinced that the Devil made compacts with anyone and everyone willing to do his bidding, and wrote that: 'No one need think that the world can be ruled without blood. The civil sword shall, and

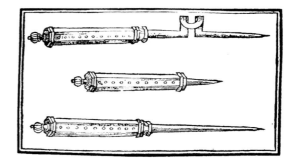

The dastardly tools of the witch-pricker. In the hands of a Witchfinder, these devices could prove condemning. With a retractable 'prick' the witch-pricker could easily find a place on the body of the accused where a good stab caused no pain or blood, this was taken to be 'the devil's mark' and could well lead to their conviction and execution.

Here we see a woman, accused of witchcraft, about to be examined and 'questioned'. Once stripped naked she will be subjected to various tortures until the authorities elicit from her the confessions they desire. Depicted here are the finger pillory, branding irons, fiddle, flail, restraints, pincers and even part of a rack (on the right). The title of this nineteenth-century engraving is "You are going to be tortured so much the sun will shine through your body"

must, be bloody'. Accordingly, although Luther and his followers may have rejected the pope and many of the precepts of the Catholic Church, they were as quick to latch on to the *Malleus Maleficarum* as to pick up the Bible.

By 1530, Catholics and Protestants were competing not only for the hearts and minds of Christian Europe, but also to see who was most efficient at exposing the army of the damned. Undoubtedly this was at least partly an attempt by each side to prove they were more dedicated to carrying out the work of God than the other. After nearly a century of ecclesiastic competition, neither side seemed to have made satisfactory headway so Christian Europe went to war with itself. Between 1618 and 1648 the staunchly Catholic Habsburg rulers of Austria and Spain warred with Protestant Sweden, Denmark, the Netherlands and Catholic France. Germany, divided between Catholics in the north and Protestants in the south, went to war with itself. In England, where most of the Catholics had already been persecuted out of existence, the Puritan government took their own little Holy War to staunchly Catholic Ireland where English forces imposed Protestantism at sword point and, in retaliation, the Irish murdered English civilians left and right. In 1642, bands of Irish rebels burned and stoned to death English men and women, forcing children to murder their parents, mothers to kill their own children and men to murder their entire families before they, themselves, were consigned to the burning post.

As part of this campaign of seemingly unending unholy terror, the universal hunt for witches was ratcheted up along with the fighting, and the torture used to extract confessions increased in frequency and ferocity. By the mid-point in Europe's religious wars – commonly referred to as the Thirty Years War – witches were no longer being burnt a few at a time, but by the dozens and hundreds. In Protestant-controlled Geneva, Switzerland 500 were burned in less than three months; one Catholic Bishop in Bamburg, Germany burned 600 and another in Wirtzburg did away with no less than 900. In Savoy, Italy 800 were condemned to the stake at a single, mass trial. But the record for cruelty is unquestionably held by German theologian Benedict Carpzov who, over the course of his career, is credited with signing death warrants for more than 20,000 women and men. In all fairness it must be considered that witch hunting did not take place everywhere. Some communities, indeed some entire districts, were

This image depicts the burning of several heretics in Schwarzenburg, Switzerland. These scenes may have lacked some of the grandeur and spectacle of the Inquisitional *auto-de-fe*, but the end result was nevertheless just as horrid and brutal.

spared its horrors, but once the mania took hold, it inevitably spread like a virulent cancer.

On 7 April 1611, a seventy-year-old housewife from Ellwangen, Germany, by the name of Barbara Rufin, was arrested on charges of desecrating the Eucharist – the wafers used in the Christian service of Communion. There is no doubt that Frau Rufin was a cantankerous sort; even her husband often referred to her as a witch. Over the days of her incarceration and interrogation more and more of her neighbours came forward to insist that Barbara was, indeed, a witch; among them was her daughter-in-law, with whom she argued frequently and violently. No matter how much evidence piled up against her, Rufin refused to admit to practicing witchcraft. By 12 April the inquisitors decided the only thing left was to torture the 'truth' out of her. On the first day of torture she was racked twice, for fifteen minutes at a time. By the end of the third day, after enduring a total of seven rackings, she confessed. On 16 May she was beheaded with a sword – a standard form of execution in Germany at the time – and her body was publicly burnt. But it seems that before she met her end Frau Rufin had offered the names of some of her accomplices. When questioned as to the accuracy of her statements, those who had testified against Rufin were certain that the others were witches as well. The hunt for witches in and around Ellwangen instantly spiralled out of control. By the end of the year more than 100 women and men had been murdered in seventeen mass executions; the following year an additional 150 fell victim to the Ellwangen hysteria. Every name volunteered by every suspect and informant was written down in the inquisitor's log book and passed on to the pertinent authorities. One woman volunteered the names of twenty-nine others, another offered up two dozen names. When, joy of joys, a name cropped up more than once it was sufficient cause to order an immediate arrest. Some of those accused found themselves arrested and tried nearly two decades after being named.

The process of interrogating a suspected witch was always the same; the accused was asked questions so leading and cleverly worded that no matter how they answered they appeared guilty. 'Who seduced you into witchcraft?' If the answer was 'no one' it was concluded that they had willingly volunteered. Written confessions were as conveniently standardised as the questions. All this was formality, of course. There was never any doubt that the accused would be found guilty; we know this because records indicate that inventories of the accused possessions (which would be confiscated by the court or Church after their execution) began almost immediately after the suspects were arrested.

In 1615, three years after the Ellwangen panic began, three priests were arrested, tried and executed on charges of baptising infants and adults in the name of Satan. At least this explained how there came to be so many witches in the Ellwangen area. There were hundreds of similar cases of snowballing witch panics all over Europe in the years between 1525 and 1675, but this one instance should be sufficient to indicate the general course of events.

It is important to note that the Thirty Years War ended in 1648, the same year England's Puritan Parliament began passing draconian laws against almost everything, and only months before King Charles I was led to the block. It may have taken them a while to get around to dealing with threats as small as putting on theatrical performances and playing cards, but from the earliest days of the Civil War, the Puritans in government had been meting out self-righteous justice to the perceived agents of Satan. As late as 1665, Sir Matthew Hale, Lord Chief Justice would say he had 'no doubt at all that there were such creatures [as witches]' and promptly sentenced two women to be hanged solely on the testimony of a third woman who insisted the accused had caused her children to 'cough extremely and brought up crooked pins and once a big nail with a very broad head'. Seeing a handful of pins and a nail was all the proof Hale needed. But even the forces of good sometimes need a little help, and during the all-encompassing chaos of the English Civil War this help came in the form of the most notorious witch hunter of all time, Matthew Hopkins.

Prior to March 1644 Matthew Hopkins was nothing more than a clerk for a shipping company and part-owner of a tavern in the town of Mistley, Essex. But among the tavern's regular patrons was John Thurlowe, head of Oliver Cromwell's spy ring and this gave Hopkins an 'in' with the government and allowed him to gauge which way the political wind was blowing. When a lonely, cantankerous, one-legged old woman named Elizabeth Clarke was accused of witchcraft, Hopkins – undoubtedly aware that Mrs Clarke's mother had been hanged as a witch – ordered her arrest without any real authority to do so. Then, with the help of a local thug named Jack Stearne, he proceeded to question Mrs Clarke. Knowing that torture was illegal, Hopkins stripped the old woman naked, deprived her of food, drink and sleep and forced her to hobble up and down her cell, on her crutch, until she collapsed. According to the written report that Hopkins submitted to the court along with Clarke's confession: 'In March 1644, she and some seven or eight of that horrible sect of Witches living in Essex . . . with diverse Witches of other towns who had their

solemn sacrifices and there offered to the Devil'. For good measure, he insisted that the widow Clarke had 'three teats about her, which honest women do not.'

With half a dozen more witches now named, and more names pouring forth with each round of torture, Hopkins added three new members to his team, including Mary 'Goody' Phillips, an expert witch-pricker. Unlike most prickers, who had to poke and prod for hours until the victim confessed or failed to feel pain, Hopkins supplied Phillips with a prick with a retractable needle; it was completely painless and appeared as though the needle was being sunk deep into the victim's flesh. It was a cheap stage trick, but it purchased the lives of dozens of women.

Pricking was not the only way Hopkins could identify a witch; he insisted he could tell just by the way a woman threw her hair over her shoulder or how she interlaced her fingers whether or not she was having sex with the Devil. In a matter of months Hopkins was the talk of southern England and even the reactionary parliamentarian newspaper *The Scottish Dove* lauded his work, claiming that under Hopkins' questioning: 'The witches do confess they had been in the King's Army and have sent out their hags to serve them ... His Majesty's Army, it seems, is beholding to the Devil'. Other papers ghoulishly reported on the supposed offspring brought about by the Devil's coupling with witches. Some described limbless Cyclopes while others insisted they were two-headed, eight-limbed cats with human hands. No wonder then that requests poured in from all over East Anglia for the services of Matthew Hopkins, who now styled himself Witch-Finder General of England.

Hopkins not only charged 'by the head' for every witch discovered, but in many places he ordered local authorities to levy special taxes to pay his expenses and his helpers' wages. But it must have seemed like it was worth every penny because everywhere Matthew Hopkins went dozens of witches would be discovered, arrested, tortured into confessing, tried according to law and publicly executed. Of thirty-four women slated for trial at Colchester in July 1645, four died in prison, one (a teenager) was released when she agreed to testify against the others, and the remaining twenty-nine were hanged.

Some of the confessions elicited by Hopkins demonstrate that not only can a person be tortured into confessing to almost anything, but just how willing the public and courts must have been to accept such obviously forced testimony. Margaret Wyard insisted the Devil came to her bed in the guise of a handsome young man with blond hair, but

Opposite: The frontispiece to *Discovery of Witches* (1647) by Matthew Hopkins, Witch Finder General of England. He kept Elizabeth Clarke awake in her cell for four days. These are the animal 'familiars' which she reported seeing in that time. Based on this testimony, she was executed for witchcraft.

Elizabeth Chandler claimed that when he came to her it was in the shape of 'roaring things' that 'slithered into her bed in a puffing and roaring manner'. Disagreeing with both of these was the testimony of an old woman who said her demonic lover was nothing less monstrous than two gigantic beetles. It is hardly surprising that Hopkins' victims would confess to anything. In his notes on the torture of the septuagenarian Rev. John Lowes, who at first staunchly denied any wrongdoing, Hopkins wrote: 'We kept him awake several nights together while running him backwards and forwards about his cell until he was weary of life and scarce sensible of what he said or did'. Hardly surprising then that Rev. Lowes finally confessed to giving birth to, and suckling, four little demons as well as conjuring up a storm that caused a ship to sink, with a loss of fourteen lives. Lowes' retraction did him no good and no one ever checked to see if a storm, and the associated shipwreck, had taken place. Rev. Lowes was hanged in August 1645.

By late autumn of that year, Hopkins had brought about the executions of nearly 200 people, had an equal number behind bars and no one knows how many had died in prison. When Hopkins offered to visit the village of Great Staunton in Huntingdonshire, however, all did not go as planned. A member of the town council showed Hopkins' letter to the local vicar, John Gaul, and Gaul promptly denounced Hopkins from the pulpit, and in a pamphlet, where he said: 'Every old woman with a wrinkled face, a furrowed brow, a hairy lip, a squeaking voice or a scolding tongue, having a ragged coat on her back and a dog or cat by her side is not only suspected but pronounced for a witch'. Soon, even some in Parliament began questioning Hopkins' tactics, if not his motives. One unbiased London newspaper wrote: 'Life is precious and there is need of the greatest inquisition before it be taken away'. By Christmas, Hopkins' services were no longer being requested and his reign of terror was over. In nineteen months he had judicially taken the lives of more than 230 people.

Samuel Butler's satire *Hudibras* commented on Hopkins's activity, saying:

Has not this present Parliament
A Lieger to the Devil sent,
Fully impowr'd to treat about
Finding revolted witches out
And has not he, within a year,
Hang'd threescore of 'em in one shire?
Some only for not being drown'd,

And some for sitting above ground,
Whole days and nights, upon their breeches,
And feeling pain, were hang'd for witches.
And some for putting knavish tricks
Upon green geese and turky-chicks?
And pigs, that suddenly deceast
Of griefs unnat'ral, as he guest;
Who after prov'd himself a witch
And made a rod for his own breech.

The last line refers to a tradition whereby disgruntled villagers caught Hopkins and subjected him to his own 'swimming' test: he floated, and therefore was hanged for witchcraft himself. However, it is believed by most historians that Hopkins actually died of illness (possibly tuberculosis) in his home. The parish records of Manningtree in Essex record his burial in August of 1647.

Matthew Hopkins may have been the most notorious of the witch hunters, but he was neither the first nor the last. Four years later, in 1649, a Scotsman named John Kincaid – the most celebrated witch-pricker of his day – was called to Newcastle-upon-Tyne where he was paid 20s for every person he could get convicted of witchcraft. On his arrival in the city, the town crier walked the streets calling for informers to present their suspicions to Kincaid at the town hall. Of the thirty women accused of practicing the black arts, twenty-seven were convicted and executed.

By the late 1650s, England had grown tired of witch hunting, Puritans and Oliver Cromwell's brand of law and order. Cromwell himself died in 1658 and Richard Cromwell, his son and heir, known even to his father as 'Tumble Down Dick' was unable to hold the Puritan government together. In 1660, King Charles II was recalled from exile and meekly handed his late father's crown. Being a fun-loving sort of guy himself, Charles repealed the Puritanical laws against gambling, drinking, dancing and general merry-making. He also had the rotting bodies of Cromwell and his cohorts exhumed and hanged as an example to others who might feel the urge to chop off a monarch's head. In a move toward religious tolerance, he severely limited the power of courts to try people on charges of blasphemy, heresy and other religious offences. The British court system in general, however, was still weighted heavily against anyone brought before the bar. Defendants were not permitted to present witnesses on their behalf nor have counsel to represent them – that was supposed to be the judge's job – and only the crown had a prosecutor to plead its case. Unfortunately, in far too many instances the judge did little more than bolster the case for the prosecution.

All too aware that the cards were stacked against the accused, juries often leaned as far in the defendant's favour as the court leaned toward their conviction. To prevent conviction, and the subsequent imposition of some unspeakably nasty punishment of a defendant, juries were likely to massively underrate the seriousness of a crime or the value of goods stolen in a robbery. Perjury, it seems, became a full-time profession with professional 'witnesses' and jurors vying to sell their services and testimony to the highest bidder. Known as 'Straw Men' these paid, expert witnesses wandered up and down in front of courthouses with bits of straw tucked into their shoe buckle – a subtle but easily recognisable form of advertising. Naturally, judges were well aware of such goings on, and were quick to sequester juries and threaten them with incarceration and starvation if they returned a verdict not to the court's liking. This process of brow beating juries into cooperation reached its height during the short-lived reign of James II, Charles II's younger brother, who ruled between 1685 and 1688. James' court system, along with much of the government, was run by Judge George Jeffreys. The best description of the horrible Jeffreys came from the late King Charles, who had once said the judge possessed: 'no learning, no sense, no manners and more impudence than ten whores'. King James, on the other hand, loved him.

Like a scene from some cheap horror movie, Jeffreys draped the walls of his courtroom with scarlet tapestries and accepted only one plea: 'guilty'. Anything else was a complete waste of the court's precious time. Even minor offences brought horrific punishments. Anyone foolish enough to stand up to Judge Jeffreys went to the block. Anyone impious enough to disagree with King James was sent down to Jeffreys, who sent them to the block. Anyone accused of petty crime would inevitably meet the hangman. When Jeffreys sentenced Sir Thomas Armstrong to the block without the benefit of trial, Armstrong demanded his right to due process. Jeffreys snapped back: 'Then that you shall have, by the Grace of God.' Turning to his bailiff he added: 'See that [the] execution be done on next Friday following the trial'. When the handsome and popular young Duke of Monmouth accused King James of poisoning King Charles to grab the throne, Jeffreys went after Monmouth and his supporters, hunting them down and dispatching them to the noose or block by the hundreds.

At 10 a.m. on 15 July 1685, an armed guard escorted the Duke of Monmouth from the Tower to Tower Hill where he was to mount a scaffold draped in black bunting especially for the occasion. Along the route, more than 3,000 of the young duke's supporters had gathered to witness the grisly spectacle. So fearful was the king of an attempt to rescue his nephew that he had ordered the guard to shoot Monmouth dead if there were any disturbances in the crowd before the execution was complete. For a man about to die, the duke's manner was unnervingly calm and composed. When the entourage mounted the scaffold, the two bishops who accompanied the condemned man began a prayer. Although Monmouth dutifully repeated their words, he refused to pray for the salvation of the king, only muttering 'amen' when they had finished. In a break with established custom, he refused to make a final speech, handing a prepared statement to one of the bishops to read to the crowd. As he approached the block, he also refused the customary blindfold.

Before kneeling to place his head on the block, Monmouth calmly bent down and pulled the executioner's axe from under a pile of straw. Lifting it up, he ran his finger along the edge and turned to the headsman, the notorious Jack Ketch, asking if he thought it was sharp enough to do the job properly. Staring at his victim with disbelief, Ketch was even more astonished when Monmouth handed him the exorbitant sum of 6 guineas, saying: 'Pray, do your business well. Do not serve me as you did my Lord Russell. I have heard you struck him four or five times; if you strike me twice, I cannot promise you not to stir.' He then turned to one of his servants and told him that if Ketch did a clean job he was to receive six more guineas. With that, he knelt down and placed his head on the block.

Ketch, unnerved by Monmouth's calmness and casual attitude, completely bungled the job. When the first blow only grazed the back of the duke's head, he turned his blood-covered face upward, staring directly into Ketch's eyes. Two more blows had still not finished the horrid job and in anger and frustration Ketch threw down the axe, declaring that he would pay 40 guineas to anyone in the angry crowd who could do the job better. It was only when the Sheriff of Middlesex, who was standing on the platform, demanded that Ketch finish his job or be killed on the spot, that he retrieved the axe and struck another ill-aimed blow. According to an eyewitness, 'the butcherly dog did so barbarously act his part that he could not, at five strokes sever the head from the body'. Finally, in exasperation, Ketch used his belt knife to sever the duke's head from his body and put the condemned man out of his misery.

By now, the crowd's anger had turned to fury. Their young hero had been butchered. Pushing and shoving their way past the ring of guards, they stormed the scaffold, dragging Jack Ketch to the ground, threatening to tear him limb from limb. Before the guards could control the situation and rescue the executioner, dozens of people had dipped their handkerchiefs in Monmouth's blood as though he were a holy martyr to the Protestant cause. To make the already grotesque situation even worse, Monmouth's family now realised that the duke had never had his portrait painted. After retrieving the body, they had the head sewn back on the stump and propped up long enough for an artist's rendering to be made. Only then was the body returned to the Tower of London for burial in the chapel of St Peter ad Vincula.

When a man named Titus Oates was arrested on charges of perjury in the summer of 1685, Jeffreys sentenced him to be paraded around the courts of Westminster and the Royal Exchange with a placard around his neck describing his crime. Then he was flogged through the streets from Newgate Prison to Tyburn. As if this weren't enough, on every 9 August, for the rest of his life, Oates was to be locked in the pillory at Westminster; on every subsequent 10 August he was to be pilloried at Charing Cross and on 24 April at Tyburn.

In mid-December of that same year, Jeffreys passed sentence on a woman convicted of petty theft. As she was hauled from the court, Jeffreys addressed the executioner who was about to lead her to Tyburn. 'Hangman, I charge you to pay particular attention to this lady. Scourge her soundly, man; scourge her till the blood runs down. Tis Christmas, and a cold time for madame to strip; see that you warm her shoulders thoroughly.' For such gross judicial misconduct the king rewarded Jeffreys with the title of baron, a seat in the House of Lords and the post of Lord Chancellor. By 1688 it had all become too much for Parliament to bear. King James was ousted from the throne and George Jeffreys was clapped in the Tower of London. A few months before he drank himself to death the following year, Jeffreys made a telling comment about justice under King James II. Defending his own reign of terror, Jeffreys said: 'I was not half bloody enough for him who sent me hither.'

When James was replaced on the throne of England by his daughter Mary and her husband William of Orange, the dual monarchs took the first, tentative steps on the long road to judicial reform. Many of the cruellest forms of corporal punishment were outlawed and at least reasonable proof was required before a person could be sentenced to the gallows. Tragically, leniency, like severity, did nothing to deter criminals from committing crimes, and public humiliation still retained an important role in setting an example as to the cost of transgression.

The English legal system, along with all its flaws, was carried to the American Colonies by those who left the mother country to build a new life in the New World. Because so many of those who settled in the New England colonies were adherents to the severe, Puritanical belief system that dominated England in the 1600s, the laws in that region dealing with morals, Godliness and, not surprisingly, witchcraft, were more stringent than they were in the more southerly colonies of Virginia and the Carolinas. Although the immigrants insisted they fled Britain and Europe to escape religious persecution, the religious freedom they sought was only to extend as far as their own small group; those of other beliefs were hounded and tortured mercilessly. When Quakers moved into Massachusetts and settled beside the Puritans, they were welcomed as warmly as the *Conversos* and *Moriscos* were in inquisitional Spain.

When a Quaker named William Bond was arrested for his faith he was, according to an account written down in 1703 and purportedly taken from a deposition made by Bond's jailer:

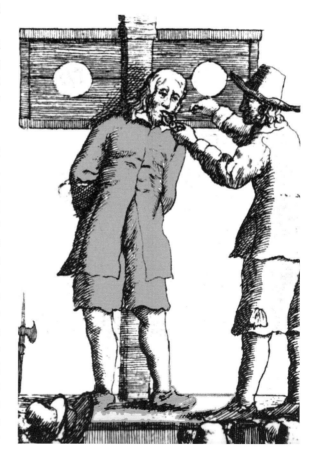

Burning a hole through the tongue

> put in irons, neck and heels ... and so kept in irons for the space of sixteen hours ... and all this without meat, whilst his back was torn with whipping ... yet [the jailer] laid on him with a pitched rope twenty blows over his back and arms, with as much force as he could drive, so that with the fierceness of the blows the rope untwisted and [the jailer's] arms were swollen with [the effort] ... presently the jailer ... got a new rope [and] gave [Bond's] broken, bruised and weak body fourscore and seventeen [ninety-seven] blows more, foaming at the mouth like a madman ... he gave him in all 117 blows with a pitched rope, so that his flesh was beaten black, and as into jelly, and under

his arms the bruised flesh and blood hung down, clotted as it were, in bags.

In seventeenth-century Massachusetts (which was a particular stronghold of Puritanical faith) idolatry, blasphemy and adultery were all punishable by death. Anyone in Massachusetts who denied the existence of God was subject to having a hole bored through their tongue with a hot iron and even such trivial transgressions as smoking tobacco and wearing unseemly clothes could lead to a fine and turn in the stocks or pillory. When a certain sea captain named Kimble returned from a three-year voyage he was immediately arrested and clapped in the stocks for being so lewd as to kiss his wife on the doorstep of their home: they were outside, so the kiss had been public and, to compound the offence, it had taken place on a Sunday. But all these things are trivial when compared to what happened in the sleepy village of Salem, Massachusetts in the spring of 1692.

The affair that came to be known as the Salem Witch Trials began when two bored, nasty-minded teenage girls accused the local minister's West Indian slave of being a witch. They posed in grotesque positions, made ugly faces, jerked and twitched and swore up and down it was all Tituba's fault. It got the adults' attention and probably seemed like fun. Soon eight of the girls' friends were imitating their posturing and pointing fingers at several other old women in the village. It might have gone no further than that, but when the girls' accusations were backed up by one of their mothers, a member of the prominent Putnam family, it all got completely out of hand. Now the centre of attention and being pressed for details, the girls' well-rehearsed performances soon had their mothers convinced that they, too, had seen witches flying across the sky on broomsticks. Obviously the girls could not admit they had been lying all along, so they kept accusing more and more people of being witches and the accused were rounded up and locked in chains.

Word of such accusations spreads quickly and it was only a matter of weeks before Massachusetts Governor Phips had appointed well-known Puritan fanatic Cotton Mather to assemble a special court of enquiry. Mather and three close friends sat on the five-judge panel which was headed by one of the most rabidly superstitious witch hunters in history, William Stoughton. The only member of the court not among Mather's cronies was Nathaniel Saltonstall and after only a few sessions he walked away in disgust at the way the proceedings were being handled.

Opposite: This illustration by Howard Pyle shows the arrest of an old woman in Salem Massachusetts on the charges of witchcraft. It was the result of an hysteria which swept through the small community like the plague and left a legendary trail of destruction in its wake.

By the time the court convened, more than 100 people had been arrested and incarcerated on charges of witchcraft; among them were Sarah Good and her four-year-old daughter Dorcas. They were thrown into a tiny cell together and the young girl (Dorcas) was chained to

a wall – possibly because she was small enough to slip between the narrow gaps between the bars of the cell.

Another was eighty-year-old John Proctor who had been arrested because he dared protest the entire proceeding; if he denied that the accused were witches he must also be a witch. Bravely, Proctor refused to enter any plea to the absurd charges and was sentenced to the gallows. Another man who refused to plea was Giles Corey. Corey refused to answer any plea – either guilty or not guilty. The prosecutors were determined to make him talk. So in an effort to force him to confess, Corey was pressed to death under an old door on which more and more stones were heaped. Periodically he would be asked whether he was ready to enter a plea, but with utter contempt, he merely replied '... more weight ...' And so more weight was added until Corey's old ribs eventually shattered.

The trials dragged on from mid-June through most of September and before they were over, nineteen women and one man had been hanged, and four women had died in prison. Four-year-old Dorcas Good, whose mother had been hanged, went insane and never recovered. Two dogs were also hanged, having been convicted of being witches' familiars.

The story of Salem is similar to those in Ellwangen, Germany and Essex, England with one notable exception. None of those accused of witchcraft, with the notable and tragic exception of Giles Corey, were tortured into making a confession. They were undoubtedly badly treated and poorly housed, but they were not beaten, pricked, starved, racked, or subjected to any of the other tortures previously associated with witch hunts in Great Britain and Europe. There was also a considerable, and immediate, backlash against what happened in Salem. Cotton Mather's own father, Increase Mather, denounced the court in a pamphlet entitled 'Cases of Conscience', wherein he said: 'It were better that ten suspected witches should escape than one innocent person should be condemned'. Massachusetts minister John Hale had a similar reaction. 'It can not be imagined that in a place of so much knowledge, so many in so small [a] compass of land should abominably leap into the Devil's lap at once.' Thanks to the public outcry, the remaining women awaiting trial were released in January 1693 and by the middle of that month the General Court of Massachusetts ordered a day of fasting, prayer and soul-searching in memory of what had taken place at Salem. In 1702 the proceedings of the special court at Salem were declared unlawful and four years later, Ann Putnam Jr, one of the girls who had instigated the hysteria,

publicly apologised for the suffering she had caused a decade earlier. Half a century later, Salem was officially renamed Danvers.

The case of Salem, Massachusetts may have been the first instance in which individual reason actually helped halt the public insanity of a witch hunt, but it is important to note that there have always been a few brave souls willing to risk the noose or the stake to stand in opposition to accusations of witchcraft and the torture associated with this, and most other crimes. As early as 1563, Dr Johann Weyer, physician to the Duke of Cleves (who was, in turn, the nephew of Henry VIII's fourth wife, Anne of Cleves) wrote a treatise entitled 'To Prevent a Shipwreck of Souls', in which he said:

these wretched women, whose minds have already been disturbed by the delusions and arts of the devil and are now upset by frequent torture, are kept in prolonged solitude in the squalor and darkness of their dungeons, exposed to the hideous specters of the devil, and constantly dragged out to undergo atrocious torment until they would gladly exchange at any moment their most bitter existence for death, are willing to confess whatever crimes are suggested to them rather than be thrust back into their hideous dungeons amid ever-recurring torture.

Nearly a century later, Lutheran minister Johann Faber of Esslingen, Germany wrote that the 'almost inhuman practice of torture might force even the innocent to confess ...'

Around this same time, Jesuit Priest Friedrich von Spec said:

Even when judges claim that a witch had confessed without torture ... in reality they were tortured, but only in an iron press with sharp-edged channels over the shins, in which they are pressed like a cake, bringing blood and causing intolerable pain, and this is technically called without torture, deceiving those who do not understand the phrases of the inquisitors. Some inquisitors would even tell their victims the names of those they wished them to denounce; they would also inform them of what others had said about them, so they would know what details to confess. Once arrested, there was no hope for the accused witch, even if she survived the torture. It is assumed that a woman cannot endure two or three tortures unless she is a witch. If to endure in great torment, one grinds her teeth, compress her lips and holds her breath, they say she laughs. Some faint under torture and they call it sleep. If the devil causes a man to hallucinate, it did not necessarily mean that he was a heretic;

while if accomplices confessed to impossibilities, this was not [in reality] an indictment even against one who otherwise confessed.

Following the Salem witch trials of 1692 it began to dawn on governments on both sides of the Atlantic that there were deep-seated problems in the judicial system that would have to be addressed if western civilisation was not to devour itself. But change never comes easy. The last execution for witchcraft in England took place in 1716 when Mary Hicks and her ten-year-old daughter were hanged. The last witch burning in Scotland came eleven years later. By 1736 most British statutes against witchcraft had been repealed but the suspicions and fear lingered. Nearly a century later, in the early 1800s, there were still people in Great Britain being arrested on charges of having lynched or drowned old women suspected of witchcraft. The last recorded case of 'swimming' a suspected witch took place in England in 1825 when a mob of lunatics from Wickham Skeith, Suffolk, seized an itinerant peddler named Isaac Stebbing and threw him into the local mill pond to see if he would sink or float. Tragically for Stebbing, he refused to stay down long enough to drown and it was only thanks to the intervention of the local vicar that he was not lynched. A similarly tortuous course toward enlightenment and reform took place in every European country where the witch craze had once gripped the population with its unreasoning fear and associated horrors. How many individuals – most of whom were elderly women – perished at the hands of witch hunters could not be accurately estimated even if the records were complete, which they are not. Should the death toll include those who died under torture or passed away locked in some dungeon while they awaited interrogation? Best-guess estimates on the overall toll of judicial murder during the age of witch hunts range from as low as 200,000 to as high as 1 million. Considering the population of Europe as a whole during this period, the number of judicially imposed murders could run as high as one out of every 200 persons.

4

REFORMS OF THE EIGHTEENTH AND NINETEENTH CENTURIES

B y 1700 the craze for hunting down witches had largely faded thanks to the dawning realisation that confessions extracted by torture, and the acceptance of hearsay evidence by courts, bore little resemblance to convictions achieved by objective judicial process. At the same time, torture was still a generally accepted form of punishment for a vast variety of crimes, despite the fact that there had been voices crying for the elimination of corporal punishment and mutilation for more than a century. Late in the sixteenth century, French statesman and essayist Michel de Montaigne wrote:

> ... all that exceeds a simple death, appears to me perfect cruelty. I could hardly persuade myself, before I saw it with my eyes, that there could be found souls so cruel ... who for the sole pleasure of murder would commit, hack, and lop off the limbs of others; sharpen their wits to invent unusual torments and new kinds of deaths ... What right then, but that of power, can authorize the punishment of a citizen, so long as there remains any doubt of his guilt? Either he is guilty, or not guilty. If guilty, he should only suffer the punishment ordained by the laws, and torture becomes useless, as his confession is unnecessary. If he be not guilty, you torture the innocent; for in the eyes of the law, every man is innocent whose crime has not been proven.

Similarly, in 1624, a Dutch thinker named Johannes Grevius insisted that no true Christian would ever contemplate the use of torture on anyone for any reason, be they a fellow Christian or a follower of another faith.

Reform always comes hard and progress toward change is halting at best. The path toward the elimination of torture came as much through public rejection of the grisly spectacle of burning, branding and dismemberment as it did through judicial reform, but even public sympathy with the abstract concepts of what was fair and right was often at odds with the physical reality of life in a crime-ridden world.

By 1700, London had become one of the fastest growing cities in the world. With a population of more than 600,000 it was the hub of a vast and expanding empire; housing foreign traders, migrant workers (many of whom were perpetually unemployed), swarms of soldiers who flooded into the city between foreign military engagements and gangs of idle rich kids with nothing better to do than find new ways of getting into trouble. It was, in short, much like any modern city with a serious crime problem. Among the worst offenders were street gangs like the Mohocks. The Mohocks were only one of more than a dozen gangs plaguing London in the first decades of the eighteenth century, but their habits were typical. Unlike most modern street gangs, the Mohocks and their contemporaries were not poor and directionless; they were rich and shiftless, relying on their parents' money and social position to keep them out of prison. Their violence was appalling. Roaming the streets at night they alternated attacks on the unwary and helpless with violent bouts of drinking and brawling among themselves. Selecting their victims at random, gangs gouged out eyes, hacked off noses and ears and stabbed people to death with near impunity. Women were shoved head-first into tar barrels, which were then set on fire and rolled down the street. In one instance, a Mohock named Plunket went to his wig maker to collect his new peruque. When the proprietor refused to lower the agreed-upon price, Plunket picked up a razor and slashed the man's throat.

Combine the semi-organised violence of gangs like the Mohocks with the random violence of a city filled with unemployed workers and demobilised soldiers and any plea for reform will quickly be drowned out by public cries for order and safety at any cost. Hangings of convicted criminals drew the same cheering crowds that had formerly gathered to see witches executed and traitors hanged, drawn and quartered. During the hey-day of the Mohocks, England still imposed the death penalty for no less than thirty-two crimes including high treason, petty treason, piracy, murder, arson, burglary, house-breaking, assault, highway robbery, horse theft, stealing anything with a value greater than 1s and any form of robbery. In each case – except high-treason committed by a nobleman, where the punishment was beheading – the sentence was either transportation to the Colonies or death by hanging – and all hangings were public. Lesser crimes brought a term of incarceration in one of the growing number of prisons but although torture was no longer a routine part of punishment, imprisonment was hardly better than many of the old physical mutilations.

For centuries, prisons and dungeons had been the breeding ground for a mysterious plague known as 'gaol fever'. Probably a catch-all term for a vast variety of contagions spawned in the filthy, disease-ridden mass cells, since the 1500s gaol fever had occasionally broken out, taking the lives not only of uncounted numbers of inmates, but of guards, prison wardens and citizens at large. In 1577 it had swept Oxford and killed more than 300 people in forty-eight hours. Eleven years later it claimed 500 lives in Exeter. By the early 1700s, thanks largely to the increased numbers of prisons and burgeoning prison populations, gaol fever was still alive and well. Following the 1728 arrest of the wardens of London's Marshalsea and Fleet prisons on charges of murdering and robbing their prisoners, a commission was established, under the direction of General James Oglethorpe, to investigate prison conditions and make recommendations for improvements that might help eliminate both rampant corruption and the constant threat of gaol fever. What Oglethorpe and his board found was shocking in the extreme.

Eighteenth-century prisons, like some of their modern counterparts, were privately owned, profit-making ventures; but rather than billing the government for their services, it was the prisoners themselves who bore the cost of their incarceration. Inmates at London's Newgate Prison were charged three guineas for admission, half a guinea per week for a bed and additional fees were charged for candles, eating utensils and food. In the case of the Marshalsea and Fleet prisons, prisoners were even charged for the manacles they wore and were routinely tortured in an effort to extract money from their families. If a prisoner could not pay his bill, he was simply kept inside until someone paid his way out or he died: whether they had been convicted of any crime, or their sentence had run its course, was irrelevant.

Oglethorpe's commission heard of prisoners fighting with each other, and the rats, for scraps of rotten food; of cells that had open sewers running through them and of prisoners who could not afford a bed being forced to sleep on the wet floors. One testimonial told of a man who had taken his dog to prison with him, to protect him from the rats: the rats had killed and eaten the dog. Another report concerning the horrible floggings routinely administered to prisoners said: 'I saw a man walk across the yard with the blood that had run down from his lacerated flesh squishing out of his shoes at every step ... and the ants were carrying away great pieces of human flesh that the lash had scattered on the ground'. Other tales were too horrible to detail and Oglethorpe's report annotated them only as 'indescribable nastiness'. The committee completed its report and handed it to Parliament who filed it away and conveniently forgot about it. Fortunately, there were concerned citizens, members of the judiciary and even of the government, who took a more enlightened, hands-on approach to legal reform.

In 1748 – ten years after the Oglethorpe commission – a ten-year-old boy named William York was convicted of the stabbing to death of a young girl and sentenced to be hanged. The Home Secretary interceded on William's behalf and sentenced him to prison for ten years on the condition that, upon his release, William would join the navy. At issue was not the crime (William had been duly convicted of that) but the effectiveness of capital punishment, particularly in the case of one so young, in preventing others from committing similar crimes. Four years after William York's ordeal, Horace Walpole – a well-known political pundit, essayist and gossip – was attacked by a gang and shot in the face while strolling through Hyde Park. Writing of the event to a friend, he decried, 'what a shambles this country is grown'. The same day Walpole wrote his letter, seventeen men were hanged at Tyburn but it did nothing to slow London's crime rate. One of the many factors contributing to London's soaring crime rate was the growing instance of organised crime and criminal gangs. Unlike the Mohocks, these were hardened criminals who banded together to increase the effectiveness and profitability of their activities.

Only months before Walpole's encounter, the problem of organised crime had been addressed by Henry Fielding (a London magistrate and author of the novel *Tom Jones*) when he wrote: 'Officers of Justice have owned to me that they have passed by such criminals with warrants against them without daring to apprehend them; and indeed they could not be blamed for not exposing themselves to sure destruction'. Lambasting the system of punishment, as well as the impunity with which criminals operated, Fielding referred to England's prison system as 'prototypes of Hell' where criminals could exchange information

and form gangs. To fully appreciate Fielding's statements it is necessary to understand that as late as 1751 neither London, nor anywhere else in England, had anything remotely resembling an organised police force. Local citizens patrolled the streets as an unpaid public service but it did little, if anything, to deter crime. It was a situation Henry Fielding and his brother John decided to do something about. In 1753 they convinced the government to fund an organisation that became known as the Bow Street Runners. With the Fielding brothers serving as commanding officers and magistrates, the Runners investigated reports of criminal activity, looked for clues, interviewed witnesses and, with a little luck, apprehended the guilty party. In retrospect this seems an obvious way to fight crime, but the Bow Street Runners were the first professional detective force in Great Britain's long history.

With the Fieldings leading the way toward reform, John Howard took up General Oglethorpe's fallen banner in 1755 and again insisted that England could not possibly call itself a progressive nation until it reformed its prison system. Like Oglethorpe, Howard decried the complete wastage of human life imposed by a system that shackled men and women to a wall when they could be taught a trade, or

This example of a public pillory shows how popular this sort of spectacle could be given productive work to do. What Howard included in his report, that Oglethorpe had not, were numerical statistics. Of 4,375 inmates polled, half of them were found to be in prison because they were unable to pay their debts. Most hardened criminals – at least those who had not been hanged at Tyburn – had been transported to the colonies, flogged, pilloried, or branded. Howard concluded his report by stating that most of the people who were incarcerated were either debtors; were awaiting trial; had been imprisoned for misdemeanours or were simply too poor to buy their way out of jail. He also cited an earlier report which stated that more than 5,000 people died in British jails every year from starvation. It took John Howard nearly twenty years to get the government to listen, but in 1774 he finally convinced Parliament to investigate conditions in Britain's prisons. As they had done when General Oglethorpe carried out his study more than forty-five years earlier, the new report was quietly shelved and ignored, despite the fact that more and more international voices were calling for the world to rethink the manner in which it dealt with society's misfits.

In 1764, Cesare Beccaria, an Italian lawyer from Milan, published a treatise entitled *Crimes and Punishments.* In his paper, Beccaria said the best way to fight crime was through prevention rather than punishment; that everyone was entitled to a speedy trial and that the use of torture, either to extract a confession or as a means of punishment, was futile. The work must have caught someone's attention; it was translated into twenty-two languages and went through six Italian editions in only eighteen months. Five years later, an English magistrate expressed similar sentiments when he wrote: 'it is scarcely to be credited that by the laws of England, there are above 160 different offences which subject the guilty parties to the death penalty'. Compare this to the thirty-two hanging offences in force only seventy years earlier, and the fact that the number of capital crimes would continue to rise until, by the end of the century, they would top-out at a staggering 220. Predictably, however, nobody seemed willing to take action on reforming the system; not even when King George III personally established a fifteen-member cabinet to review each and every death sentence passed in England – excepting those where the conviction had been for murder. Each case may have been carefully reviewed, but the numbers of hangings continued to increase as the list of capital offences grew. The best anyone seemed able to do was devise more efficient ways of hanging people. In 1760 a new 'drop' method was proposed. Rather than simply hauling the condemned into the air and allowing them to kick and thrash until they slowly strangled, the drop was supposed to ensure a speedy death

by breaking the victim's neck. The first man given an opportunity to try out this advanced technology was the Earl Ferrers, but the trap failed to open properly, the Earl was left to choke to death and business continued as usual at Tyburn's hanging tree.

Finally, in 1783, it was decided that public executions did more to excite a ghoulish populace than it did to eliminate crime. Henceforth, hangings would no longer be public affairs and on 7 November 1783 the last man was hanged at that cherished institution, the Tyburn Tree. While reformers may have taken some small comfort at this de-glorification of execution, even as respected a personage as Dr Samuel Johnson – compiler of the first English language dictionary and conversationalist extraordinaire – thought it signalled the end of civilisation. 'The age is running mad for innovations', he cried, 'even Tyburn is not safe. Executions are intended to draw spectators. If they don't, they don't answer their purpose. The public is gratified by a procession; the criminal is supported by it.' Eight years later, in 1791, gibbeting was outlawed as was the public flogging of females – women could still be whipped as punishment for some crimes, but the sentence could not be carried out in public.

For all its flaws and failures, the eighteenth century had witnessed some laudable progress in the way criminals, and suspected criminals, were dealt with. New rules of procedure made hearsay evidence less acceptable, and torture to elicit a confession had been outlawed. Adding to this was the fact that defendants were prohibited from offering any evidence in court; if no statement from a defendant was admissible, then a confession extracted by torture had no value. By 1827 a law had been passed whereby a plea of 'not guilty' was automatically entered any time a suspect refused to plead either guilty or not guilty – it was a distinct improvement over 'pressing' a plea out of a suspect. Similarly, in the newly established United States of America, the Fifth Amendment to the Constitution guaranteed that no-one could give self-incriminating evidence.

Although uncounted thousands of Englishmen and women were convicted of capital crimes during the 1700s, less than one out of three were actually hanged. Deportation to the American Colonies (or, after America's Declaration of Independence in 1776, to Australia) was considered a more humane alternative to execution. Prisoners, however, did not always see it this way and on more than one occasion convicts insisted they would rather swing than be transported. There was certainly justification for their fears. Conditions onboard prison ships were comparable to the worst dungeons of the Middle Ages. Between 1750 and 1755 alone, the bodies of more than 2,000 dead prisoners were dumped into New York harbour, thousands more floated in other American harbours and who knows how many human carcasses had been tossed overboard at sea. The value placed on a deported criminal's life is made clear by the fact that the British government offered anyone willing to help establish colonies in Australia a grant of 4,000 acres of land, forty cows and forty convict-slaves. Captain Arthur Phillip, first governor of New South Wales, Australia, wrote to the Crown asking: 'if the convicts commit either murder or sodomy, may I sell them to the natives for meat?' We do not know what answer he received.

Despite the perils of transportation and the less than progressive attitude of their guardians, the overall success of deportation brought about its own sort of reform of the English penal system. When the British public learned that thousands of prisoners were helping to build roads and improve the physical infrastructure of newly established towns in America and Australia, they began insisting that prisoners in Britain be given similar productive tasks to perform.

Outside Great Britain, similar changes in the treatment of law breakers were also coming about. Ecclesiastical courts were slowly losing their power to impose physical punishments on individuals whose crimes were more of the spirit than of the flesh. Even the more traditionally structured nations were slowly stripping away the power of local noblemen and war-lords, forcing them to hand over suspected criminals to government-controlled courts who followed rules set down by a central judiciary. Integral to this process of reform was the slow abolition of torture. In most cases, as had been true in Great Britain, torture as a means of extracting a confession was stricken from the books before it was abolished as a form of punishment. In 1721, Elector Frederick I of Prussia decreed that torture could only be used after he, personally, had reviewed the case in question. In 1754, Frederick II – known as Frederick the Great – outlawed torture altogether. In 1734, Sweden became the first country to outlaw the use of torture in any form, for any purpose. Between 1738 and 1789 the Kingdom of the Two Sicilies did away with torture as did Austria between 1769 and 1776. Thanks largely to the work of Milanese lawyer, Cesare Beccaria, Italy banned torture in 1786 and the Netherlands followed suit between 1787 and 1794.

In 1801, Czar Alexander I of Russia was made aware of a case wherein a prisoner had confessed to a crime under torture but had later been proven innocent. On 27 September, the Czar decreed that his government must, henceforth:

> ensure with all strictness throughout the whole Empire that nowhere in any shape or form … should anyone dare permit or perform any torture, under pain of inevitable and severe punishment … that accused persons should personally declare before the Court that they had not been subjected to any unjust interrogation … that finally the very name of torture, bringing shame and reproach on mankind, should be forever erased from the public memory.

Spain only followed suit in 1812, the same year it belatedly abolished the Holy Office of the Inquisition and the horrors that had accompanied it since 1484.

Like Spain, France seemed more reluctant than most of her continental neighbours to adopt penal and corporal reforms. As late as the mid-

eighteenth century, a man convicted of the attempted assassination of King Louis XV was condemned to having the offending hand lopped off before molten lead and boiling oil were poured on the bleeding stump; and this was only the prelude to the real sentence. Horses were tied to each of the man's limbs and then whipped off in all directions in an attempt to dismember the felon. As his joints proved stronger than the horses, the executioner stepped in and loosened the man's arm and leg joints with a knife. As late as 1791, victims were still being boiled in oil and only because Voltaire refused to stop writing about the inequities of the French judicial system were the rack and flogging abandoned in 1789. The year 1789 was significant to the history of French punishment in at least one other way as well. On 14 July of that year an angry mob stormed Paris's Bastille prison, signalling the downfall of the monarchy. As brutal and bloodthirsty as the revolution and the ensuing Reign of Terror were, the Revolutionary Assembly did manage to outlaw the use of torture in criminal investigations. Despite the tens of thousands of innocent people who were sentenced to death in the name of the Revolution, those found guilty of less egregiously treasonous offences than suspicion of being a closet monarchist or addressing their neighbour as 'Monsieur' rather than the more politically correct 'Citizen', were simply condemned to being dressed down by the court with the following words: 'Your country has found you guilty of an infamous action: the law and the tribunal strips you of the quality of French citizenry.' Unlike the British, who sent their outcasts to the American Colonies or Australia, the French did not seem to care where the condemned went so long as they left France. For those found guilty of truly anti-revolutionary offences there was a far more famous, and infamous, end in store, but this particular institution of the Reign of Terror had its beginnings long before the fall of the Bastille and the rise of 'La Revolution'.

On a balmy Paris day in May 1738 a heavily pregnant woman was so shocked by the sight of a man having his limbs shattered on the wheel that she had to be carried home after going into premature labour. Both mother and son survived their ordeal with no apparent side effects. She and her husband named the boy Joseph: the family name was Guillotine. Forty-eight years later, in 1785, Joseph Guillotine began experimenting with mechanical methods of separating a man from his head – other nations had used such devices before, as we saw with the Halifax Gibbet, but since none of the previous inventors had been French, beheading machines had never seemed acceptable to the French. By October 1789, the Revolutionary Assembly had taken power and Joseph Guillotine managed to arrange an audience to explain the principal of his machine. The supposedly instantaneous death by decapitation seemed to be in line with the new French policy of abolishing torture. Maximilian Robespierre – the Machiavellian head of the Committee of Public Safety who would send uncounted thousands to their death in the name of liberty – openly wept because he insisted that the thought of harming another human being was abhorrent to him, and it should be obvious to anyone that Guillotine's beheading machine was entirely painless. More importantly for the egalitarian-minded Revolutionary Assembly, citizen Guillotine's machine would be used on all malefactors regardless of their social class. An equal death for all French citizens.

It took the revolution two and a half years to pass a bill decreeing that all executions in the Republic would take place on the machine rapidly becoming known as Madame Guillotine (as well as 'The People's Avenger', 'The National Razor', 'Saint Guillotine' and 'The

Opposite: It was the French physician Joseph-Ignace Guillotine who first promoted a law that required that all executions (even those of commoners and plebeians) be carried out by means of a "machine that beheads painlessly". An easy death – so to speak – was no longer to be the prerogative of nobles. After a series of experiments on cadavers taken from a public hospital, the first of these machines was put up in the Place de Greve in Paris on 4 April 1792, and the first execution (in this case of a common highwayman) took place on the 25th of April. Soon this invention was to become the hallmark of the years 1792–94. It is worth noting here, that the entire motive behind its invention and use was to do away with the more torturous aspects of public execution. Death was intended to be swift and painless ... or at least that was the idea.

Science quickly now discovered a new and surprising fact (confirmed by modern neurophysiology): a head decapitated by a swift slash of an axe or guillotine knows that it is a beheaded head whilst it rolls along the ground or into the basket. Consciousness survives long enough for such a perception. After the execution of Louis XVI and Marie Antoinette on 21 January 1793, the "machine" (called only thus until this date) became known as "la louisette" or "le louison"; only after 1800 did the term "la guillotine" become established.

Patriotic Shortener') and almost immediately the ungainly device began popping up all over France. The first victim of the first guillotine was Nicholas-Jacques Pelletier, whose execution for theft had been delayed specifically so he could try out the Revolution's new toy. To make the most of the occasion – and the least of the fountains of blood that inevitably followed the fall of the blade – the machine had been painted red and Pelletier was dressed in matching hues. Almost instantly variations on the guillotine sprang up everywhere. Some had multiple blades and others, like multi-seated privies, were designed to accommodate more than one victim at once. Miniature replicas of the death machine appeared as children's toys capable of decapitating anti-revolutionary sparrows. Diminutive guillotines adorned the dinner tables of revolutionaries and, when made of glass and porcelain, were filled with perfumes. Robespierre, himself, draped one in blue buntings and made it an object of worship in a newly invented 'religion' dedicated to the 'goddess of reason'.

Those less imbued with the true spirit of the revolution, however, began to ask disturbing questions: Did it really kill as quickly as its inventor claimed? On more than one occasion a victim's head was seen to roll its eyes and try to speak as it tumbled across the scaffold amid a fountain of blood. When Charlotte Corday – sentenced to death for having murdered revolutionary pamphleteer Jean-Paul Marat – was beheaded, the executioner picked up her head and slapped her face. Before life flickered out, Corday looked at her killer and scowled. One wonders what Maximilian Robespierre's reaction was when his own turn came to meet the National Razor. Given its reputation and association with the Reign of Terror, it is hardly surprising that the Guillotine never gained wide acceptance outside of France.

While 'Madame Guillotine' was tidying up resistance to the revolution at the rate of thousands a week, London was doing away with its own miscreants at the paltry rate of one hanging every fortnight, but the array of crimes which lead to the king's gallows was still growing. By 1820, people were being hanged for such horrific offences as stealing a single piece of wood, defacing Waterloo Bridge and impersonating one of the old-age pensioners at Chelsea Barracks. Sickened by the inability of England to reform her own judicial code, subjects of the Crown took matters into their own hands – at least when called up for jury duty. When a man was charged with having stolen a £10 banknote the jury valued the piece of paper at 39s – a misdemeanour. When another man was charged with stealing a sheep, the jury only found him guilty of stealing the wool – also a misdemeanour. Similarly, a horse thief was found guilty of the petty crime of stealing horse hair.

Still, as handy as England's judges were with the gallows, progress was being made in other areas. Since torture as punishment had been made illegal, when a person was convicted of a crime that called for branding, the condemned was asked to hold a slice of ham while the bailiff pressed a cold branding iron against the slab of meat. Undoubtedly the symbolic act was followed by a stern lecture, but it was a lot less painful than the alternative. Like branding, flogging slowly went the way of the dinosaur. The last known case of judicially imposed flogging in Great Britain took place in Scotland in 1817 and in 1820 the whipping of women was abolished. Two years later the flogging of men was also outlawed, but the practice would continue as a standard disciplinary measure in the Royal Navy until 1881.

In a truly forward-looking move, Warwickshire courts began imposing one-day sentences on youthful offenders in 1820. As part of this imaginative early-release program, the youth had to promise to go home at the end of the day and their parents swore to guarantee the child's future behaviour. It was a far cry from one generation earlier when a child caught stealing a loaf of bread would have been hanged. When these one-day sentences were first imposed they were officially

These restraints show a technological refinement and humanitarian development from their medieval ancestors. We see a lead cuff (top) for locking about a prisoner's wrists and leading them from place to place. Wrist shackles (centre) have built in locks and rounded edges, making them marginally more comfortable to wear than earlier examples. And the ankle fetters (bottom) exhibit similar properties. These devices developed as a result of the move toward incarceration and imprisonment in favour of private or public torture for judicial punishment.

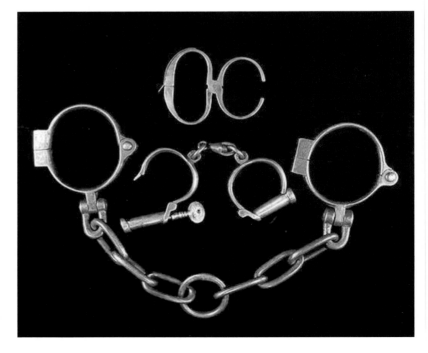

unrecognised, but their unquestioned effectiveness was carefully followed by the best legal minds in London.

These heartening statistics should not be taken to indicate that centuries of abuse ended with a few enlightened judges or the single stroke of a pen. In 1823, Grey Bennet testified before the House of Lords that he was aware of at least 6,959 cases of whippings that had taken place inside England's prisons over the previous seven years. By and large, however, British prisoners were being released from their shackles and chains and put to work cleaning up the squalid conditions in which they lived. Some prisoners spent shifts on treadmills which ran ventilating fans that helped freshen the fetid air and remove collected moisture from jail cells. Similar treadmills were used to pump sewage out of prisons and pump in clean water and still others were used to operate flour mills. It may not have taught the inmates a useful trade but it was a vast improvement over being chained to the wall of a damp dungeon.

In 1829, London became the last major city in Europe to receive a police force. Under the guiding hand of Sir Robert Peel (who had established a similar force in Ireland in 1812), the London Metropolitan Police – commonly known as 'Peelers' or 'Bobbies', after their founder, or as 'Coppers' after the copper buttons on their uniforms – began tackling the crime problem at its source. The earlier crime could be detected, and the sooner criminals realised that there was little chance of escaping the long arm of justice, the sooner the honest people of London – and eventually the citizens of every town and city throughout Great Britain, Europe and the rest of the world – could sleep in relative ease.

Despite the best efforts of social reformers everywhere, the twin problems of dealing with crime and meting out punishment have never been adequately solved. No matter how harsh, or how lenient, judicial systems are, criminals still haunt every corner of the planet. How we, today, deal with them is still being examined by our court and legislative systems and will continue to be debated for the foreseeable future. How non-European countries and societies have sought to deal with these interconnected problems, at various times in the past, will be examined in the next chapter.

TORTURE AROUND THE WORLD

B ased on what we have seen so far, it might easily be construed that torture was somehow limited to the Western World. This would be an incorrect assumption. Torture and cruelty are not limited to any specific culture, geographic area or time period. Wherever weak, fearful people struggle to retain their grip on power, there is an almost unlimited capacity to inflict pain and suffering in the name of the greater good. Consequently, this chapter will deal with a few select cultures, scattered across the planet and through the centuries, where torture has been accepted as an integral part of the social structure. With these broad parameters in mind, it seems only logical to begin with that most ancient of human cultures, China.

Among Western nations China is perceived as a place brimming with strange and exotic methods of inflicting an unimaginable array of tortures. Considering what we have already seen of Western civilisations it would be erroneous to credit the Chinese with a greater sense of cruelty than the rest of the world. It is fair to say, however, that the Chinese attitude toward torture remained unchanged for a longer period of time than it did among Western nations. Until the early years of the twentieth century, the Chinese system of judicial punishment was based on the Tang Code of law, instituted some time around 200 BC. This continuity gave the Chinese slightly more than two millennia to perfect their approach to inflicting pain, and perfect it they certainly did.

Old China, like most early civilisations, had a strictly delineated class system and punishment was meted out according to a person's social status. Slaves who committed bodily assault on a free man or woman

Twentieth-century Chinese postcard depicting prolonged execution by exposure through confinement in bamboo cages. Whether the weight of these unfortunate men is being supported entirely by their necks or whether their ankles have also been locked within restraints is unclear from the image.

were executed, while a free man who killed a slave – be it his own or someone else's – could receive no greater punishment than a single year of imprisonment. If a nobleman killed a slave, or even a free commoner, they were subject to no punishment at all. For the bulk of society – that is to say the entirety of the free population below noble rank – there was a sliding scale of punishments determined not only by the severity and nature of the crime, but also by the social status of the accused. For those of a higher rank who assaulted, robbed or murdered someone of a lower rank, the punishment was considerably less than it was for someone of a lower social rank who committed the same offence against a person of higher rank. If this seems like a shockingly medieval approach for a civilisation as enlightened as China, we must take into account that Chinese society was based on a rigid sense of order and propriety. Crime in any form disrupted that order and it was essential that social balance be restored lest the fabric of society unravel as chaos ensued. The Tang Code was every bit as concerned with guaranteeing the perpetuation of the proper order of things as it was with punishing wrongdoers.

To make this complicated system workable, the Code was divided into two sections; the first dealt with basic principals of civil and criminal law, and the second with portioning out the proper penalties for every conceivable type of crime – taking into consideration the various circumstances under which it may have been committed as well as the social class of both perpetrator and victim. Because the

Chinese are a philosophical people, the Code also contained lengthy justifications as to why one punishment was more appropriate for a given offence than another. If this seems impossibly complex, at least it ensured that justice was portioned out according to law rather than the whim of the presiding judge, as was so often the case in Western Europe. To make this system work as efficiently and impartially as possible, the guilt of the accused had to be established beyond any shadow of doubt, and the only way this could be accomplished was through a confession. In all fairness to what is about to come, it should be mentioned that those who confessed to the crime prior to their trial – thus saving the court a lot of time and money – were subject to receiving a much lighter sentence than those refusing to confess even in the light of overwhelming evidence of guilt. Today we would call this plea-bargaining. For those who obstinately refused to confess, there were a variety of ways to make them reconsider.

One such method of confession-extracting torture was called 'kneeling on chains'. The prisoner's thumbs and big toes were bound together, behind their back, forcing the entire weight of their kneeling body to fall on the toes and knees. As if this weren't uncomfortable enough, a coil of sharp-edged chain was placed under the suspect's knees, inflicting excruciating pain and lacerating the knees, sometimes cutting so deep that it severed the tendons. If it was allowed to continue long enough, permanent damage would be done to the knee joints.

Even if such torture was not employed, a few days, or weeks, in a Chinese jail should have been enough to loosen the tongue of even the most recalcitrant prisoner. While prisoners were allowed to roam free in communal cells during the day, at night each man was locked into their bunk with a device nearly identical to the stocks. The prisoner was laid on their back, on their bunk, and their feet were locked in a stock-like device attached to the foot of the bed, making it impossible for the prisoner to shift position or turn over in their sleep. Just to make sure the victim did not, somehow, wriggle out of the stocks, their hands were locked in manacles attached to the wall with chains and another chain, attached to the bunk, was pulled tight across their chest and locked into place. There are no accounts of prisoners escaping from Chinese jails during the night.

When a confession was finally elicited and sentence had been duly passed, lesser crimes were often punished by the imposition of a fine, as they were in most other societies. In China, however, this fine might well be accompanied by a loss of social rank. In instances of petty crime, this loss of position might only be temporary; for more

The Chinese punishment of 'kneeling on chains'. Although not precisely an image of what is described in the main body of the text, this beautifully rendered painting should serve to illustrate the sort of punishment being described.

Here we see a Chinese version of the prison cell. Whether attempted escapes were commonplace is unknown, but this prisoner has been secured by wrist, ankle and neck to his cell bunk, which was also presumably contained behind some sort of locked door or cage and would have had armed guards as well.

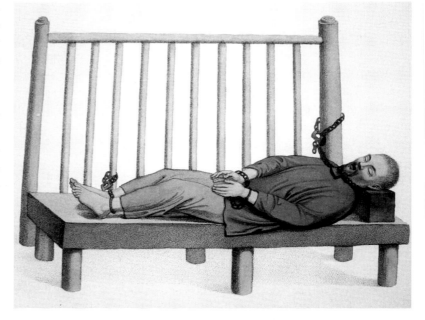

serious offences it could be permanent. If the judge considered a fine or loss of rank too severe a punishment, the guilty party might simply have their ears twisted. Two burly guards held the prisoner immobile while grabbing his ears and twisting with all their might; not hard enough to tear the flesh, but certainly hard enough to leave a lasting impression. For slightly more serious offences such as petty theft, public drunkenness or insulting someone of a superior social rank, a good flogging might be imposed and this was always carried out immediately – in the courtroom. To determine the proper number of blows, the judge again referred to the Tang Code. The crime might call for the use of a light whip or a heavy whip and could, depending upon the nature and circumstances of the incident, demand anywhere from 10 to 100 blows. The punishment must precisely fit the crime. When the severity of the flogging had been determined, the punishment was inflicted with a whip made of lengths of split bamboo. While it may not have broken the skin, enough pain and damage were inflicted that the prisoner's entire back and rump were soon a mass of subcutaneous blood-blisters.

One possible alternative to a sound whipping was for the convict to be forced to wear a pillory-like collar known alternatively as the *fcan hao*, *cangue*, *tcha* and *ea*. Like the European pillory, this device consisted of a massive wooden collar into which the victim's head was locked. In this case, however, the collar was not mounted on a stake. Rather, it was just a chaffing, cumbersome collar the prisoner was forced to wear for a proscribed period of time. To make the punishment even more uncomfortable, the outer rim of the collar was sometimes fitted with three iron spikes, making it impossible for the condemned to lie down or rest his head. Generally, if someone did something which warranted being locked into this collar, they had also been bad enough to receive a flogging; so they were first whipped and then pilloried.

As a vast country populated by people who spoke many different languages, translators were an integral part of Chinese society. For interpreters who knowingly mistranslated either their boss's words, or those of another party, a special punishment was devised. The convict was forced into a kneeling position with a thick bamboo rod placed behind their knees. When their knees were on the ground and their full weight on the bamboo rod, a guard would stand on either end of the rod. The pain was excruciating but no permanent, physical damage was inflicted. Special punishment was also reserved for women convicted of the crime of 'lack of modesty' – a polite way of saying prostitution. For this particular crime, the prisoner was forced to kneel while small

This image comes from a twentieth-century postcard of Chinese prisoners of war wearing the cangue, which served very much like a portable version of the European pillory.

slivers of wood were placed between her fingers. Heavy cord was then wrapped around the fingers and drawn tighter and tighter, forcing the knuckle bones against the wood. Note that during the majority of these punishments the prisoner was made to kneel. This subservient posture not only showed deference for the judge, but was yet another form of humiliation inflicted on the guilty party.

No matter what form the punishment was to take it was customary, in this highly ritualistic society, for the prisoner to grovel before the judge – on their knees, of course – and beg for forgiveness, understanding and leniency. Whether or not this ceremonial display of repentance had any effect on either the court or the sentence is open to debate but there are instances where the prescribed sentence would undoubtedly have brought even the most hardened criminal to the point of begging. One of the most shocking, non-capital crimes in old China was reserved for Buddhist monks convicted of having sexual relations. There was only one punishment for this crime. A hot iron rod was driven through the neck muscles of the victim and a length of chain was then threaded through the raw, charred hole and tied around his neck. Like a dog on a horrible leash the monk was led through the streets of town, naked, begging for money. Only when a court-specified amount of cash had been collected was the poor wretch released and returned to his monastery. There were even harsher, non-capital punishments, one of the more common being blinding. The condemned was held down while a guard rubbed their eyes with a cloth soaked in lime. In a matter of minutes the eyes were entirely eaten away.

In addition to covering a myriad of lesser civil and criminal offences the Tang Code also dictated the nature of, and punishment for, what was known among the Chinese as 'abominable crimes'. There were only ten of these but the terms in which they were couched allowed a fair amount of latitude in determining exactly what acts might constitute an abominable crime. According to the Code, these crimes included: plotting rebellion, plotting sedition, plotting treason, resistance to authority, depravity, great irreverence, lack of respect for a parent, discord, unrighteousness and incest. In the first case, plotting rebellion, simply being involved in discussions with other rebels was sufficient for conviction. For the next two offences, the seditious or treasonous act must actually have taken place for the accused to be found guilty. For all three crimes, decapitation was the only possible punishment but the sentence did not end there. Under the assumption that such dastardly plots are never carried out alone, a person found guilty of one or more of these offences was also assumed to have confided their plans to their relatives and household. Consequently, a collective punishment was inflicted on the condemned man's family. His father and sons over fifteen years of age were strangled; younger sons, brothers, grandfathers, concubines and servants were sold as slaves and all female relatives were driven into exile. A similarly grim,

This nineteenth-century engraving was one of the earliest depictions of Chinese justice to which Western Europe was exposed. It would have probably seemed a cruel and barbaric torture to nineteenth-century Western civilization who had moved on to imprisonment and penal reform.

collective fate was visited on the extended family of anyone convicted of murdering three or more members of their family.

Because the family unit was so central to the Chinese way of life, crimes against the family were considered as heinous as crimes against the government; it was an affront to the natural order of things and therefore must be punished by the harshest means possible. Plotting to kill one or both parents, or either grandfather, was punishable by death, as was the act of striking a parent. In fact, if a child wrongly accused a parent of a criminal act the child was put to death for their audacity. Even if the accused parent was subsequently convicted of the crime, the child was sentenced to 100 blows with a heavy whip and three years in prison for exposing their parent's dishonour. Curiously, because familial order could only be maintained when children obeyed their parents, hitting a child, or turning them in for the commission of a crime, was not considered a punishable offence. As harsh as this all sounds, the Tang Code did make exceptions. Punishment for crimes against the family was always less severe and sometimes suspended altogether when the convicted party was under seven years of age, or over ninety. Those between seven and fifteen and those between seventy and ninety were exempt from torture and physical punishment, and could redress all but the most severe crimes by paying a fine. The mentally and physically handicapped were exempt from all forms of torture and those who were the sole support of aged or physically handicapped parents often had their sentences commuted so the parents were not made to suffer for their children's crimes.

In those instances where the death penalty was imposed, but where beheading was not called for, as it was in cases of treason, sedition or plotting rebellion, the method of execution could vary greatly. Looking at the nature of these executions one can easily believe that the condemned might have been a lot better off if they had tried to kill the emperor and been hauled off to the block. One method

This image shows a Chinese variation on the brodequin. While the victim is stretched out on his stomach (presumably so that he might be flogged or be subject to other torments), the torturers are driving wedges into the slats which hold his legs in order to break the bones of his ankles. It is likely that this was done more as a painful punishment than as a means of extracting a confession.

involved stretching the prisoner on a rack-like device before the guards kicked and stamped on him until all his bones were broken; then they beat him to death with heavy clubs. In addition to beheading, being stomped to death and strangulation, there was a particularly grizzly form of execution reserved primarily for those unwise enough to kill their father. In what was known as *Ling Che*, translated alternately as 'Death by a Thousand Cuts' and 'Death by Slicing', the condemned was, quite literally, carved up like a Christmas turkey. Having centuries to perfect this particularly nasty form of execution, the torture master could make it last as long, or short, a time as the crime and the judge warranted. Once the prisoner had been hauled to a public place and tied down to a table or framework, the executioner appeared with a covered basket containing the tools of his job; a collection of razor-sharp knives, each one marked with the name of a specific body part. Sliding his hand inside the basket, the executioner withdrew a blade at random and proceeded to hack off the designated part. A leg muscle might be cut away, or the ears or, if the condemned was extremely lucky – or the victim's family had sufficiently bribed the torturer – the 'heart knife' might be withdrawn first. A description of such an execution comes to us from an English visitor to China, Sir Henry Norman, and runs as follows:

> Grasping hand-fulls from the fleshy parts of the body, such as the thighs and the breasts, [he] slices them off. The joints and the excrescences of the body are next cut away one by one, followed by amputation of the nose, the ears, the toes and the fingers. Then the limbs are cut off piecemeal at the wrists and ankles, the elbows and knees, the shoulders and hips. Finally, the victim is stabbed in the heart and his head cut off.

Far more than just an unimaginably painful death, the *Ling Che* was intended to dishonour the victim and make it impossible for him to rejoin his ancestors in the after-life. It was a horrible punishment in the here and now, with an eternal punishment to follow.

Like the Chinese, their off-shore neighbours, the Japanese, developed a rigid system of punishment wherein honour, and the loss of honour, were as integral to the judicial system as was punishment itself. Also like the Chinese, the Japanese punished minor infractions of the law by whipping the miscreant with a bamboo whip and/or with an elaborate system of fines. When the crime was serious enough to warrant death, however, the highly developed sense of personal

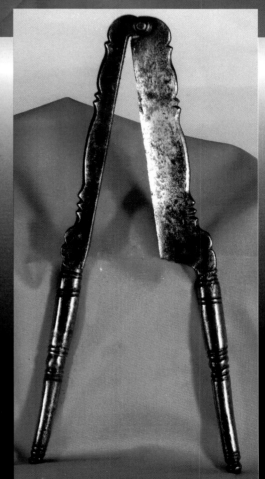

Top: This crucifix conceals a dagger. The purpose of this implement was supposedly to aid in the redemption and dispatch of a heretic who was being publicly executed by the office of the Inquisition, perhaps during an auto-de-fe. If the victim would recant their 'transgressions' and embrace the cross (in some way) the Inquisitor might be willing to have mercy on them and kill them quickly with the dagger rather than let them die slowly and painfully in the flames.

Right: This simple yet exquisitely made implement would be used to sever parts of the victim. It could be used in a variety of ways from tongues to lips to nipples to finger joints, etc. As this is such a beautifully made example, it is likely that this item may have been originally intended for a different purpose such as the *Izmail* used by a *Mohel* in the Jewish ritual of circumcision.

Left: Most people will be familiar with the story of the Man in the Iron Mask supposedly about the twin brother of King Louis XIV of France.

That story was inspired (at least in part) by objects such as this . . . known as Branks or masks of shame.

Above: This collar, with its suspended bell, would have been worn by a number of different individuals singled out for public humiliation. Whether a penitent or a troublesome guild member, this item would have been locked around their neck and they would have been led through the streets while being whipped, assaulted or otherwise tormented by the raging populace.

Left: Masks of shame – or Branks, as they were more commonly known – came in a wide variety of fantastical forms. Their variation is dependent in part on the imagination of the craftsman who constructed them and in part due to regional differences or variety of offence.

Here we see a variety of fantastical branks. Clockwise from top left: a donkey mask with a sealed mouth; followed by a boar's head; then the mask of a monarch or pope; and finally what appears to be an ass or sheep. Centre is a German postcard depicting a shrewish wife being publicly shamed for the 'house dragon' she is seen to be.

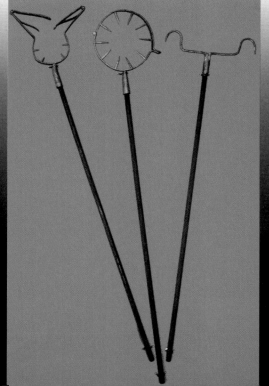

These devices are known as 'neck-catchers' and would have been used in a variety of ways and for a variety of reasons. They might be used to lead a prisoner from his holding cell to the torture room and back. They might have been used to escort a condemned man or woman to their place of execution, or they may have been used to parade criminals through the streets. It is clear to see that once the device surrounds someone's neck, there is very little hope of escape or independent action other than to cooperate with whomever has hold of the pole. In the detailed image at the top of the page you can appreciate the ingenious mechanism which allows for the device to be easily slipped about someone's neck, but with little hope of them getting out. Using this device a victim could be coordinated and coerced even without any actual contact.

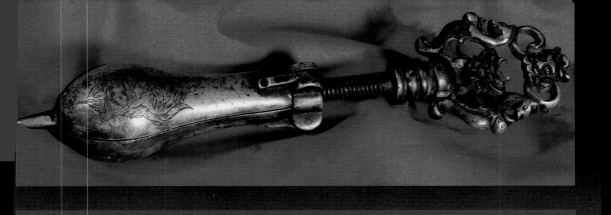

This is the innocently named 'Pear'. But this devilish device is anything but innocent. The operational mechanism (clearly demonstrated by the two images below) works by twisting the filigree handle so that the 'petals' of the pear open outward and can only be contracted by reversing the screw mechanism. This would have been inserted into the vagina or anus and then cranked open with obvious horrific results, or even have been inserted into the mouth and cranked open until the teeth shattered and the jaw dislocated. It is yet another example of where the artistic, beautifully designed and crafted device hides a dark and sinister purpose.

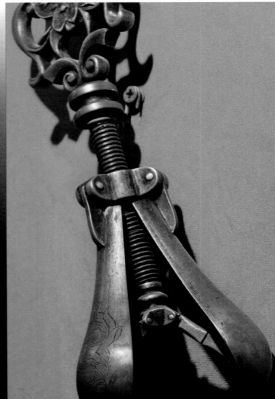

These images depict various forms of restraint. At the top of the page to the right you can see depicted both shackles and manacles for the wrists and ankles as well as a set of thumbscrews or thumbcuffs in the centre of the grouping.

Below that is a headcage which would have been used as a restraint device as well as a form of public humiliation (similar to the brank shown earlier and the scold's bridle discussed later).

And at the bottom of the page we see two very well-preserved examples of thumbscrews. While the thumbscrews in the image at the top of the page have a loop to serve as an attachment point for restraint, those at the bottom of the page are likely to have been created for the sole purpose of inflicting pain.

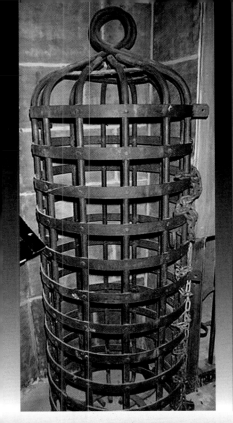

Here we see a variety of iron cages. These are properly referred to as gibbets, though the term can be somewhat confusing as hanging gallows and very early guillotines were occasionally called gibbets. Whether bodies were placed in these devices following execution for public display or a living victim was locked within to die of exposure, it was public spectacle which encouraged the use of these devices.

Gibbetting was common law punishment, which a judge could impose in addition to execution. It was most often used for traitors, murderers, highwaymen, and sheep-stealers, to discourage others.

The structures were therefore often placed adjacent to public highways. Although the intention was deterrence the public response was complex. Samuel Pepys expressed disgust at the practice. There was Christian objection that persecution of criminals should end with their death. The sight and smell of decaying corpses was offensive, and regarded as 'pestilential', so a threat to public health. In some cases, the bodies would be left until their clothes rotted or even until the bodies were almost completely decomposed, after which the bones would be scattered.

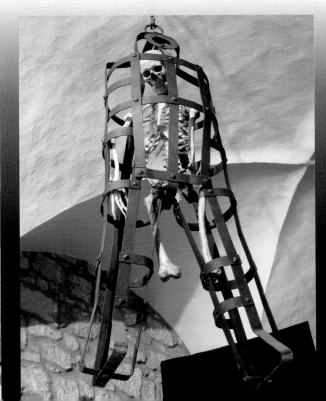

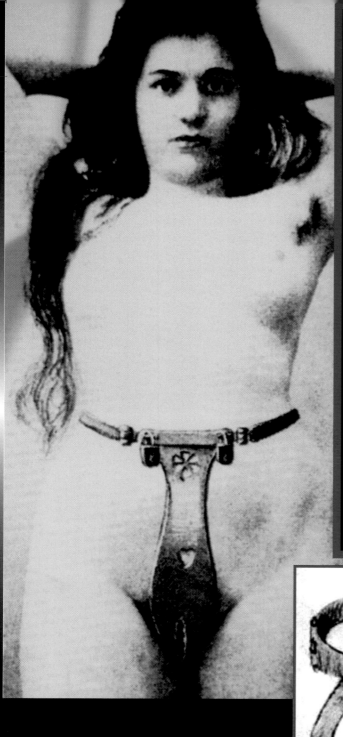

The first known mention of chastity belts in the Western world is in Konrad Kyeser von Eichstätt's *Bellifortis*, (*c.* 1400) which describes the military technology of the era. The book includes a drawing (see below) that is accompanied by the Latin text: 'Est florentinarum hoc bracile dominarum ferrcum et durum ab antea sic reseratum.' ('These are hard iron breeches of Florentine women which are closed at the front.')

The common myth about early chastity belts is that they were used by crusaders travelling to the holy land, to insure the fidelity of their wives who awaited their return. This seems rather implausible, since those early belts were very uncomfortable, and it seems very unlikely that they could be worn for extended periods of time. Another, more plausible, theory suggests that the belts were used by the women themselves to protect them against rapes during times such as the surrender of a city following a siege.

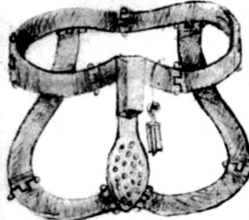

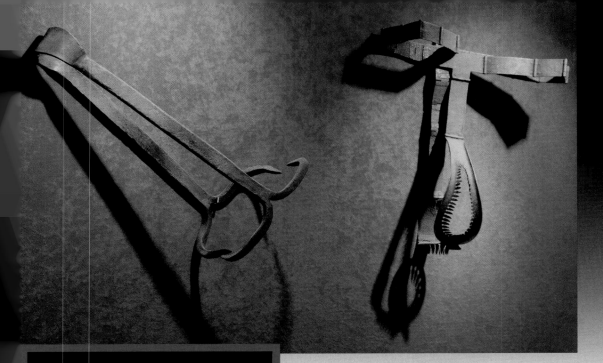

'Girdle of Purity'. 'Girdle of Venus'. 'Florentine Girdle': some of the names of the device better known as the Chastity Belt. While not an object used in the dungeon, the belt was responsible for more than its fair share of anguish. The image on the right depicts a design in which the front (vaginal) opening is quite small in order to allow fluids to escape but only very small objects could enter. The example depicted on the right of the top image, however, has a larger opening but one which is studded with very sharp teeth.

Above on the left is an entirely different sort of torture device designed specifically for female anatomy. This device is referred to as a breast ripper. This item was used both as a punitive and an interrogational device. Punitively, it was used red-hot to mark the breast of unmarried mothers. In an inquisitory nature claws were used,

Here we have a truly spectacular piece of craftsmanship. Whether or not chastity belts were locked on women by men who were worried about their fidelity or by the women themselves as protection against rape, it is open to interpretation whether these devices fall into the category of torture. But no matter which interpretation you take, there is no denying the beauty of the design and workmanship of this gilded example.

We may be tempted to consider these objects as barbaric relics of a distant past, but consider the following: In April, 2002, the Uwe Koetter Jewellers company of Cape Town, South Africa completed and delivered a spectacular diamond and pearl-encrusted chastity belt made of gold to a British customer. The belt reportedly cost 160,000 African Rand and was a wedding gift from a husband-to-be for his bride to wear at their wedding.

This instrument, sometimes referred to as 'the throne' was a pillory-like chair designed to hold the victim upside down by his feet. As you can see in Goya's illustration (left) the victim, once locked into place, would often have been flogged (note torturer in shadow on the left of the image) or have water poured into his mouth to choke him (note pitcher). Additionally, in the process of inquisition there would be a questioner (centre) and a scribe recording any statements the victim may have been able to make. This device was favoured by inquisitors in areas where the law permitted only one torture session of any given subject. With this device they could declare that they only inflicted one session – even if that session may have lasted for weeks on end. If done carefully, not only would these excruciating tortures have been non-lethal, but they would also have not left any noticeable marks on the body of the victim.

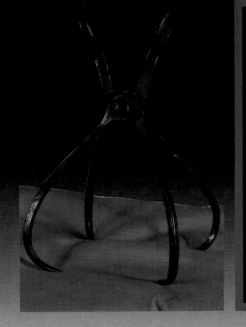

Right: A prisoner being subjected to this device would have been strapped down before having this forced into his or her mouth and then screwed open. This would result in broken teeth, followed by a broken jaw and then finally (if they were strapped face down) damage to the vertical vertebrae at the back of the neck. Not only could this torture be inflicted upon them, but they could be left in the grip of the jawbreaker for any length of time.

Above: This device is known as both the 'witch's spider' and the 'Spanish Spider'. These four-pronged, scissor-joined claws were basic tools in the torture dungeon. They served, both red-hot and cold, for the lifting up of the victim by the buttocks, breasts, belly or head, often with two prongs in the ears or the eyes. They can still be found in the Third World today, especially for the interrogation of women.

Left: There are many types of bonds that tie humans to inhuman burdens: leg irons, arm irons, belts, and collars in great variety. This example is typical of the idiomatic ball and chain. The prisoner locked within this iron collar would be forced to carry this weight about with him for a long time; weeks, years, perhaps even for the rest of his life. This particular stone weighs 27 lbs (over 12 kg).

Furnished with spikes on all sides, this device (above left), which weighs more than 11 lbs (5 kg) is locked around the victim's neck, constantly and systematically eroding the flesh of the neck, shoulders and jaw to the bone. Infection, gangrene, sepsis and finally the erosion of the bones themselves (especially the exposed vertebrae) can prove fatal. The spiked necklace (top right) served a similar function. In the bottom right image we can see an example of a *cilice belt*. While these could be (and were) employed by torturers, they were more commonly self-imposed for the purposes of self-mortification. Whether worn around the torso or around a thigh or bicep, these devices furnished with sharp barbed spikes (222 in this example) on the inside were, and in some circles still are, dear to religious self-mortifiers. Below left we can see an example of a coat of thorns. Rather than serving as a punishment, this is found to be worn in certain parts of the world by torturers or executioners themselves, it certainly would have been helpful in dissuading any victim from readily fighting back.

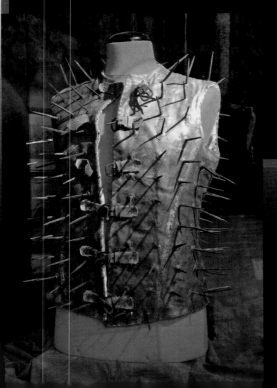

The punishment of the spiked barrel is fairly straightforward. A victim would be stripped naked and forced into a cask (such as those pictured here) with hundreds of inward-facing spikes. The cask would then be sealed and rolled down a hill or around the town or even thrown into the ocean to be tossed and rolled and thrown by the waves crashing on the shore. It should be apparent that there would be little hope of surviving such an ordeal.

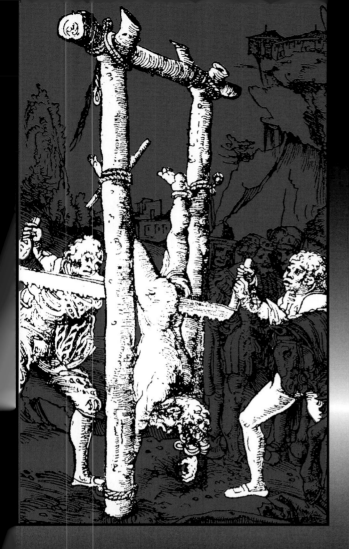

There is not much that needs to be said about the torture of the saw after examining the accompanying illustrations. The implement pictured below is a common four-hand two-man saw used by woodsmen and carpenters through the centuries.

History abounds in martyrs who suffered this fate, one that may be worse even than being burned at the stake with a slow, small fire, or being repeatedly dipped into boiling oil. Owing to his inverted position, which assures ample oxygenation of the brain and impedes the general loss of blood, the victim does not lose consciousness until the saw reaches the level of the lungs or the heart.

The Bible (II Samuel 12:31) tells us that David exterminated the inhabitants of Rabbah by putting man, woman and child 'under saws, and under harrows of iron, and under axes of iron, and made them pass through the brick-kiln'.

Perceived (along with the axe and the stake) as a method of execution to be wielded by the righteous, the saw was often meted out to homosexuals of both sexes though predominantly to men. There are various records of this sort of gruesome punishment being carried out in Spain, Germany, France and Italy – among others – until as recently as the nineteenth century.

The images above (based on a woodcut done by Lukas Cranach in 1548) and on the following page clearly show this method of torturous execution in action.

honour peculiar to the Japanese played a large part in ridding society of its worst offenders. Among the Japanese, high-ranking men and women were often given the opportunity to commit *hari-kari* (ritual suicide) rather than face the humiliation of public execution. Death was more acceptable than dishonour and death at one's own hands more acceptable than death at the hands of someone else. For crimes such as treason, where such respectable ends were not likely to be an option, the 'Death of Twenty-One Cuts' mirrored almost exactly the Chinese practice of *Ling Che*. Compare this description of the Death of Twenty-One Cuts – given by English traveller Richard Jephson, around 1865, when it was imposed on the captured rebel leader Mowung – with that of the *Ling Che*, above.

> With superhuman command of self, the unhappy Mowung bore silently the slow and deliberate slicing-off of his cheeks, then of his breasts, the muscles of upper and lower arms, the calves of his legs, etc., etc., care being taken throughout to avoid touching any immediate vital part. Once only he murmured an entreaty that he might be killed outright – a request, of course, unheeded by men who took a savage pleasure in skillfully torturing their victim.

Another equally cruel means of dispatching those convicted of capital crimes was to wrap their bodies in bundles of twigs and set them alight. This crowd-pleasing variation on the old European custom of being burnt at the stake provided the added attraction of watching the poor creature dance around wildly, in excruciating pain, while they were cooked alive.

In Japan, like China, torture was an acceptable means of convincing accused criminals to confess to their crimes and, as was true in the West during the Middle Ages, of making reluctant witnesses provide testimony. Such judicial torture often employed a split-bamboo whip, but unlike the whip used in China to administer punishment for minor infractions of the law, the Japanese whip was constructed so the sharp edges of the bamboo pointed outward, slicing as deep

He we see a combination of the torture of the pulley and of flogging with 'the broom'. Depending on where that cord binding his wrists leads, the victim here might be subjected to any one of a number of horrific torments.

into the flesh of the victim as razor blades. By judicial order, the flogging could last until the victim volunteered to speak, or up to 150 lashes. Beyond that point, further punishment would almost certainly have resulted in death. Another method of loosening tongues and refreshing faulty memories was known as 'Hugging the Stone'. In this basic but brutal torture, the accused was forced to kneel in a pile of knife-sharp flint fragments while heavy stones were piled in their lap.

Yet another such torture, known as *Yet Gomon*, mirrored almost exactly that used by the Spanish Inquisition. Here, the prisoner's wrists were bound behind their back and they were lifted into the air by means of a rope, where they were either left to dangle and dislocate their shoulders or dropped, by degrees, and have them jerked out of the sockets in a matter of seconds. This grizzly torture could only be employed in cases of murder, arson, theft, robbery and forgery of a document or an official government seal.

Taking Japan's long history into account, it seems that the seventeenth century was a period of particular judicial brutality, specifically in relation to the persecution of individuals who adopted Christianity. It seems especially eerie that religious persecution in Japan would so closely mirror, in both intensity and time period, the activities of the Spanish Inquisition. Here, as in Spain, men, women and children were murdered in an orgy of religious intolerance. Some were humiliated by being stripped naked before being thrown from a cliff or tossed into the boiling, natural cauldrons created by Japan's numerous active volcanoes. Other accused Christians had their limbs roped to four oxen which were then driven in opposite directions, ripping the victim to pieces. In September 1622, fifty Christians were simultaneously burnt alive in the city of Nagasaki. How very much like an inquisitional *auto-de-fe* this gory spectacle must have been. Precisely forty years after this particular mass execution, an equally terrible persecution of Christians took place in the same city. On this second occasion, September 1662, two European chroniclers, Francois Caron, a Frenchman and Joost Schorten, a Dutchman, were on hand to record the events.

They forced the women and more tender maids to go upon their hands and feet ... through the streets; that done, they caused them to be ravished ... by villains and then throwing them so striped and abused, into great deep tubs full of [poisonous] snakes and adders. Binding the [young men] about with combustible matter ... and also their fathers ... [they] set fire to them, whereby they underwent inconceivable torments and pains: some they poured hot scalding water continually upon them [and] tortured them in that manner till they died, [some of] which endured two or three days ... hundreds of them being stripped naked, and burnt in the foreheads [branded] that they might be known, and driven into the woods and forests, all men being commanded by proclamation, upon fear of death, not to assist them with either meat, drink, clothing or lodging. Once a year they precisely renewed their inquisition, and then every individual person must sign in their church-books, with his blood, that he renounces Christianity.

As it was in both the Orient and Europe, the system of juris prudence and punishment on the subcontinent of India was inextricably linked to both religion and maintenance of the social structure. In India, however, it was religion itself which dictated the shape of the social hierarchy. Hinduism, the official religion of untold millions of Indians, had its origins long before the first Hindu texts, the *Vedas*, were written down sometime around 1000 BC. Integral to this belief system was a rigid, inflexible division of social classes known as *castes*. The original caste system, in descending order, from top to bottom, ran as follows: the *kshatriyas*, the *brahmans*, the *vaishyas* and, at the bottom, the *shudras* (known as untouchables). Although originally the highest social order, by 500 BC the exalted position of the *kshatriyas* had been overtaken by the *brahmans* and, once in power, the *brahmans* did everything they could to retain control of the system. Integral to maintaining their hold on society was controlling all governmental and judicial functions and, through these offices, making it both impossible and illegal for those of lower castes to climb the social ladder. More than forty ethnic sub-groups were declared 'impure' and their treatment at the hands of their *brahman* masters, and the mogul emperors who controlled vast swaths of Indian territory, was no better than one would expect for subjugated peoples living in a primitive society.

Conveniently for the *brahmans*, the *Vedas* texts, and the later Laws of Manu, both provided as much support for the repression of the lower classes as the rules of the Spanish Inquisition did for the cruelties inflicted on Jewish *conversos* and Moorish *moriscos*. Like their very un-Christian counterparts in Spain, the *brahmans* insisted that only through ample punishment could the undesirable and criminal classes be 'saved' or, in this case, find a better incarnation when reborn into a new life here on earth. As was true of burning heretics and witches, the belief was that the more suffering that accompanied a person's punishment and/or death, the greater their chances of being 'purified'. Add to this the vast size and fractured political structure of old India and what emerges is a system of injustice haphazardly applied at the whim of hundreds of local rulers.

As was true of their early medieval European counterparts, when there were no witnesses to verify charges, Indian courts routinely relied on trial by ordeal to decide right from wrong or, as the Indians put it, *dharma* from *adharma* – justice from injustice. In Europe this often took the form of the accused being forced to reach into a cauldron of boiling water and extract a hot stone; the Indian incarnation having the suspect bury his arm, or arms, in a pot of cow dung mixed with boiling oil. If he pulled out his arm with no ill effects, he must, therefore, be innocent. Even more pernicious were trial by poison and trial by fire. In trial by poison, the accused had to thrust their hand into a covered basket containing a poisonous snake in an attempt to retrieve some small object. If they could fish around long enough, find the object and extract it without receiving a fatal bite, they were declared innocent. In trial by fire, they were required to walk across a bed of red-hot coals without having their feet blistered. Less painful at the time, but no less random, was the drawing of lots. The words *dharma* (justice) and *adharma* (injustice) were written on leaves, small pieces of parchment, or other objects and then placed in a jar from which the accused would extract one at random. *Dharma* says you are innocent, *adharma* declares guilt.

In instances where there were witnesses to a purported crime, providing testimony was not an option. As in the rest of the world, reluctant witnesses were routinely tortured until they remembered things 'correctly'. In at least one creatively sadistic instance, Indian authorities took a novel approach to forcing a witness to testify. Knowing that a man will often feel more concern for his family than for himself, local officials seized a potential witness's infant son, threw him in a bag containing a furious cat and threatened to beat the bag with bamboo poles if the man did not speak. Both his memory and willingness to testify instantly reappeared.

In all fairness to the Laws of Manu, it should be noted that in cases of petty crime the proscribed punishment for a first offence was a simple warning and, if the situation warranted, a fine commensurate with the offence. A second offence might either involve a much stronger dressing-down or some minor punishment and a considerably stiffer fine. A third appearance before the local justice would understandably bring a crushing fine often accompanied by some form of corporal punishment severe enough to leave a lasting impression. Continued offences and the person would be considered a hopeless criminal and physical mutilation would be imposed.

Mutilation, whippings and physical abuse were common at nearly all levels of society – the *brahman* class, local chieftains and emperors being almost always exempt. Masters beat their slaves, parents beat their children and courts beat incorrigible, small-time criminals. For more serious offences, as well as for recidivists, there were more creative punishments. While local versions of such now-familiar implements of torture and humiliation as the stocks, the rack, branding with hot irons, prolonged duckings in the local pond, starvation and forcing limbs into boiling oil or water were all employed as widely in India as in Europe and the Far East. There were also local variants on torture.

Memorably, the Indians seemed to excel in the use of sleep deprivation as a means of extracting confessions. Despite its use by Matthew Hopkins for eliciting confessions from suspected witches as discussed in Chapter 3, this inexpensive, non-lethal and highly effective form of torture would not be adopted by the West for many centuries after it had become a standard practice in India. The physical reality of India's hot, humid climate also provided opportunities for breaking a person's spirit and health not available to Europeans. If being pulled behind a cart and whipped was nasty, embarrassing and painful in Europe it could, quite literally, kill a person in India. Also unique to the climate are a selection of wildlife that will gladly inflict torture when given an invitation. A person tied to a tree and smeared with honey will attract an army of carpenter beetles and red ants that can gnaw their way through the skin in a matter of minutes. Unchecked, they will completely devour a human being over the course of a day. Much like the Chinese punishment for prostitution – whereby a woman's fingers were squeezed between slivers of wood – the Indians extended this procedure to crushing the feet of a convict, or suspect, between two heavy boards. We have seen many instances where a prisoner had their thumbs, or limbs, bound so tightly with cord that the flesh was cut through to the bone; in India a similar torture was inflicted by wrapping a digit or limb with a hot wire which was then doused with cold water. Instantly, the searing heat of the wire ended, only to be replaced by deep cuts made when the hot metal contracted.

Indian torture masters were every bit as skilled with a humble length of rope as was the Spanish Inquisition. Prisoners' heads were bound with ropes (either around the temple or by the throat) and the other end tied to their feet, either by forcing the man's head forward past his knees, or bending him backwards as far as his spine would allow. Alternatively, one leg might be pulled so far forward that it nearly touched the victim's shoulder, and tied in that position. For a truly satisfying moment of sadism, the torturer might then force the man to stand on his free leg, beating him savagely each time he fell over. The arms and legs might be interlaced in grotesquely painful ways and bound in that position or heavy, sharp rocks might be tied to a prisoner's back, making it impossible for him to stand erect and impossible for him to lie down. Horrible as all these tortures are, the pain and physical exhaustion they inflicted were inevitably increased if the procedure was carried out under the blazing Indian sun. A report by British commissioners, assembled in 1855, recounts one such torture session imposed on a man and his son for failing to pay a land tax. 'Both men [had] their legs tied together, and their heads tied to their feet in a stooping posture; their hands were tied behind them, and stones placed upon their backs; in which posture they were made to stand from six in the morning until noon. It will hardly be a matter of surprise that the father died the following month.' In a similar incident, a man who was unable to pay a tax of one rupee, four annas (then the equivalent to six British pence, or about twenty modern American cents) had his hands tied behind his back and his head bound to his feet with a rope for two hours. The 1855 report mentioned above, which was delivered to Parliament that same year, contained the following paragraph:

Among the principal tortures in vogue in Police cases we find the following – twisting a rope tightly around one arm or leg so as to impede circulation; lifting [a man] up by the moustache; suspending by the arms while [the hands are] tied behind the back; searing with hot irons; placing scratching insects, such as the carpenter beetle, on the navel, scrotum and other sensitive parts; dipping in wells and rivers till the party is half suffocated; squeezing the testicles; beating with sticks; prevention of sleep; nipping the flesh with pincers; putting pepper or red chilies in the eyes, or introducing them into private parts of men and women;

these cruelties occasionally persevered until death sooner or later ensues.

Like the Chinese, the Indians found more interesting uses for bamboo than making it into fishing rods. Two stout bamboo poles could be tied around a person's chest and squeezed tighter and tighter until the ribs cracked. Fingers could be crushed between bamboo rods or, more creatively painful, the fingers of one hand could be tied tightly together and sharp-edged splints of split-bamboo driven between them with a mallet.

All the accounts given above were carried out by legitimate governmental bodies but in the far-flung provinces, where petty war lords and minor moguls reigned supreme and uncontested, these 'official' tortures were inevitably augmented by locally devised punishments, many of which were supremely cruel. In at least one village in the Cuddalore district, the local favourite seemed to be hanging a miscreant by the heels, binding his waist tightly with a rope and then stuffing red-hot chilli powder up his nose. The precise results of this ghastly procedure were omitted from the official British report, saying only that they were 'too revoltingly indecent to be referred to'. In 1718, the local mogul of Bengal, named Murshid Aly Khan, forced those who would not, or could not, pay their taxes, to drink a mixture of water buffalo milk and salt until they died of diarrhoea.

In a torture reminiscent of one practiced in ancient Greece, victims of unrestrained, remote Indian justice were sometimes bound and sewn up inside the hide of a freshly slaughtered water buffalo. As the skin dried and shrank in the blazing sun, it slowly squeezed the life out of the poor wretch. If the weather was cloudy, or if it was the rainy season and there was insufficient heat to shrink the skin, the condemned was simply left to lie in the open until they died of thirst or the insects devoured them.

If India is home to innumerable strange and deadly insects and serpents, it is also the land of that great, placid beast the elephant and inevitably these gentle, two-ton giants were employed as unwitting assistants in the administration of various forms of torture. Like a piston-driven variation of the rack, a man whose leg was chained to an elephant's hind leg could find his limb ripped from its socket when the animal was instructed to do no more than walk across a courtyard: a 400lb leg, moving forward with enough force to propel an elephant, exerts an amazing amount of pull. In a grizzly finale to this performance, it was common to have the elephant end

Execution by elephant was a novel means of dispatching convicted criminals and was, so far as we have been able to determine, unique to India as a judicial punishment. This illustration (found in an illustrated Victorian English magazine) should not require any further explanation to show how this method of execution was carried out.

the miscreant's suffering by instructing it to step or sit upon on the prisoner's head.

If nearly every culture on the planet has suffered unspeakable tortures at the hands of their leaders, the people of Africa can legitimately be said to have suffered twice; first under the laws of their own societies, and later under the harsh dictates of slave masters who used them as forced labour.

For its part, Africa has never been blessed with cohesive government. Since the dawn of time it has been ruled by local chieftains and petty war lords who only knew how to retain their precarious hold on power through terror and corruption. Such politics make for unhappy and rebellious peoples who can only be held in check by increasingly harsh measures. If justice in tribal societies was harsh, that which took place between competing groups was even harsher. Although it was never universally practiced, some African tribes, particularly those in the Niger and Cameroon regions, punished prisoners of war by eating them. Sometimes these captives were merely slaughtered, cooked and devoured while on other occasions, and in other places, they were slowly cut away a piece at a time; forced to watch as their captors taunted them and devoured chunks of their body until they finally bled to death. The reasoning and motivations behind cannibalism are nearly as many and varied as the tribes which practiced it and are far too complex to go into here. The authors have, however, covered this practice in detail in their book *Eat Thy Neighbour: A History of Cannibalism* (Sutton Publishing, 2006). As was true with inner-tribal relations, punishment within given tribes was often meted out with unparalleled cruelty; the method of torture being dictated by the specific nature of the crime and the rules of the tribe.

Among the most appalling crimes in many African societies was that of adultery, and the punishments were even more terrible than the practice of stoning to death imposed on adulterous women by the ancient Hebrews. Among the Ibo tribes of Nigeria, a couple caught *en flagrante delicto* were forced to have sex before a crowd of onlookers. When they reached climax, they were tied together in a final embrace before having a sharpened stake driven through their bodies. The impalement was carefully calculated so as not to kill them immediately and the pair were then carried through the village while being spun around the pole like human propellers. The end of this march-of-death was the local river, where the couple was thrown into the water near a nest of crocodiles, there to meet their bloody ends amid thrashing tails and snapping serrated jaws. Amazingly, this same tribe had at least two additional forms of punishment reserved for adulterers. In the first alternate punishment, the condemned pair were paraded through the village and taken to a grove of sacred trees where they were laid on top of one another and bound together, the man's head in the woman's crotch and vice-versa. Then they were strung up in the trees in such a manner that the man's head was facing downward. In this position they were simply left until they died; the man usually dying first as he

A young African boy submits to an ordeal test by a witch-cleansing cult. Where the causes of illness and misfortune are seen as supernatural, witch-finders remain commonplace.

was hanging upside down. In the final punishment for sexual relations outside wedlock the accused pair were tied to two stakes, situated about 4ft apart and arranged so the couple faced each other – the better to watch their mutual destruction. Over the next day they were given no food but were allowed to have all the water they wanted. The water, of course, had been highly salted and in a matter of hours under the hot tropical sun both parties were severely dehydrated and voraciously hungry. When the man was asked if he wanted something to eat it would have been nearly impossible for him to have said anything but 'yes'. With that, a guard hacked off a piece of the woman's breast and fed it to her lover, carefully staunching the wound so she would not bleed to death. This process was repeated, back and forth – the utmost care being taken to keep both victims alive for as long as possible – until one or the other expired from shock and blood loss. The survivor was then allowed to live for as long as they could make the carcass of their beloved last. Ritually enforced, mutual cannibalism. One can only assume that other crimes among the Ibo were met with equally creative forms of sadism.

If African tribal law was almost universally harsh and cruel, it is hardly any wonder that enslaved tribesmen and women expected, and received, no better treatment at the hands of the European slave traders who began exporting them to Spain, Portugal and the Caribbean Islands in the early 1500s. In retrospect it seems almost beyond belief that the so-called civilised people of Europe would trade in captive human beings as though they were cattle.

As late as the mid-seventeenth century, the English attorney-general said: 'Negroes, being pagans, might justly be held in slavery, even in England itself'. We can assume this was not meant to imply that if these poor creatures converted to the saving grace of Christianity they should immediately be given their freedom. But there was no widespread need for slave labour in Great Britain or Europe. The workforce was required on European-owned 'New World' plantations. If their destination alone were not a sufficient death sentence for enslaved Africans, the trip across the ocean – where they were packed like cord-wood in the holds of ships – was unspeakable enough to claim the lives of anywhere from one-fifth to one-third of the average 'cargo' of slaves.

The sugarcane grown on Caribbean plantations was turned into rum, and as the demand for rum increased back home in England and Europe, the demand for slaves rose commensurately. In 1655, the British captured the island of Jamaica from the French. Three years later they imported a modest 1,400 slaves to work in the fields. By 1670 the total import of human beings had risen to 8,000. By 1720 it had reached 80,000 and by 1775 – the year prior to the American Colonies declaring their independence – it had skyrocketed to 190,000, reaching 250,000 just prior to 1800 and topping out at a colossal total of 314,300 by the time Parliament outlawed the trade in 1824. Note that owning slaves was not outlawed, just importing them from Africa. Even if these hundreds of thousands of people had suffered

Here we see the systematic and ritualized decapitation of enemy soldiers in the aftermath of some sort of tribal warfare. While it may not adhere to the modern ideas espoused by the Geneva Convention for the treatment of prisoners of war, this is a merciful end in comparison to Greek, Roman and early European treatment of captured enemies.

no tortures worse than being hauled across an ocean to live out their lives in bondage the slave trade would still rank as torture on a scale that would have impressed even Nero or Genghis Khan. Of course, the horrors of slavery did not end with forced emigration, separation of families and hard labour.

When human beings can be purchased as cheaply as 30 English Pounds per head there is little incentive for being nice to the help. Overseers and armed guards watched over the slaves day and night; the slightest infraction of the rules being universally met with severe whippings. Considering the mentality necessary for one man to purchase another, it might not stretch credulity to hypothesise that some of the slave owners and overseers may have taken a sadistic pleasure in flogging another human being until their back resembled ground beef. And it was not only the brutes in the field who tortured the slaves; the landowners and, on occasion even their wives, engaged in such brutality. The following account took place on the Jamaican plantation owned by an English couple by the name of Earnshaw, and the slave in question was a woman named Eleanor Mead.

> Her mistress, Mrs Earnshaw, who is described by some as a lady of humanity and delicacy, having taken offence at something which this slave had said or done, in the course of an argument with another slave, ordered her to be stripped naked, prostrated on the ground, and in her own presence caused the male [slave] driver to inflict upon her bared body 58 lashes of the cart whip ... One of the persons ordered to hold her prostrate during the punishment was her own daughter, Catherine. When one hip had been sufficiently lacerated, in the opinion of Mrs Earnshaw, she told the [slave] driver to go round and flog the other side.

One might assume that the good Mrs Earnshaw may have had more in mind than punishing Eleanor for arguing with another slave. Possibly Mr Earnshaw liked Eleanor more than was proper, and if his wife had confronted him with her suspicions it would have been Mrs Earnshaw, not the slave woman, on the receiving end of the whip. This may, of course, not be the case at all, but it is a fact that the constant punishment of slaves helped prevent slave couples from marrying. Why? If it is painful to watch fellow prisoners being tortured, how much more painful it must be if the victim is your husband, wife or child? Why would the plantation owners care if their slaves married or not? Because it was cheaper to buy an already grown-up slave freshly imported from Africa than to bear the expense of rearing one from birth until they were old enough to be sent into the fields. How far did such grotesque examples of destroying family life among slaves go? In testimony before the British Parliament, a Protestant minister named Peter Duncan testified as follows:

> In the year 1823 I knew of a slave driver having to flog his [own] mother. In the year 1827 I knew of a married Negress having been flogged in the presence of ... her husband ... Merely because this Negress would not submit to satisfy the lust of her overseer, he had flogged and confined her for several days in the stocks.

As heart-wrenching as Rev. Duncan's testimony is, it cannot be automatically assumed that all men of the cloth stood bravely in opposition to slavery. In St Anne's, Jamaica, in 1829, the Rev. G.W. Bridges was charged with maltreating a mixed-race slave woman. It seems the good reverend had invited a guest for dinner and ordered this particular woman to prepare a turkey dinner for the occasion. For whatever reason the guest did not show up and Bridges took out his anger on the cook. After tearing off all of her clothes he bound her hands and hung her from a conveniently placed hook in the ceiling. Then he whipped her with a bamboo rod until – according to testimony presented at his trial – 'she was a mass of lacerated flesh and gore'.

While it has always been considered unforgivable for one person to whip another's horse or dog, it seems as though it was perfectly acceptable to whip another man's slaves. If the beating was severe enough to cause permanent damage, or even kill the victim, providing an equivalent, replacement slave would almost always compensate for any hard feelings.

Not surprisingly, whippings were not the limit of punishment forced on the victims of slavery. Offences large and small could be punished by branding, or they might be branded for exactly the same reason a cow is branded – to establish ownership. For slaves prone to running away, there were always chains and shackles secured to the bunkhouse walls and ball-and-chains that could be worn in the fields. There were also iron collars with foot-long spikes projecting in three or four directions, nearly identical to those we found being used in ancient China. Of course, if a slave simply refused to accept bondage and

A slave is bound to a lashing post. Here she will await flogging or branding or whatever other torments her captors may devise, though she is also under threat from the rising tide and from the crocodiles pictured on the left-hand side of the image.

continued to run away, his or her owner was completely within their rights to hack off one of their legs. A late eighteenth-century traveller through the Jamaican town of Paramaribo stated that during his stay in the town he saw: 'No less than nine Negroes [who] had each [had] a leg cut off for running away'.

It should come as no surprise that now and again the slaves rose in revolt against their masters. Such an event occurred on the island of Santo Domingo in 1791 and the ensuing carnage was beyond belief; each side doing their level best to massacre the other in the most abominable ways they could think of. When one of the rebel leaders was captured he was hauled through the streets of town, standing in the back of a cart while on his way to execution. He was not tied there, his feet had been nailed to the floorboards of the wagon. In an eerie echo of the medieval European practice of being broken on the wheel, the man's limbs and ribs were smashed to pieces before he was thrown, still alive and screaming, onto a roaring fire.

Equally barbaric tortures were used by Europeans on the slaves worked to death in the African colonies. In Dutch-held Surinam, a slave convicted of a capital offence was first hooked through the ribcage with a wrought-iron hook, the opposite end of which was attached to a chain. The poor wretch was then hoisted up on a gallows, or a convenient tree, and left to dangle until he died of exposure or suffocation brought about by a ripped diaphragm. As late as 1900 slaves in the Belgian Congo were 'questioned' by being hoisted into the air by ropes tied around their armpits.

Once suspended, heavy weights were then tied to their feet and a saw-horse-like structure was set between their legs. If they refused to talk, or cooperate, or if the exercise was purely disciplinary in nature, they were dropped onto the horse so that their genitals were crushed and their pelvis shattered.

The hatred engendered by the long nightmare of slavery did not magically end when slavery was abolished. Tortures very much like those recounted above were still being inflicted on the people of Haiti – by their own leaders – well into the second half of the twentieth century.

Most of us comfort ourselves with the belief that torture no longer exists and therefore has no influence on the modern world. Nothing could be further from the truth for two reasons. First, events of the past are relevant in the modern world because if we forget them, or deny them – as some Spanish still deny that the Inquisition was as horrible as it really was and some revisionist historians refute the reality of Adolf Hitler's death camps – then we are doomed to repeat the cruelties of the past until the end of time. Secondly, and more ominously, the use of torture is alive and well. It exists in Zimbabwe, in Iran, in Afghanistan, Cuba, in Saudi Arabia and dozens of other nations and places around the globe. If there is a moral to be had in all of this it is that no matter what justification is used for torture, its practice and use is rooted in only one thing – the maintenance of power of one group over another. Even in instances such as the Spanish Inquisition and the great witch hunts – where God and the protection of the faith were employed as moral justification for torture and corporal punishment – the underlying factor was inevitably the wielding of personal and political power over a perceived – and almost certainly imaginary – enemy. So long as any society or nation is ruled by fearful leaders, torture will always be an issue. So long as general populations delight in the blood-sport of 'harsh justice', shamefully avert their eyes from things they would rather pretend did not exist or tacitly accept whatever their government tells them, torture, brutality and man's inhumanity to man will follow as surely as thunder follows lightning.

This is an example of the judas cradle upon which a victim would be sat ... their hands (and sometimes feet) securrely bound and weights (such as the one pictured here) locked around their ankles pulling them down deeper onto the unrelenting spike.

Section III

AN ENCYCLOPEDIA OF TORTURE

In the previous sections of this book we investigated a variety of torture methods as they occurred within the historical context of their times and geographic locations. In order to keep to our historical structure, we found it necessary to skim over many types of torture and, in some cases, eliminate specific torture devices and techniques altogether. In this section, which is divided into various methods of torture and sub-divided by specific types of torture, we hope to present a more comprehensive description of those tortures covered in the previous sections and also explain many types of torture previously unmentioned. Here then, submitted for your approval (or disgust), is a catalogue of cruel, bizarre and often outrageous punishments employed by mankind over the centuries.

1

TORTURE BY BURNING AND BRANDING

BRANDING

From Classical Rome through most of the eighteenth century, searing a convict's flesh with a hot iron was considered a valid way to ensure that miscreants would endure perpetual punishment by being ostracised from respectable society. If a person's shame was irrevocably burned into their skin (usually on the hand or face) they would never be able to hide from their past convictions; indeed, when a person appeared in court they were required to hold up their hand to determine if they bore brands from previous convictions – hence the custom of holding up the right hand when being sworn in for testimony. The type and location of brands varied with the country and manner of the crime, but here are a few examples. Rome branded recaptured, escaped slaves with an 'F' for *fugitivus* and in eighteenth-century England those who spoke out against the government were branded with 'SL' for seditious libeler. A rogue's hand was branded with an 'R', thieves with a 'T', liars bore the letter 'F' for falsehood and vagabonds (now referred to as the wandering homeless) were marked with a 'V'. Perjurers' foreheads were permanently decorated with a 'P' and those who took the Lord's name in vain received a 'B', for blasphemer, in the same place. Military deserters' armpits were branded with a 'D' and soldiers convicted of bad conduct received a 'BC' in a similar location. There were many other common brands

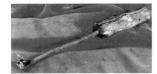

Branding iron

Branding iron

and innumerable local variations as well as different letters designating these same offences as applicable to various languages. The French also adopted the practice of burning a convict's sentence into their skin, hence someone sentenced to hard labour received a 'TF' brand meaning *travaux forces* and those condemned to perpetual hard labour were marked 'TPF' for *travaux a perpetuite*, and a thief might be branded with a 'V' for *voleuse*.

BORING WITH A HOT IRON

Similar to branding (see above). Throughout the Middle Ages and until the end of the eighteenth century, petty criminals were routinely subjected to having holes burned through various parts of their bodies with a hot iron, not unlike a small fireplace poker. Liars, perjurers and blasphemers were likely to have a hole burned through their tongues while petty thieves and drunkards were more likely to have a hole seared through one, or both, of their ears. See also the section on Chinese torture for the punishment meted out to libidious monks.

Brazen bull

BRAZEN BULL

This ingenious study in depravity was unique to the ancient Sicilian city-state of Acragus (now known as Agrigentum) during the reign of the tyrant Phalaris. The eponymous device was no more than a hollow, life-sized statue of a bull with a door in its side large enough to shove a man into the belly of the statue. When the victim had been jammed in place and the trapdoor locked, a fire was lit beneath the statue, heating it red hot. The screams of the condemned man could be heard through the open mouth and nostrils of the figure and were supposed to sound like an enraged bull.

Gridiron

BURNING

Throughout history many crimes have led men and women to the burning stake, but this fearsome practice found its greatest acceptance during the religious persecutions and witch hunts that lasted almost continually from the early 1500s through the late 1600s. In both cases, because the crimes involved were considered to be crimes against

God and the Church (be it Roman Catholic or Protestant) considered the act of burning a person condemned for heresy, or consorting with the Devil, as the only sure means of purging the evil from their souls. Horrible as being burned alive must have been, religious and civil authorities agreed that it was better for the body to suffer than for the soul to be condemned to eternal damnation. It was commonly believed that by making the person endure the unimaginable torments of hell while still on earth, they might at least stand some chance of eternal salvation. So many who witnessed such an horrific act as burning at the stake would not have viewed it as a gruesome spectacle, but rather as a charitable act of mercy and potential redemption inflicted upon some poor soul 'for their own good'. It should also be noted that many of those who were burnt at the stake had already been strangled to death before their bodies were consigned to the flames. This small act of mercy was considered a courtesy to be bestowed upon those who at least showed some sign of repentance, but were too depraved and evil to be accepted back into decent society.

Burning at the stake

The process of burning was relatively straightforward. The condemned was led to the place of execution where a mound of brushwood, bundles of twigs and logs had been piled around a large wooden stake. The victim and a guard then mounted the pyre and the victim was chained to the stake and, usually, had their clothing smeared with grease, oil or tar to help fuel the flames. Before the pyre was lit, a priest asked the condemned to affirm their faith in God and offered them a cross to kiss. An eyewitness account describes what happened next. The story comes from England, the year was 1555 and the victim was Rev. Dr John Hooper, Bishop of Gloucester who had been condemned for refusing to convert from the Church of England to Roman Catholicism.

Burning the feet

Command was now given that the fire should be kindled, but owing to the number of green [twigs] it was some time before the flames set fire to the reeds. Another fire was soon kindled of a more virulent nature ... he now prayed with a loud voice. 'Lord Jesus, have mercy upon me; Lord Jesus, receive my spirit.' And these were the last words he was heard to utter. But even when his face was completely black with the flames, and his tongue swelled so that he could not speak, yet his lips went till they were sunk to the gums; and he knocked his breast with his hands until one of his arms fell off, then continued knocking with

Burning at the stake of Thomas Tomkins

the other while the fat, water and blood dripped out at his finger ends. At length, by renewing of the fire, his strength was gone ... Soon after, the whole lower part of his body being consumed, he fell over the irons that bound him, into the fire, amidst the horrible yells and acclamations of the bloody crew that surrounded him. This holy martyr was more than three quarters of an hour consuming; the inexpressible anguish of which he endured as a lamb ... his nether parts were consumed and his bowels fell out some time before he expired ...

BURNING SULFUR

Toward the end of the great age of witch hunts, German inquisitors sometimes tortured suspected witches by placing a lump of sulfur under one or both armpits and setting it alight. Considering that sulfur burns so furiously that even water can not extinguish it, and that major veins and arteries lie embedded beneath the arms, this could well have been not only unimaginably painful but terminal.

THE CAULDRON

Apparently devised by the Spanish Inquisition, the cauldron consisted of nothing more than a large kettle which was turned upside-down on a victim's stomach. Beneath the cauldron were several mice, or one or two rats. A charcoal fire was then lit on the upturned bottom of the pot and as the vessel heated to red-hot the frantic rodents sought the only possible route of escape by clawing and chewing their way into the victim's stomach.

The cauldron or fire bowl

FRYING AND ROASTING

From the days of ancient Assyria until early eighteenth-century France, people have been heaved into gigantic frying pans and roasted like living chops. This account of frying comes from the Roman chronicler Gallonio and describes one such execution which took place during Emperor Nero's persecution of the Christians (64–68 AD).

The frying pan ... was filled with oil, pitch or resin, and then set over a fire; and when it began to boil and bubble, then were the Christians of either sex thrown into it ... to the end that they might be roasted and fried like fishes ...

The Romans occasionally roasted one of their victims on a gridiron, a grate-like construction that functioned like a massive barbeque grill. Supposedly St Lawrence the martyr was dispatched this way in the year 258. Similarly, during the Spanish Inquisition, there are reports of Inquisitional victims being put into gigantic pans and slid into huge ovens like roasts.

Roasting alive

HOT WIRE

While binding various parts of the body with cords and ropes was common in many places and times, the Mogul Emperors of India took this torture one step further and bound their victim's thumbs, fingers or hands with hot wires. As though the pain of the searing wire burning its way into their flesh were not enough, once the wire was in place it was doused with cold water, causing it to contract and cut its way still deeper into flesh and bone.

SPANISH CHAIR

The Spanish Inquisition seemed never to run out of creative ways to inflict pain on their victims. The Spanish Chair looked like nothing so much as an old-fashioned wicker garden chair, with the exception that it was made entirely out of iron. The open spaces of the back, seat and between the arms and legs were filled with chain mail and metal restraints at the wrists, ankles and across the chest held the victim in place. In some cases this chain mail was fitted with sharp spikes that dug into the victim's flesh. Once strapped and spiked into place, the agony was increased either by placing a brazier of hot coals under the seat, or exposing the victim's feet directly to a live fire. To prevent the feet from burning away too fast, they were sometimes basted with oil or fat. While it would be comforting to say that this little horror was limited to the Spanish Inquisition, the truth is that it was widely adopted throughout Germany, France, much of Central Europe and even, according to some sources, Great Britain, and remained in use until well into the 1700s.

Trial by ordeal

TRAIL BY FIRE AND WATER

During the Dark Ages and early Middle Ages, Trial by Ordeal was a perfectly acceptable means of determining whether or not a person was guilty of a specific crime. Despite the fact that the outcome was as random as throwing dice, Trial by Ordeal was accepted by the Church, governments and the populace at large as an incontrovertible means of establishing the truth – primarily because it removed the flawed element of human judgment and left the outcome firmly in the hands of God. In Trial by Fire the accused was required to walk barefoot over anywhere from three to nine red-hot ploughshares, pick up a glowing hot iron bar and walk three paces or, alternately, place their hand inside a super-heated glove of chain mail. When the ordeal was over, the damaged part of the body was salved with ointment and wrapped in a linen bandage. Three days later the bandage was removed; if no blisters had appeared the accused was deemed innocent. If, on the other hand, there was obvious blistering the judgment was 'guilty'. Trial by Water involved the accused plunging their hands (sometimes swathed in protective layers of linen cloth) into a vat of boiling water in order to extract a large stone from the bottom of the pot. As with Trial by Fire, the hands were salved and bandaged and examined after three days.

2

TORTURE BY CRUSHING, SMASHING OR BREAKING

BOOTS

This particularly nasty little device first appears in the historical record around the year 1590 and was used in different forms and shapes throughout Britain, Europe and the Orient for centuries. The British and European version of the boot was generally an iron, boot-shaped shell designed to fit over the foot and lower leg of the victim. Once in place, wooden wedges were driven between boot and leg until the limb crushed to the point where blood, muscle and even bone marrow oozed from the cracks and out around the top of the boot. As though that were not enough, sometimes the boot was applied red-hot, searing the flesh before the crushing began. In India, the boot consisted of little more than two boards, lashed to either side of the victim's foot, after which the ropes were twisted so tight that the ankle bones, and eventually the entire foot, was crushed.

BREAKING ON THE WHEEL

The wheel in question might be no more than a standard wheel taken from an oxcart or wagon, or it might be as elaborate as a custom-made device resembling a wheel mounted on a low pole (or axle) permanently set into the ground in such a manner that the wheel and support pole

A version of the boot

The wheel

looked like a circular picnic table. To this wheel, those condemned to an especially brutal death were tied in a spread-eagle position. In front of a cheering crowd the executioner proceeded to inflict as many varying painful tortures as possible until the victim died. Common among the tortures used on the wheel were having great pieces of flesh ripped from the body with plier-like pincers (sometimes heated red-hot), having every joint and limb shattered with iron bars or wooden mallets and having the hands, feet, arms and legs lopped off with axes. As life ebbed from the victim and the spectacle seemed nearly over, the executioner would strike off the poor wretch's head. A particularly elaborate variation on the wheel used by the Romans involved a wide, drum-like wheel mounted about 1ft above the ground on an 'A' frame, so as to resemble a Ferris wheel. The outside of the wheel was set with multiple spikes and it was to the face of these that the victim was tied. Beneath the wheel, mounted into the ground was a second set of spikes. When the wheel was turned the victim was ground to pieces between the two sets of spikes.

BRODEQUIN

Brodequins

Used primarily by the French, the *brodequin* was a shallow, three-sided box, or trough, made to fit snugly enough around a man's legs so that the legs were compressed tightly together. When the legs were in place they were securely bound with ropes. Next, wooden wedges were driven between the victim's knees and ankle balls, shattering the delicate bone ends. Additional wedges were often driven directly into the soft tissue of the thighs and around the shins.

PILLIWINCKES

Finger pillory

A uniquely Scottish device, the pilliwinckes (alternatively spelled pilliwinks) were a device for crushing the fingers not unlike the thumb screws (see below in this section). Whatever their precise appearance, written descriptions indicate that they caused the fingers of one hand to be bent palm-ward from the rear-most joint where they were held in a flat position while the device was slowly tightened to the point where the fingers were crushed. Whatever their exact nature, they were universally described as 'a grievous torture'.

PRESSING

Pressing was used specifically as a method to force reluctant suspects into confessing their crimes. Under medieval and later law, a full confession was necessary before the government could confiscate the property of the convicted party. Without such a confession the suspect's personal property would remain in the family even if the party in question was found guilty. To help ensure a confession, the slow and painful torture of pressing was instituted. According to the official act:

Finger screws

> the prisoner shall be remanded to the place from whence he came, and put in some low, dark room; there he shall lie without any litter or anything under him, and that one arm shall be drawn to one quarter of the room with a cord, and the other to another, and that his feet shall be used in the same manner, and that as many weights shall be laid on him as he can bear, and more. That he shall have no sustenance but the worst bread and water, and that he shall not eat the same day on which he drinks, not drink on the same day on which he eats; and so he shall continue till he die.

Obviously the point was to make the poor wretch talk long before he expired, but in some instances the accused held out until their ribs were crushed. Such was the case of Margaret Clitheroe who, in 1586, was accused of providing sanctuary for a Jesuit priest. After a quarter of an hour of pressing, during which time nearly 900lbs were piled on her, Clitheroe's ribs literally exploded through her sides. Another case where the victim held out until his body was crushed under the weight took place during the Salem Witch Trials of 1692 when Giles Corey was pressed to death for refusing to confess that he was a witch. In a slower, more prolonged pressing, in 1776 Thomas Spiggot endured more than a week of daily increased weights. In his delirium Spiggot believed his head was being crushed but, in truth, it was only the increased blood pressure that caused the pain in his head. Finally, after a total of 400lbs had been piled on top of the door laid on Spiggot's back, he agreed to confess. In India a variation on pressing involved tying two stout bamboo poles to the front and back of a victim's chest and then, usually with the aid of ropes, pulling them tighter and tighter until the ribs were crushed. In this instance the purpose of the exercise was not to make the victim confess but to maim them so horribly that they were assured of a slow, agonising death.

A version of the brodequin

The wheel

Scavenger's daughter

A sketch of the scavenger's daughter in use

SCAVENGER'S DAUGHTER

Named for its inventor, Leonard Skeffington (whose name was later corrupted to 'scavenger'), Lieutenant of the Tower of London during the reign of Henry VIII, the scavenger's daughter was a torture device made of iron bars that had been roughly formed into an 'A' shape with a loop at the top large enough to be locked around a man's neck, two loops at the mid-point (approximately where the cross-bar of the A would be) manacled the wrists and two more loops as the lower ends of the A, into which the victim's knees could be locked. The device was short enough that the body had to be bent forward far beyond its normal limits – usually by having the torture master's assistant straddling the victim and pressing down on his shoulders – before a man could be locked into it. The chest was forced to the knees and the stomach to the thighs until the victim was virtually doubled into a ball. The unnatural extension of the spine caused blood to gush from the victim's ears, nose and mouth. If left on for more than a few minutes the scavenger's daughter could permanently dislocate the spine and fracture the breast bone and ribs. Alternatively called Skevington's Gyves, the Iron Shackle, the Spanish A-frame and the Stork, there are only a very few accounts of this device ever being used. A make-shift variation on the Scavenger's Daughter was employed by Britain's Royal Navy where it was referred to as 'Tying Neck and Heels'. In this procedure, the victim would have one musket laid across his shoulders and another placed beneath his knees. The two guns were then pulled towards each other with the aid of ropes and several strong sailors. The damage was nearly identical to that inflicted by the Scavenger's Daughter.

SCHNEIDEN

As far as we are aware, this is a uniquely German device, first recorded in 1530 and also known as the *Kranz*. It was, in effect, no more and no less than a jaw crushing machine. The *Schneiden* took the form of an iron skullcap held in place by a heavy leather chinstrap. Once in place the strap could be tightened with a ratchet. If pulled tight enough the victim's teeth were shattered, his jaw broken to pieces and the pressure on the skull became so intense that it felt as though it would explode. To make the pain more unbearable the torture master might amuse himself by tapping on the metal cap with a small hammer.

Headcrusher or schneiden

THUMB SCREWS

This infamous device was designed to place increasing amounts of pressure on the knuckles of both thumbs simultaneously. The victim's thumbs were inserted into an 'M'-shaped frame of iron or wood and locked into place by means of a bottom plate which was screwed into place by a small crank or wing nut. As the nut was turned, the lower plate pushed ever harder on thumbs, squeezing them against the top bar of the frame. When the victim agreed to give the right answers the pressure was released; if they refused to cooperate, the pressure could be increased until the knuckles were shattered. In India, a torture similar to the thumb screws was devised, wherein the fingers of the accused were crushed between bamboo rods. Alternatively, the fingers of one hand were bound tightly together with cord and bamboo wedges were driven between the knuckles of the fingers, slicing through flesh, tendon and bone, crushing the knuckles and breaking the fingers.

Thumb screws

3

TORTURE BY CUTTING, PIERCING, TEARING AND IMPALING

AMPUTATION

From the dawn of history criminals and enemies of the state have been subjected to having varying parts of their bodies lopped off both as a punishment and as a visible warning to those who would emulate their transgressions. Ears, noses, lips, hands, feet and entire legs have been publicly hacked away, leaving the victim permanently maimed and unable to earn an honest living.

Typical of this practice was medieval France where felons were often sentenced to have their feet amputated; thieves lost their left ear for a first offence, the right for a second and their life for a third. Similarly, under King Louis XII (reigned 1498–1515) anyone found guilty of eight offences of blasphemy had their tongues ripped out. Under English King, Canute (reigned 995–1035) adulterous women had their nose and ears cut off. The most elaborate ceremony associated with corporal amputation came about during the reign of England's Henry VIII (1509–47).

The Sergeant of the Woodyard brought the chopping block and cords with which the prisoner's hand was to be bound into place. The Master Cook handed the knife to the Sergeant of the Larder who would cut off the offending hand. The Sergeant of Poultry cut off the head of a chicken whose body would be shoved over the stump (apparently to prevent infection), the Yeoman of the Scullery tended

Shears for amputation of digits, ears, noses, tongues, etc.

Thirty-four pirates beheaded in twenty-seven minutes

then pull out the victim's lungs, careful not to rip them loose. The results, at least until the victim died a few excruciating hours later, gave the appearance of a pair of flapping, bloody wings – hence the name of the torture.

DEATH BY ONE THOUSAND CUTS

See *Ling Che*, below, in this section.

FLAYING

Executioner's beheading sword

The idea of tearing the skin from a living human being may be as old as cruelty itself, but it first occurs in the records of medieval Europe around 1100 AD. How late this grim practice was still imposed is unknown, but records show that as late as 1366 the Count de Rouci was skinned alive for having betrayed Lyon, France to the English. Generally, the victim was tied, upside-down, to a square frame, in a spread-eagle position. The executioner would then ring his ankles with a sharp knife and make an incision down the inner surface of each leg, again ringing the genitals, and continue the slit down the victim's stomach and chest. Beginning at the ankles, the skin was then stripped away from the victim much like a hunter skins an animal after shooting it. If the pain of having one's skin ripped from the body, and exposing the sensitive inner flesh and muscle to the air, were not horrific enough, by the time the peeling process reached the stomach the intestines were likely to tumble out and fall over the victim's face. Once nearly devoid of skin, the victim would be left exposed until they died of shock and blood loss.

HANGING, DRAWING AND QUARTERING

Hanging, drawing and quartering, that uniquely medieval sounding torture, was probably devised in 1241 by England's King Henry III. The best description of the process would seem to be in the words read out when a judge imposed this particularly gruesome execution on someone who had been convicted of treason. He announced to the court that the condemned was:

to be taken from the prison and laid upon a sledge or hurdle, and drawn to the gallows or place of execution, and then hanged by the neck until he be half-dead, and then cut down; and his entrails [are] to be cut from his body and burned by the executioner; then his head is to be struck off, his body divided into quarters and afterwards his head and quarters to be set up in some open places as directed.

Not mentioned in the official wording are several details worth noting. After being hanged the victim was awakened as much as possible by having water thrown onto his face; otherwise he might miss what was to come. Next, before he was disembowelled, his private parts were cut off and tossed into the waiting fire – this was to show that traitors would not be allowed to reproduce (even if he thought he would have time or opportunity prior to his decapitation). The disembowelling (technically the 'drawing' part of the sentence as the bowels were said to be 'drawn out from the body') if done by an experienced executioner, could be accomplished without the victim losing consciousness. Then, while the poor wretch was still screaming, the executioner would reach inside the trunk of his body, rip out his heart, hold it up before the cheering, jeering crowd and cry out: 'Behold, the heart of a traitor!' The records indicate any number of hanging, drawing and quarterings where the victim remained conscious, screaming and praying right up until the point where either their heart was pulled out or their head was struck off. The various cuts of carcass mentioned in the official sentence – the head and four quarters of the body – were then parboiled with bay leaves and cumin seed as preservatives and given a liberal coating of tar before being affixed on a pike and used to decorate town gates and bridges throughout the kingdom. Records show that these well-preserved cuts of corpse could last for decades before the elements and the crows reduced them to mere bones. The last recorded hanging, drawing and quartering in England took place on 20 September 1586 when seven of fourteen men convicted of plotting the murder of Queen Elizabeth were dispatched in this manner.

Early guillotine

HERETICS FORK

This creatively painful device was designed to make the life of an accused heretic even more miserable than it already was. The instrument itself looked like a leather dog collar with the business end of two table forks

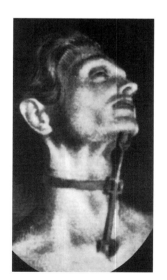

Heretic's fork

Heretic's fork

attached to it at right angles. When the collar was latched around the victim's neck, the forks were situated so that one jabbed him beneath the chin and the other rested in the hollow at the bottom of the throat where it joins the collar bone. If the prisoner attempted to lower or even move their head, the tines of the fork bit deep into the flesh, impaling the tongue and digging into the throat. The tines were not long enough and not situated at such a position that they would kill, but were undoubtedly amazingly painful.

IMPALING

Impalement takes no special skill. The only equipment necessary is a victim and a pole stout enough to support his body. In practice, the usual means of impaling was to place the victim on the ground, or a convenient table, and ram the pole as far up his rectum as possible without ripping his head off. The pole and its writhing decoration was then set into a hole in the ground where it could be seen by all and sundry. If the executioner managed to miss the heart, the victim could remain alive, shrieking in agony, for several hours. History's most famous practitioner of this macabre art form was undoubtedly Prince Vlad II of Walachia (reigned intermittently 1448–76), known properly as Vlad Dracula (that is Vlad, son of the dragon, in honour of his father, Vlad Sr, upon whom the Order of the Dragon had been bestowed) or, more frequently, Vlad Tepes, meaning Vlad the Imapler. Although there have been others who impaled their enemies, Vlad took it to extremes, decorating the no-go zone around his castle with the carcasses of thousands of Turkish enemies. Needless to say, the Turks subsequently left Vlad and his territories off their list of places to visit.

Impaling

IRON MAIDEN

That uniquely Germanic invention, the Iron Maiden, originated in the town of Nuremberg at some point in the high-middle ages; probably in the 1400s. The item in question – known in German as the *Eiserne Madchen* – looked very much like an Egyptian mummy case, its outer surface carved with the likeness of a woman. The inner surface of both the door and case were set with 4–6in-long spikes. When a victim was pushed into the case and the door was closed they would inevitably

Iron Maiden

and unavoidably be pierced from all directions at once. The purpose however, was not always to kill instantly. The spikes were carefully measured so that they would not pierce to the heart. Presumably, now and again someone would open the case and see if the victim had reconsidered his situation; consent presumably leading to extraction and at least the possibility of survival. The Iron Maiden was never a mass-produced, commercially available item and consequently each model differed slightly. Some were meant to kill instantly and some had long spikes conveniently located so as to pierce the eyes and enter the brain. Although the Maiden is most associated with medieval Germany, it is hardly surprising that it was adopted by the Spanish and Italians. Equally unsurprising is that someone thought of a similar device long before the Middle Ages. The earliest known version of such a device comes down to us from ancient Sparta where the local dictator, Nabis, commissioned an iron statue of his wife, Apega. The statue was so designed that its spring-loaded arms could be opened to expose a nasty set of spikes. When Nabis felt an interview was getting nowhere, he would have his victim shoved into his wife's arms, which would then snap shut, crushing the man against the spikes. Presumably, as the spikes would have been located at about chest height, extraction and survival were not options.

Iron Maiden

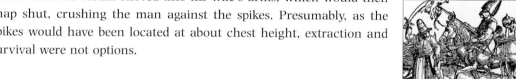

Impaling of infants

LING CHE

Translating roughly as Death by One Thousand Cuts, the Chinese *Ling Che* may well be the most lingering and painful death imaginable. According to tradition, the victim was tied to a table while the executioner appeared with a cloth-covered basket filled with knives, each knife bearing a symbol denoting a particular portion of the body. Reaching under the cloth he would extract a knife at random and slice off the specified body part. Fingers, calf muscles, breasts, thigh muscles, nose, eye lids, it was all in the luck of the draw. Given the right random set of circumstances the torture could go on for hours on end. Inevitably, one knife was marked with the symbol for the heart. When this item appeared the victim's suffering would end in a matter of seconds. Presumably, there were instances where the condemned man's family bribed the executioner to find the heart knife immediately. An almost identical torture was practiced in Japan where it was called Death by Twenty-One Cuts, presumably based on the possible number of knives involved.

Decapitated heads following Chinese execution of pirates

Pass (or cradle)

PASS (OR CRADLE)

This little grotesquery seems to have been unique to the Germans and may have been intended for towns that could not afford an Iron Maiden of their own. Looking disturbingly like an over-sized baby's cradle the *Pass* was a large, rectangular wooden box with rockers affixed to the bottom. The interior surfaces of the 'cradle' were set with sharpened iron spikes; when the victim had been stripped naked and lowered into the *Pass*, it was rocked violently back and forth. The results seem too self-evident to require description.

PENDULUM

Pendulum

Any reader who would be drawn to pick up this book and read thus far will undoubtedly be familiar with Edgar Allen Poe's story entitled 'The Pit and the Pendulum'. It tells a macabre story in which a man is cut in half by a giant clockwork pendulum with a weighted blade whose edge was as sharp as a razor. As the clockwork winds down the pendulum slowly descends, a fraction of an inch at a time, allowing the victim to see his own horrific death coming toward him over the course of several hours. The story may be fictional but the device was all too real and was yet another bizarre invention thanks to the creativity of the Spanish Inquisition.

We have found that sometimes the torture of the pulley also known as suspension *or garrucha* or *Squassation* was occasionally referred to as the pendulum. This seems to have been especially so when the torture victim had heavy weights attached to their ankles or toes and were made to swing back and forth while suspended in the air. For more on this variation see *garrucha* below.

PINCERS

Pincers

Ripping strips of flesh from victims' bodies with pincers, which looked and worked much like an over-sized pair of pliers, was a common form of pre-execution mutilation employed across much of Continental Europe throughout the Middle Ages.

Although the English seem not to have used the pincers, the French, Germans, Dutch and others found them quite attractive. In some instances the pincers were heated red-hot as a means of increasing the pain. In France, if the victim was not to be put to death, the gaping wounds left by the pincers were further tormented by having boiling wax or hot lead dumped into them.

Pincers at work

PRICKING

Invented as a means of determining whether or not a woman was a witch, pricking involved jabbing the victim with an iron needle mounted on the end of a wooden handle.

According to the theory of the day, a witch had places on his or her body, properly known as *stigmata sagarum*, which, thanks to the intervention of the Devil, were impervious to pain. In practice, everyone has small places where there are few nerve endings, particularly on the back. Alternately, when a victim has been jabbed often enough, the nervous system will simply shut down. Some witch hunters, notably the notorious Matthew Hopkins, the self-styled Witchfinder General of England, carried a witch-prick with a retractable needle. When the device was pressed against the victim's flesh, the needle retracted into the handle, making it appear as though they had been jabbed, but with so slight a pressure that it often went unnoticed.

Skewers for pricking

SAW

There is really very little that can be said about this method of torture which is not abundantly clear in the accompanying images. Obviously this is a form of execution, but it is one that would be slow and painful. It should be noted, however, that in the images where the victim is suspended upside-down and the torturers/executioners begin cutting them in half at the groin, the victim (owning to the fact that the brain is maintained with a supply of blood and oxygen) will remain alive throughout the horrific ordeal until the saw reaches the heart or lungs.

Sawing

Aftermath of a scalping

SCALPING

Although it may extend back into the mists of history, the practice of scalping is first recorded in the annals of that doughty Viking king of southern England, Canute (reigned 995–1035). Centuries later, the practice was revived by the French – who were busily trying to wipe out every English settlement in the New World – and explained the practice to their American Indian mercenary forces as a means of proving how many English men and women they had killed. The Indians were paid on a per-head basis and scalps were much easier to transport than complete heads. It should be noted that scalping, itself, is not necessarily fatal. A scalping victim may live, but the exposed top of their skull will forever be exposed to the air and will need constant applications of oil to keep the skull bone from drying out.

4
TORTURE BY RESTRAINT

ANCHOR

This cruel instrument of restraint forced the prisoner into a humiliating posture of submission. The use of this device for prolonged periods in damp dungeons would sometimes result in permanent deformity of the spine. Different models of this device can be found in the chamber of torture at the Castle of Kwidzin in eastern Poland.

BILBOES

Much like the hobbles used to keep horses from wandering, the bilboes were nothing more than two ankle shackles set at opposite ends of an 18in-long iron bar. Apparently deriving their name from Bilbao, Spain, where they were reputedly invented, the bilboes could either be used to keep prisoners from running away or, by the addition of a chain, secure the victim to a post, a wall, or any other permanent fixture.

BINDING

One of the surest, quickest and cheapest methods of making a person suffer is to immobilise them with rope restraints. The tighter the victim is bound, the greater their suffering. This rather obvious fact

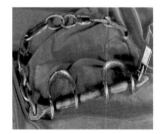

Bilboes

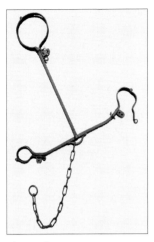

The anchor

has undoubtedly been recognised throughout history and in every geographic location on the globe, but some people seemed to excel at the art of binding with the express purpose of inflicting the greatest possible amount of pain. In India prisoners were bound in impossibly unnatural positions, such as having one leg tied to their opposite shoulder and pulled as tightly as possible or by placing a noose around their throat, the other end of which was pulled down his back and tied to his ankles; any attempt to move would nearly strangle him.

From Henry VIII's England comes the case of Mark Smeaton, the court minstrel who was accused of dallying with Queen Anne Boleyn. To induce a confession, Smeaton's head was encircled with a knotted rope, the knots being arranged so they rested over his eyes. When the rope was twisted tight the pressure compressed Smeaton's eyes until they exploded. On a smaller scale, the Spanish Inquisition often bound a victim's thumbs together with a small cord which was wrapped so tightly that blood spurted from beneath the thumbnails. The Inquisition were masters of the rope and more of their inventive rope-based tortures are described below.

GARROTTE

Death by strangulation has always been around but in medieval Spain the practice became a standard means of execution for criminals of all sorts. The *Garrotte*, the official mechanism employed in Spanish judicial strangulation, took the form of a small stool attached to a short post. The victim was bound hand and foot and seated on the stool before a metal collar, which was attached to the post, was fixed around their neck. At the back of the collar was a crank, or screw which, when turned, drew the collar tighter and tighter until the victim's neck was slowly pulled onto a metal spike which protruded from the post. In theory, the spike punctured the cervical vertebrae, killing the victim in seconds; in practice the victim was usually strangled to death.

IRON COLLAR

Iron collars, attached to the end of a length of chain which was, in turn, attached to a ring mounted into the wall of a dungeon or prison cell, have been a favourite form of restraint since the invention of iron. They kept prisoners firmly in their place and could be used to haul them around as the need arose. Occasionally the victim was kept a bit too firmly in place. In Carlisle Castle, in the north of England, the chain from collar to wall was so short that if the prisoner happened to roll out of bed they were almost sure to strangle themselves. A popular variation on the collar was the 'jaggs', known in Holland as '*joungs*' and in France as the '*Carcan*'. The collar was the same as always, but rather than being mounted in a cell it was attached to a church wall or the local market cross, thus allowing religious transgressors to be exposed to public humiliation while they contemplated their sinful life.

LITTLE EASE

Although not technically a restraint, Little Ease was a notoriously small cell in the Tower of London. So tiny was Little Ease that a prisoner shoved inside had no room to either stand up nor lay down, being forced into a perpetual crouching position. Although Little Ease is the best documented place of tight confinement, one can assume that many such hell-holes existed in the Middle Ages and well into the eighteenth or nineteenth century.

PORTO

Yet another of the Spanish Inquisition's notorious rope tortures, the *porto* consisted of a rack-like wooden bed in which a series of holes had been drilled at strategic locations. When the victim was laid out on the bed, ropes were threaded through holes located on either side of both arms and either side of his thighs. With the help of a windlass, the ropes were pulled so tight that they dug through flesh and muscle tissue, often tearing their way to the bone. One variation on the *porto* was to have the ropes attached to the wall rather than to a wooden bed. The prisoner was seated on a small stool, the ropes threaded through wall-mounted iron rings, conveniently located at the hands, arms and waist. When the ropes were pulled tight enough the stool was kicked away and the prisoner dangled from the wall until he was ready to cooperate.

Chinese garrotte

Partial drowning

WOODEN HORSE

This torture, predominantly employed by the Spanish Inquisition could be used alone or as a part of the *Tormento de Toca*, described under the section 'Torture by Water'. The 'wooden horse' in question was a shallow box, much like a trough, large enough for a man to lie down in, that was either fitted with legs or placed on a table. At the point inside the trough where a victim's waist would be, an iron bar extended from one side to the other. When a man was placed in the trough this bar would rest in the small of the back, preventing him from lying flat on the bottom of the box. Once in position, the victim was securely bound with small ropes threaded through holes in the bottom of the box. Ropes were usually placed around his arms, thighs and shins and then pulled so tight – sometimes with the help of cranks – that they would cut through the flesh and cut nearly to the bone. At his point, if the torture master chose to administer even further agony, any one of several forms of water torture, described elsewhere in this section, was begun.

5
TORTURE BY PUBLIC DISPLAY, SHAME AND HUMILIATION

AUTO-DE-FE

Used as an adjunct to the Spanish Inquisition's memorably cruel punishments of torture and burning at the stake, the *auto-de-fe* (literally 'act of faith' in Spanish) was a public ceremony where both the condemned and those who had repented their 'heresies' were forced to parade through the streets of town in vast processions while displaying physical signs of their particular transgressions. Some wore signs around their neck with their crime written for all to read while others, who had recanted and were to be spared the burning post, wore inverted flames sewn to the back of their gowns. Those who were to be burnt wore upright flames. When the parade reached the appointed place, the entire assembly took part in a religious service before the condemned were handed over to secular authorities to be run through a nearly instantaneous justice mill before being tied to a burning post and set on fire.

BRANKS – MASKS OF SHAME OR INFAMY

(See also Scold's Bridle.) These devices (which are closely related to the scold's bridle described below in this section) existed in a wide variety of fantastical and sometimes downright artistic styles from about

Auto-de-fe

Brank

1500 to 1800. They were used to punish those who, by their words, had transgressed against the prevailing conventions. In the course of four centuries, countless women decried as 'scolds' and 'shrews' because domestic slavery and incessant pregnancy reduced them to neurasthenia and frenzy were thus humiliated and tortured; political power thus held up to public ridicule the petty disobedient and the nonconformists; ecclesiastical power thus punished a long list of lesser infractions. The overwhelming majority of victims were always women, and the operative principle was *mulier taceat in ecclesia*, 'Let the woman be silent in church' – 'church' here meaning the ruling ecclesiastical and secular hierarchies, both constitutionally gynaecophobic. The sense was thus: 'Let the woman be silent in the presence of the male'. The victims, locked into the masks and staked out in the town square, were also treated roughly by the crowd. Painful beatings, besmearing with faeces and urine, and serious, sometimes fatal wounding (especially in the breasts, anus and vagina) was their lot.

CANGUE

Chinese double cangue

This Chinese device, alternately known as the *fcan hao*, *tcha* and *ea*, was a massive wooden collar worn by those condemned to display their crime in public for a prescribed period of time. The donut-like *cangue* was made in two sections, held together by a hinge, which could be opened up to allow the victim to place their head into a hole in the centre. The collar was then closed and locked into place. The *cangue* made it impossible for the wearer to lie down or, in the most extreme and unusual instances of size, even to walk or stand up without risking breaking his neck. Not to mention the complete impossibility of reaching one's own mouth to eat or drink, thereby having to rely on the charitable compassion of others.

CHUCKING STOOL

Chucking stool

Devised some time prior to the Norman Conquest of 1066 (when it was known by its Latin name *cathedra stercoris*), this uniquely English form of humiliation was reserved for women who simply could not, or would not, learn how to control their sharp tongues. In the words of the day, it was: 'a seat of infamy where strumpets and scolds, with bared feet and head, are condemned to abide the jibes of those who pass by'. The chucking stool itself was no more than a wooden arm-chair mounted on two poles, much like an open sedan chair of the eighteenth century. A hole was cut in the bottom of the chair and the victim's skirts were hoisted up, leaving her exposed rump visible for all to see while she was paraded through the streets of town.

DRUNKARD'S CLOAK

Devised by King James I of England (and quite possibly having been brought into use while James was still reigning in Scotland as James VI) the drunkard's cloak (occasionally referred to as the 'barrel pillory') was a perfect example of letting the punishment fit the crime. Nothing more than a large beer keg with the bottom knocked out and a hole cut into the top large enough for a man's head to fit through, those convicted of habitual public inebriation were forced to wear the 'cloak' whenever they went out in public for a specified period of time. Sometimes additional holes were cut into the sides so the victim could use their hands to help support the barrel's weight. To prevent the victim from simply stepping out of the thing a locking collar of wood or metal was placed around their neck. While this may seem laughable, anyone who has ever tried to lift a full-sized, 36-gallon wooden cask knows how heavy they are. The drunkard's cloak was not only a horribly chaffing thing, but its weight could easily tear the muscles connecting the neck to the shoulders. There are records of the cloak remaining in use as late as 1690 when Samuel Pepys, then Secretary of the Royal Navy, mentioned it in his diaries.

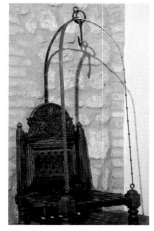
Chucking stool

Drunkard's cloak

DUCKING STOOL

See 'Ducking' in the section 'Torture by Water'.

FIDDLE AND FLUTE

These contraptions served as a sort of portable or mobile pillory (see below). Once the victim was locked into them they could be paraded through the streets whilst being led by a chain and collar around their necks, etc. Sometimes they might even be trapped within these

Drunkard's cloak

The fiddle

Iron fiddle

Finger pillory

devices before being exiled from a particular city. Similar in that way to the Chinese *Cangue* discussed above, the victim (or victims) forced to wear one of these contraptions would be completely at the mercy of any passers-by. Furthermore, they would be incapable of feeding themselves and would, therefore, have to rely on the charity and generosity of those same passers-by for food and drink. It seems that this too was a punishment largely reserved for women of a shrewish temperament.

JAGGS

See 'Iron Collar' in the section 'Torture by Restraint'.

PENANCE

Defined in *Webster's Dictionary* as 'an act of self-abasement, mortification or devotion performed to show sorrow or repentance for sin', penances were imposed on members of both the clergy and laity who were judged by the Church to be guilty of sins or criminal acts throughout the Middle Ages. Penances for small transgressions could be as mild as a short period of fasting and prayer or as great as taking a pilgrimage to some holy site. In worst case scenarios, such as one case where a Frenchman was found guilty of murdering his infant child, the condemned party had the body of the child chained to his back and was forced to walk all the way to Rome under the strict supervision of a priest and armed guards. Whether or not the man survived is unknown.

PILLORY, FINGER

Designed to punish those who insisted on disrupting church services, the finger pillory consisted of two boards, hinged together and attached to the wall of a church. One of the boards had four holes drilled through it, spaced to accept a person's fingers. In the opposite board were four corresponding grooves, or troughs, which closed over the fingers. It was hoped that once the hand of the offender was locked in place they would be a bit more attentive to the Word of God.

PILLORY

The pillory is a device wherein the condemned had their head and wrists locked into a wooden frame mounted on a shoulder-height post set up in a public place such as the local market square. Apparently it derived its name from a Greek phrase meaning 'to look through a door' – an appropriate description of someone with their head and hands poking through the front of the pillory. The first recorded use of the pillory took place in Classical Greece; the Anglo-Saxons called it the *healfang* (or half-hang) and it was in constant use throughout the Middle Ages – being codified as a legal form of punishment in England in 1269 by King Henry III – and continuing in use through the early nineteenth century all across Great Britain, Europe and the Americas. The pillory served as a method of punishing those convicted of minor crimes of all manners, be it public drunkenness, brawling, homosexuality, or disorderly conduct. Included in the myriad of petty offences for which a man or woman could be pilloried were, according to an eighteenth-century English statute: 'those who sell putrid meat, stinking fish, rotting birds, and bread with pieces of iron in it to increase its weight'. In the old Dutch colony of New York a man convicted of stealing cabbages was sent to the pillory with a cabbage tied to his head. While the victim was on public display – a period that could last from a single hour to more than a week – they were subjected to the taunts of their neighbours and, depending upon how offensive their crime was, frequently pelted with rotten vegetables, mud and stones. In some instances, the abuse to which a pilloried individual was subjected was so severe that they were knocked unconscious and ran the risk of strangling to death when the full weight of their bodies came down on their imprisoned neck. One such incident took place at London's Smithfield Horse Market in the eighteenth century, when two men, James Eagan and James Salmon, were pelted with stones, potatoes, bricks and dead animals.

According to an eyewitness account: 'The blows they received occasioned their heads to swell to an enormous size; and by people hanging to the skirts of their clothes they were nearly strangled'. Eagan died on the spot and Salmon died in prison a short time later. Only a few years after the Eagan/Salmon incident, a homosexual man was pilloried and was pummelled so badly that he: 'soon grew black in the face and blood issued from his nostrils, his eyes and his ears; the mob nevertheless attacked him with great fury'. When the pillory was unlocked he: 'Fell down dead on the stand of the instrument'. The

Pillory

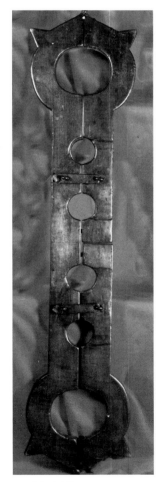

Double fiddle

Donkey – stang

Rocking horse – stang

Scold's bridle

pillory could also serve as one part of a larger series of punishments. Some who were pilloried were also whipped and others had their ears nailed to the back-board of the pillory, only to be torn free or cut off when the sentence was concluded.

RIDING THE STANG

With so many punishments specifically levied against uncouth women it seems only fair that wife-beating men and tavern brawlers should also be subjected to an equivalent humiliation – hence Riding the Stang. The stang was nothing but a length of log, or a stout pole, which the victim was forced to straddle while he was carried through the streets of his town, accompanied by merrymakers shouting, cat-calling, blowing horns and whistles to call attention to their thoroughly embarrassed captive.

Other variations on this form of torture and humiliation were put into play for military punishments, the most extreme of which is sometimes referred to as the Spanish donkey. In this case the 'stang' took the form of a wooden horse (sometimes with wheels and sometimes with rockers) and it would either have a spiked seat or perhaps even have been a simple V-shaped wedge. The malefactor would be forced to straddle the 'horse' with their arms bound behind their back and they would ride the devilish contraption while others rocked or wheeled them about. Additional torment was frequently obtained though the addition of heavy weights on the 'rider's' feet.

SCOLD'S BRIDLE

(See also Branks.) The scold's bridle, like the ducking stool and the chucking stool, was a device intended specifically to punish sharp-tongued women, and was used throughout Britain and Europe during the Middle Ages. A helmet-like cage made of iron straps, the scold's bridle was locked over a woman's head, after which she might be led through the streets of the town and exposed to cat-calls and hoots of derision. To increase the pain a metal tongue, or ball, might be forced into the woman's mouth to gag her screams or curses during the punishment. From the records of Newcastle-upon-Tyne comes this account from 1665:

There he saw one Anne Bridlestone drove through the streets by an officer of the corporation, holding a rope in one hand, the other fastened to an engine called the branks ... which was muscled over [her] head and face, with a great gag or tongue of iron forced into her mouth, which forced blood out ...

Similar devices were used during seventeenth-century witch trials to keep the accused quiet while their fate was being decided by the court.

Postcard using scold's bridle for humorous effect

SIGNS OF SHAME

A more humane variation of branding practiced in the American Colonies was the custom of having transgressors wear a sign, or placard, that made their shameful behaviour evident to anyone they passed on the street. The most famous such sign is undoubtedly the red letter 'A', sewn to Hester Prynne's dress in Nathaniel Hawthorne's novel *The Scarlet Letter*. Unlike Hawthorne's tragic heroine, the real Hester Prynne (who was tried and convicted in New Plymouth Colony in 1671) was not only convicted as an adulteress, but also as a drunkard. Her punishment was to wear both the letters A and D, denoting her double crime. In other instances, the punishment was more fully descriptive. In Boston in 1633, Robert Coles was fined 10s and sentenced to wear a sign with the single word 'Drunkard' and in 1650 a Connecticut man found guilty of insulting ministers and disrupting church services was forced to wear a sign reading 'Open and Obstinate Condemner of God's Holy Ordinances'. Similarly, Ann Boulder had to wear a sign stating that she was a 'Public Destroyer of the Peace'. Presumably, if the condemned failed to wear the sign as instructed they would be charged with more serious offences or, at the very least, given a harsher punishment for the original. This idea of 'naming and shaming' is one which is finding favour among modern contemporary exponents for crimes ranging from shoplifting to child sex offenders.

A brank in Lancaster Castle

STOCKS

Roughly similar in structure and purpose to the pillory, the stocks were a hinged, wooden restraint into which a person's ankles were locked. Also like the pillory, the stocks were of ancient origin (at least dating back to the Anglo-Saxon period) and located in public so the condemned

A postcard using punishment of stocks for humorous effect

Stocks

was exposed to constant humiliation and abuse – an indication that they were not used to punish violent criminals, but to teach people a lesson in good manners and honesty. In an English law of 1426, it states that vagrants were to be locked in the stocks for a period of three days and nights and given only bread and water. A record dating from the mid-1500s tells us that in London 'four women were set in the stocks all night till their husbands did come to fetch them' and in eighteenth-century Boston, Massachusetts, Edward Palmer was fined and sentenced to spend one hour in the stocks for stealing a plank of wood. The stocks were less physically damaging than the pillory, but to make sure the victim was not too comfortable, they were often forced to sit on the edge of a narrow board while they endured their sentence. The early medieval French added another distressing dimension to the time spent in the stocks; the bottoms of the victim's feet were doused with saltwater and a goat was allowed to lick them. It may have been hysterical for those watching but a goat's tongue is as rough as sandpaper and after a very few minutes the pain became excruciating. The humiliation associated with being put in the stocks remains with us in the phrase, 'being made a laughing stock'.

6

TORTURE BY STRETCHING AND SUSPENSION

CRUCIFIXION

Many early cultures, including the ancient Hebrews, used crucifixion as a means of executing their criminals, but it was the Romans who made this particularly slow death their specialty. How a man being crucified looks when he is hung on a cross needs no explanation; anyone who has ever been inside a Christian church is familiar with the image of Jesus suffering on the cross, but a few explanatory words of just what it was that killed the victim may be in order. Contrary to popular belief victims of Roman crucifixion were not always nailed to the cross – the weight of their suspended body would have ripped the nails through their flesh. The nails only increased the amount of pain they were forced to endure. Those condemned to crucifixion were tied to the cross while it lay on the ground and the entire affair was then hoisted upright and dropped into a hole deep enough to ensure that the cross did not topple over. In most cases there was a small platform beneath the victim's feet which allowed them to take the weight off their arms, at least temporarily. Because the entire weight of the body hung from the victim's wrists, the strain would eventually tear the muscles in their diaphragm, making it impossible to breathe. Anyone who refused to cooperate in their own death, insisting on standing on the small platform, would eventually have their knees broken with

The pulley

Gibbet

Gibbet

a long-handled sledgehammer. One way or another, sooner or later, breathing became impossible and the victim died of slow suffocation and exposure.

GARRUCHA

The *garrucha*, also known as the strappado (*estrapade* in Spanish) and as the act of 'Squassation' was one of the Spanish Inquisition's most popular forms of torture, but the same torture was used elsewhere, most notably in India and among the Japanese, where it was known as *Yet Gomon*. Although there were small variations, the basic principal of the *garrucha* involved the prisoner's hands being bound behind their back and a rope running from the wrists was threaded through a pulley attached to the ceiling or a crossbeam. When the rope was hauled in the prisoner was lifted into the air while their arms were slowly pulled from the shoulder sockets. In some cases heavy stones, weighing anywhere from 100 to 250lbs, were tied to the victim's feet as a means of increasing the pain, and in other instances the victim was repeatedly lifted and dropped to the floor, sometimes onto a mound of sharp rocks. Yet again, he might only be dropped a few feet, causing the body to jerk violently against the arm sockets. The practice seems to have been picked up by the Italians, who called it *strappare*, and the Germans who knew it as *Aufzehen*. This study in cruelty was recorded as still being in use in Italy as late as 1778.

GIBBET

The gibbet was a cage made of iron straps, invented in the sixteenth century and intended for the display of corpses after the victim had been hanged, thus providing a long-term warning to other would-be miscreants. When no proper gibbet was available, the corpse might be wrapped in chains and hung from any convenient tree. Naturally, at some point, an inventively cruel person – quite possibly Henry VIII – wondered what would happen if a condemned man were simply locked in a gibbet and left to twist in the wind until he died of exposure or starvation. Living or dead, victims of the gibbet became so numerous that they littered Europe's landscape like signposts, often being used as directional guideposts for travellers: 'Over the stone bridge, past the gibbet and on into the village'. For those unfortunate enough to be gibbeted alive there were occasional grotesque embellishments such as that recorded by an English traveller visiting Germany in the early 1600s: 'Near Lindau I did see a malefactor hanging in iron chains in the gallows with a massive dog hanging on each side by the heels, as being nearly starved, they might eat the flesh of the malefactor before he himself died of famine ...' To add variety to what could easily have become stale sport, some criminals were placed in gibbets, or wrapped in chains, and suspended over the shoreline at low tide. As the tide came in they would be engulfed by the sea.

Suspension

HANGING

Hanging is not technically a torture but a method of execution. However, until the mid-nineteenth-century invention of the 'drop method' – wherein a trap door in the floor of the gallows is sprung open, allowing the victim to fall approximately 6ft, breaking their neck – hanging was anything but the relatively swift death we often assume it to be. Those condemned to be hanged simply had a noose slipped over their head and were then hauled into the air and left to kick and dangle until they choked to death. Depending upon the weight and physical condition of the victim this could take anywhere from five to twenty minutes. In many instances, friends of the condemned helped things along by grabbing on to the victim's legs and pulling downward as hard as they could. History's most notorious place of hanging is undoubtedly London's Tyburn (located where Marble Arch now stands and commemorated with a bronze plaque set in the pavement). Having been used as a place of punishment and execution since 1196, throughout the Middle Ages and well into the eighteenth century Tyburn rivalled, and later overcame, Smithfield Horse Market as the place where the greatest number of English executions took place. In 1571, a permanent gallows, popularly known as the Tyburn Tree, was erected at a crossroads in the village of Tyburn. The 'tree' in question consisted of three stout posts, set into the ground in a triangular pattern, and rising nearly 20ft into the air. The top of these posts were then connected by three cross braces, which formed a large triangle. Over the next 212 years uncounted thousands

Gibbet

Racking and rending

of convicts would meet their end amid the jeers, cheers and cat-calls of heaving crowds of onlookers. Because of the triangular structure of the gallows, numerous victims could be accommodated at one time. The greatest number of simultaneous executions took place on 23 June 1649 when twenty-three men and one woman did what was popularly known as 'dance the Tyburn jig'. Tyburn Tree was demolished in 1783 but hanging remained universally popular well into the twentieth century.

RACK

The ladder

The rack is such a ubiquitous instrument of torture that it hardly needs any introduction. Consisting of nothing more than a flat, wooden bed on which a prisoner was laid out, the pain was inflicted by tying the victim's feet to one end of the device and their hands to ropes wound around a large windlass located at the other end. As the windlass was turned, the rope was cranked in, stretching the victim's limbs to the point where the arms could be dislocated from their sockets and/or the spine disjointed. If torture on the rack was administered carefully, in small sessions of only ten or fifteen minutes at a time and not more than twice a day, the punishment could continue almost indefinitely.

Supposedly, the rack was introduced into England around 1420 by the then Constable of the Tower of London, the Duke of Exeter, and for centuries it was commonly known as the Duke of Exeter's Daughter. Where the Duke picked up the idea is unknown, but use of the rack throughout the late Middle Ages was as ubiquitous as drinking beer. In France it was known as either *le chevalet* or *le Bane de Torture*; in Spain it was the *escalero* and in Germany the *Ladder*.

The ladder

Similar to the rack was the German torture popularly known as 'Schlimme Liesl' (Fearful Eliza). In this instance there was no wooden bed; rather the prisoner's feet were chained, or tied, to iron rings embedded in the floor while his hands were bound and pulled upward by means of a rope and pulley. In order not to waste a conveniently exposed back, punishment on this vertical rack was frequently accompanied by a severe whipping.

TORN APART BY HORSES

A person is attached to four horses, one to each limb of the body. The horses are then made to gallop in opposite directions, in the aim that the person will become dismembered. Not a very effective method unless certain tendons in the limbs are pre-cut. If they are not, then this torment would work in a way akin to the rack, simply stretching and dislocating the joints. Often an executioner would assist in the dismemberment by using a sword or an axe to cut through flesh and tendons and as such, the pull of the horses would literally tear the victim apart. (See illustration.)

Tearing apart by horses

7

TORTURE BY WATER

BOILING

How far in the past the first poor soul was boiled alive as punishment for their crimes is unknown and unknowable. The effects of boiling water (or oil or other substances) must have been obvious since the day when the first Neolithic cook inadvertently shoved their hand into a crock of boiling soup – the possibility of subjecting enemies to the same pain would have been instantly apparent. Records exist showing that the ancient Assyrian king, Antiochus Epiphanies, boiled Hebrew captives and the Romans boiled Christians in public displays of unimaginable cruelty commonly known as 'the games'. In 1531, England's Henry VIII passed a special statute declaring boiling to be the execution of choice for poisoners. This came about when the Bishop of Rochester's cook, Richard Roose, attempted to poison seventeen members of the Bishop's household. According to the records, it took Roose more than two hours to die so we can assume that he was not simply thrown into a cauldron of boiling water, but placed in a tepid bath only to have the temperature raised slowly. The Japanese took a slightly more leisurely approach to scalding their victims; they doused them with buckets full of boiling water, one at a time, over a period of days. An account from 1662 tells us that a number of Japanese converts to Christianity were killed in this manner as part of a larger mass execution.

Boiling

Ducking stool

DUCKING

Although the punishment of ducking women in the local pond came into use in southern England as early as the Anglo-Saxon period, when it was known as the *scealding* (or scolding) stool, ducking came into its own during the Middle Ages when its use spread throughout England and Europe. During this period prostitutes and shrewish women were publicly punished in ways ensured to teach them a lesson in decorum and good manners without inflicting permanent, bodily harm. One of the more popular methods of teaching a *communis rixatrix* (common scold) to hold her tongue was by giving her a good ducking in the local lake or mill pond. Slanderers and what were known as 'makebayts' (gossips) were subjected to the same treatment. The condemned was tied to a chair, or stool (commonly called a 'ducking stool' but properly termed a 'scolding stool', 'trebucket' or 'castigatory') to which two ropes were tied. Woman and stool were then heaved into the water and immediately dragged to the safety of dry land.

At some sites where duckings seem to have been carried out fairly regularly the ducking stool was permanently affixed to the end of a long, counterbalanced pole, much like a see-saw. With such advanced technology three or four stout lads could submerge and retrieve a nagging woman in a matter of ten or fifteen seconds. The main point of this exercise was to subject the victim to as much public humiliation as possible. Once she had become a figure of derision and jokes, it was hoped that her snide tongue would, hopefully, lose its sharp edge. Ducking should not be confused with the 'swimming' of suspected witches. (See below.)

Torture of the funnel

KEELHAULING

This uniquely naval punishment meant exactly what its name implies: the victim was dragged beneath a ship, along or across the keel (the backbone of the ship that extends beneath the bottom of the hull) and hauled up the other side. When a sailor had committed a crime severe enough to warrant keelhauling, a rope was looped beneath the ship and the condemned man was tied to the rope and then tossed overboard. Appointed members of the crew then hauled in the rope from the opposite side of the ship, effectively dragging the victim across the bottom of the vessel. If the rope was hauled in slowly, the condemned man might sink low enough to avoid having his back ripped to shreds by the sharp shells of the barnacles that attached themselves to the submerged portion of wooden ships, but was in danger of drowning. If, on the other hand, the rope was pulled faster, the time under water was shorter, but the chance of being slashed to pieces by the barnacles was far greater. For the most serious offences, a sailor might be condemned to be keelhauled stern to bow, along the length of the ship, rather than from side to side; this was effectively a death sentence as there is a limit to how long anyone can hold their breath. The first mention of keelhauling is found in Dutch naval records dating from 1560 and the practice was not formally abolished until 1853. Another variation of this torture involved tying a miscreant by his wrists or ankles (or both) and then dragging or 'towing' him behind a ship in full sail for a set period of time. The inability of a man to keep his head above water in such circumstances means that this would likely equate to a death sentence – even IF the waters were devoid of sharks.

Baker's punishment in ducking stool

SWIMMING

There were many ways to identify a witch but one of the more popular was to 'swim' the suspect. As in the practice of 'ducking', described above, the victim was either tied to a chair or had bound hands and feet, and tossed into a lake or pond. Unlike ducking, where the dousing only lasted long enough to thoroughly humiliate the victim, swimming required the victim to remain in the water long enough for the judge or clergymen to determine whether or not she was a witch. The prevailing theory of the sixteenth and seventeenth centuries was that water, which was the source of life and the medium used in Christian baptismal rites, was holy and, as such, would not accept an evil person into its depths. With this simple, but ultimately flawed, guideline the determination of guilt or innocence was decided upon by whether the victim floated or sank. If they floated (that is, if the water rejected them) they must be a witch and would be placed on trial as such – usually resulting in execution. If, on the other hand, they sank (and remained submerged long enough to satisfy the judges and bystanders) they must be innocent. Swimming was, invariably, a Catch 22 situation. How many innocent women and men were allowed to drown before they were deemed innocent of witchcraft can never be determined.

Torture of the funnel

Torture of the funnel

TORMENTO DE TOCA

Drowning, or choking to death, are horrible prospects that make anyone shudder to contemplate. It was this specific fear, and the pain and panic associated with it, that led the Spanish Inquisition to invent a torture known as *Tormento de toca*. In the *Tormento*, the victim was strapped down and then a length of fine-mesh cloth (usually linen) was stuffed down his throat and up his nostrils; not enough so as to suffocate him, but certainly enough to make him panic. Once the cloth was in place, a fine stream of water was allowed to trickle onto the exposed ends of the cloth, causing the moisture to be absorbed into the victim's throat and nostrils. Once the victim had nearly reached the point of unconsciousness the cloth was removed. According to eye-witness accounts, the extracted cloth was frequently covered with blood and the sensation was reported to be 'like pulling his bowels through his mouth'. In a nasty variation of this torture a funnel, rather than a rag, was forced down the victim's throat. Into the funnel more and more water was poured. Instantly the victim would start to gag and retch, but the pouring continued until the victim's stomach was bloated and distended and the water backed up into their throat and gushed from their mouth. When the victim was 'full', a noose was placed around his throat, or a gag inserted into his mouth, to prevent him from vomiting up the water. After removing the poor creature from the torture table, the torture masters rolled him back and forth across the dungeon floor, producing horrible pain in his water-filled stomach. Eventually, the gag, or noose, was removed and the victim was allowed to vomit up the water before being subjected to another round of questioning.

Presumably, some who were subjected to this horrible procedure died from ruptured stomachs or choked to death before they could answer the questions. A similar torture was used in France at the same period, although the horrible abuse of the victim seems not to have been so severe. In the first stage, known as *Question Ordinaire*, the victim had four pints of water funnelled down their throat. If this failed to elicit the desired answers the quantity was doubled and referred to as *Question Extraordinaire*.

TRIAL BY WATER

See section on 'Torture by Burning and Branding' under the entry 'Trial by Fire & Water'.

8

TORTURE BY WHIPPING

Because all forms of whipping are, by definition, similar, this section will not be broken down by method but by the types of whips used by various civilisations throughout history.

Virtually since the beginning of civilisation, whipping has been employed as one of society's most common forms of punishment. Generally it has been confined to non-lethal uses but in some instances the whip has proven as lethal as hanging or burning at the stake.

From the time of Ancient Egypt and the Babylonian king, Hamumurabi, (reigned from 1792–1750 BC) up until the present day, virtually every culture has possessed and employed at least some variety of whip to punish wrongdoers. In almost every case the number of lashes to be administered was in direct proportion to the severity of the crime; the more serious the offence the greater the number of lashes.

EGYPT

In Pharaonic Egypt, whippings were generally carried out with bundles of reeds. While this may sound like a fairly mild punishment, records indicate that in extreme cases the punishment could result in the death of the victim, usually as a result of post-punishment infection. The risk of infection setting into the dozens, if not hundreds, of open lacerations caused by a whip were a common side effect of whippings throughout all cultures until well into the nineteenth century.

Public flogging

Bastinado (caning the feet)
in Persia

PERSIA

Ancient Persian courts punished offenders with the *bastinado*, a lightweight whip made of reeds, wherein the convict had the soles of their feet slapped repeatedly with the whip. While this punishment was never considered lethal it would seem, judging from surviving records, that prolonged whippings could literally drive the victim out of their mind.

ROME

Flails

Although the Romans seldom punished free men and women with the whip, the varying types of Roman whips – each designed to inflict a different type, and degree, of physical damage – display an innovative cruelty seldom matched in history. These whips were used almost exclusively on slaves, prisoners of war, citizens of subject nations who transgressed Roman law and recalcitrant Roman soldiers. The Romans may well have been the first to make whipping a part of a greater punishment, such as by whipping a condemned person while they were being dragged to their execution. Most accounts claim that Jesus was scourged prior to his interview with Pontius Pilate, as well as on his way to the cross, with the *plumbatae* described below.

FERULA

For the most insignificant offences a simple, flat whip, known as the *ferula*, was employed and while it was undoubtedly painful and raised welts, the physical damage was temporary at worst.

SCUTICA

The *scutica* was a Roman whip made of braided strips of parchment which, like the world's worst paper cuts, could flay the hide from a victim's back with terrifying efficiency.

PLUMBATAE

The plumbatae were multi-thonged whips not dissimilar to the later cat-o-nine tails. On some occasions small lead balls were attached to the end of the thongs or thorns or tiny slivers of sharp metal were braided into the leather (in which case the whip was called the *ungulae*); any such variation was guaranteed to make the punishment vastly more painful and physically damaging.

FLAGELLUM

While nearly any whipping, if carried to the extreme, is capable of causing death, the Romans are the only society we have come across that had a whip designed specifically as a weapon of execution. Like a monstrous bull-whip, the *flagellum* could literally tear a victim to pieces. Frequently used as a combat weapon in the gladiatorial arena, the *flagellum* was also used to shred condemned groups of Christians before the leering crowds who gathered at 'the games' during the reign of Nero (54–68 AD).

CHINA

The Chinese, from ancient times until the fairly recent past, administered whippings with a whip made of lengths of split bamboo. Heavier and more substantial than the Egyptian reed whip, there is no record that the Chinese whipped to the point of death. The level of damage inflicted by Chinese bamboo whips – partly due to the limited number of lashes that were usually administered – seems to have been to turn the victim's back, or upper thighs, into a mass of welts and blood-blisters. In both China and Japan, whippings were almost universally administered while the victim was laying, face down, on the ground. During the period of the Manchu dynasty (1644–1911) the art of the bamboo whip was developed to its most effective height. Manchu flogging masters were taught how to use their whip by flogging a block of Tofu (bean curd) until they could strike it without breaking the surface.

Chinese punishment of flogging through the streets

JAPAN

Like the Chinese, the Japanese used whips made of split bamboo, but in Japan the strips of bamboo were arranged so the sharp edges of the strips were aligned outward. The effect of the razor-sharp bamboo on human flesh seems obvious enough. According to Japanese law, judicially imposed floggings could range from a few strokes up to no more than 150; but even at that point the survival of the victim was probably a matter of sheer luck.

MEDIEVAL EUROPE

From the early Middle Ages through the eighteenth century, Britain and Europe punished lesser offences with a good, public whipping. The condemned party was generally tied, or manacled, to a public whipping post – conveniently painted bright red – thus ensuring that they could not try to escape while punishment was being administered. In some cases the whipping was only one facet of a larger, more complex punishment and might come during a specified period spent in the public pillory, or the whipping might be enhanced by having vinegar or salt rubbed into the open lacerations left by the whip – while both salt and vinegar would act as defence against infection, the pain of having such astringent substances ground into open wounds could well be as painful as the whipping itself.

Flogging post

ENGLAND

The Act Against Vagrants, passed in 1530, singled out one specific group whom the choleric King Henry VIII deemed to be in particular need of hard and regular floggings. To punish these vagrants (a catch-all term generally applied to Gypsies, vagabonds who wandered aimlessly from town to town and others who simply refused to work) an additional dimension was often added to the standard public whipping. The condemned party had their hands bound and were then tethered to the back of a cart with a length of rope; as the cart was led through the streets of the town the exposed back of the victim was whipped. The punishment could last as long as it took the cart to move from one specified place to another (i.e. from the local court to the village church) or until sufficient damage had been inflicted for the blood to run freely down the victim's back and legs and leave a visible trail on the roadway.

Occasionally, even a punishment as straightforward as a whipping, could go completely, and sometimes hysterically, wrong. During the late eighteenth century, English poet William Cowper wrote a letter to a friend describing one such incident. 'The fellow', Cowper wrote,

Running the gauntlet

> seemed to show great fortitude; but it was all an imposture. The beadle [local watchman] who whipped him had his left hand filled with red ochre [a rust-coloured, dry pigment used in dyes and paint], through which, after every stroke, he drew the lash of the whip, leaving the appearance of a wound upon the skin, but in reality not hurting him at all. This being conceived by the constable, who followed the beadle to see that he did his duty, he (the constable) applied his cane ... to the shoulders of the beadle. The scene now became interesting and exciting. The beadle could by no means be induced to strike the thief hard, which provoked the constable to strike harder; and so the double flogging continued, until a lass ... pitying the beadle, thus suffering under the hands of the pitiless constable, seized him (the constable) ... and pulling him backwards ... slapped his face with Amazonian fury ... the beadle thrashed the thief, the constable the beadle, and the lady the constable and the thief was the only person who suffered nothing.

During the eighteenth and nineteenth century, the British penal system developed nearly as numerous and creative forms of the whip as the Romans and all of the whips noted below were used mercilessly by prison guards, watchmen, beadles and others in authority, in an effort to keep the rabble in line.

CHAIN WHIP

Attached to a foot-long handle were three or four lengths of stout chain of the type now thought of as 'towing chain'. The chain whip probably would not break the skin, but if wielded properly could certainly break ribs, arms and collar bones. This sort of device might be better classed as a weapon than an instrument of torture. It probably finds its inspiration in the military flail, which in turn was inspired by the agricultural threshing flail.

Flail

Flail

JAILER'S WHIP

With a short, stout wooden handle similar to that used on the chain whip, the jailer's whip was fitted with a single, 8 or 10in length of chain with a 4–6oz cast iron or lead weight on the end. There is little doubt that if properly used it could crush a man's skull like a ripe melon. As with the chain whip above, the inspiration behind this device can presumably be found in the military weapon of the flail, ball and chain, or morning-star.

BULLET WHIP

This interesting derivation on the standard whip was simplicity itself. Two or three dozen musket balls were sewn into a leather tube and attached either to a wooden handle as described above or to a simple leather strap that could be looped around the user's wrist. When rolled up it could be concealed in a man's pocket, but was as effective as a length of chain when put into action.

BRITISH ARMY

Although the British were as quick to flog disobedient soldiers as any other military establishment, it was not until the Mutiny Act of 1689 that flogging became a part of official British military policy. Standard sentence for minor infractions was established at ten lashes and anywhere up to thirty-nine could be administered for more serious transgressions. Naturally, as the whippings did little to eliminate insubordination, the number of prescribed lashes increased. By the early eighteenth century a deserter could be sentenced to as many as 900 lashes and if the desertion took place while the soldier was on guard or sentry duty it could go as high as 1,500. In October 1762, three men were convicted of dereliction of duty and sentenced, respectively to 800, 600 and 300 lashes. When such draconian sentences were imposed an army surgeon was always on hand to see that the man did not die of his wounds. If shock and blood loss became too severe, a temporary halt was called and the man taken to the base hospital where he could recover sufficiently before the remainder of the punishment was carried out. Most military floggings were carried out before the entire assembled company as a drummer beat time to keep the rhythm of the whip steady; the slower the drum beat, the longer the interval between lashes. Even as late as the Napoleonic Wars (1804–15), the Duke of Wellington himself remained convinced that his men were only effective so long as they lived under the threat of the lash. Wellington once remarked of his men: 'They are the scum of the earth. I have no idea of any great effect being produced on British soldiers by anything but the fear of immediate corporal punishment'. A member of Wellington's 1st Grenadier Guard regiment, having been convicted of insubordination, drunkenness on duty and refusal to surrender his musket to his superior officer was sentenced to 500 lashes. During the Peninsular War, carried out against Napoleon's forces in Spain, a soldier was so seriously flogged for the offence of being dirty during an inspection that he died of his wounds several days later.

As imitators of the British system, the American Colonial Army, under the Command of George Washington, suffered at least as harshly as their British counterparts. American soldiers could be mercilessly flogged for such minor infractions as wearing their hat at the wrong angle, 'malingering', swearing, not cleaning their musket properly, and not having their full compliment of ammunition.

BRITISH NAVY

Throughout much of the seventeenth and eighteenth century the British Navy was made up not of recruits or volunteers, but of 'impressed' men. Press gangs wandered the streets and prisons looking for victims who could be 'recruited' by being abducted or bludgeoned into unconsciousness only to wake up aboard one of His Majesty's ships already far from port. Considering the unwillingness of these recruits and the fact that they often had no idea what was expected of a sailor, brutal discipline was the tool of choice for teaching them the ropes – literally. When ordered to climb into the rigging, the last man up, and the last man back down, was often flogged.

For this and other minor infractions, the victim was condemned to 'Kiss the Gunner's Daughter' – that is to be bent across the barrel of a cannon while he was beaten with a 5ft length of rope, as thick as a man's wrist, that had been coated with tar.

Military flogging as punishment for pillaging

Cat-o-nine tails

CAT-O-NINE TAILS

Notorious among whips was the 'cat-o-nine tails', commonly used by the Royal Navy for formal punishments of all types. The condemned man was tied, spread-eagle, to an up-ended grating, lifted from one of the ship's hatches, while officers and crew assembled on the main deck to witness the punishment. The punishment was usually administered by the Sergeant of Marines or, if there were no marines aboard, by the boatswain's mate. It is worth noting that the cat could only be used on the open space of the main deck; the confined quarters and low ceilings of the lower decks allowed 'no room to swing a cat' – the origin of the common expression alluding to confined spaces. The 'cat' itself was a nine-thonged whip; each thong being about 2½ft in length and having two or three knots along the length of the thong. The nine braided tails cut through the skin and the knots ripped out pieces of flesh with each lash. After each lash, the punishment officer paused long enough to untangle the 'tails', lean back to apply the full force of his body to the work, take one step forward, sweeping his arm in an arc and bring the whip into contact with the miscreant. It has been said, by those who witnessed such punishment, that the bite of the cat was like having a furious hawk rip pieces of flesh from your back with its talons. The frequency with which this brutal weapon was used is made clear in the records of the Royal Navy. In 1759 alone there were four instances where 'major' floggings (more than two dozen lashes) with the cat took place. John Gazard received 600 lashes for insubordination, James Mansfield 400 for stealing, Thomas Golden and Francis French each receiving 350 lashes for desertion and 'scandalous actions', respectively.

RUSSIA

Russia may not have been infected with as many variations of the whip as the British or the Romans, but what they did have was the *knout*, introduced in the fifteenth century by Ivan III.

KNOUT

The knout was a one-handed whip like the cat-o-nine tails, but its three or four, 2ft-long thongs were made from stiff, twisted rawhide rather than cured leather. At the end of one thong was a loop to which an additional, narrow, strand of hide could be attached. This secondary thong was intended to rip small pieces of flesh from the victim during the flogging. If particular severity was intended, the entire whip was soaked in water and allowed to freeze before the punishment commenced. When asked how many lashes it took to kill a man, a Russian executioner answered that a normal man would be dead after twenty strokes, while a particularly strong man might require twenty-five.

GREAT KNOUT

The Great Knout was identical to the Knout described above, with the exception of metal hooks attached to the end of the thongs. In a matter of a few lashes the Great Knout could literally tear a man to pieces.

FRANCE

While the French used the same whips as their English cousins, they had one interesting variation, the *battoir*, which came into use during the persecution of French Protestants during the latter decades of the eighteenth and early decades of the nineteenth century.

BATTOIR

Not really a whip at all, the *battoir* was adapted from the common laundry paddle – a long-handled, mixing paddle used to stir vats of laundry while it was being boiled. To add to the nasty punishment the paddle itself was able to inflict, nails were driven through the spatulate end of the paddle, far enough that the point of the nail protruded slightly through the surface. The *battoir* was used to administer corporal paddlings to women accused of Protestant leanings or who were known to consort with Protestant men. The victim was bent forward, her skirts and petticoats thrown over her head and her bare rump was paddled until, in the words of one witness: 'blood streamed from the women's bodies and their screams rent the air'.

Flail

If this book is to amount to anything more than a litany of horror and human degradation we must try to answer the basic question: what kind of mentality does it take to willingly inflict, or vicariously enjoy, the suffering of other human beings? We saw in Chapter 4 of Section II (Reforms of the Eighteenth and Nineteenth Centuries) that over the course of a century or more, governments and individuals made valiant efforts to rectify the worst aspects of interrogation, punishment and the penal system. This seems only reasonable as, since the time of Classical Greece, there were thinking people who understood that torture, at least as a means of extracting reliable information, simply does not work. Almost anyone will confess to anything in an effort to ameliorate the pain.

Tragically, since the end of the Second World War the movement toward reform has not only slowed, but in many cases has actually reversed. Precisely to what degree the use of torture has increased is difficult to determine. In many cases the abuse of prisoners may not have increased but we are now more aware of it than we were in times past. In other instances there has been a demonstrable return to the 'bad old days'. Without doubt there are nations where the institution of torture is as pervasive as it was four or five centuries ago. In much of the Middle East and South East Asia thieves still have their hands cut off, and serious crimes still bring about beheadings, many of which continue to be carried out in public ceremonies reminiscent of the guillotining of Revolutionary France or the hangings at London's Tyburn Tree. According to Amnesty International, as late as the 1970s at least sixty countries continued to use severe corporal punishment as a means of dealing with crimes both large and small. In 1991, Barbados actually brought back the cat-o-nine tails as a means of punishing drug dealers.

For any nation, or group of people, to engage in the use of torture, a far more complex set of circumstances are required than the cruel whim of a dictator. Both the police and military must at least give their tacit consent, if not their full cooperation; the entire judiciary system must accept torture as useful and acceptable and, to some greater or lesser degree, depending upon how totalitarian the regime is, so must the people. In some cases this consent comes in the form of openly embracing torture while in others it takes the form of public denial that such goings-on take place while privately sanctioning them or dismissing the practice with a tacit acceptance. This last was the case in medieval and renaissance England, in Soviet era Russia and remains so in the United States and dozens of other countries to this day. If your immediate reaction is to deny that torture still takes place, particularly in seemingly civilised Western nations, consider the report released by Amnesty International on Wednesday, 23 May 2007. In its report AI concluded that the world is experiencing 'a human rights meltdown'. 'The politics of fear', the report said, 'are fuelling a downward spiral of human rights abuses ... The "war on terror" and the war in Iraq, with their catalogue of human rights abuses have created deep divisions that cast a shadow on international relations. The US administration is treating the world as one giant battlefield for its war on terror.'

If one asks why torture continues to exist and is still being practiced by so-called civilised nations, the answer remains much the same as it was stated in Section I of this book: weak, insecure, paranoid leaders feel safer if they can identify, isolate and destroy one or more 'enemy conspiracies'. Once this enemy (for the Spanish Inquisition it was heretics; for the Puritans of Salem, Massachusetts it was witches; for Joseph McCarthy it was communists; for Ronald Reagan it was 'the evil empire'; for George Bush it was 'the axis of evil') has been identified, its agents can be rounded up and forced to confess their crimes and the names of their confederates. The more forced and public the confessions are, the better their propaganda value. This is why Middle East terrorists force their own victims to confess in front of video cameras. Hence the witch hunts begin.

This is not to deny that the world is under threat by a more than ample number of lunatics. We are up to our eyeballs in terrorists, political fanatics, fundamentalist zealots and dangerous people of every kind imaginable. But the truth is not as simple as governments would like us to believe – the conspiracies, if they actually exist, may not be nearly as organised or pervasive as we are told to believe. But governments and military leaders need to find simple, clean-cut solutions to easily identifiable problems. The problem as they see it, or at least as they like to sell it to the public, is that there is some great conspiracy out to destroy civilisation as we know it and all we have to do is find its members and crush them. It is on such neat, well-organised assumptions that Rome persecuted Christians, the Inquisition burned heretics and Hitler sent Jews to the gas chambers. The US, Great Britain and their allies use the same justification as the basis for the 'War on Terrorism'. Of course, to be able to go after the bad guys (and spend the endless amounts of money required to do so) the governments and the military must convince their people (the voters who keep them in office) that there is a very real, identifiable, danger and that only Big Brother knows how to make the monster go away. Such convincing requires a major propaganda effort.

The first step in convincing an entire country that someone is out to get them is by identifying who that 'someone' is. Heretics must be identified and publicly humiliated, or tortured, into confessing their sins. Sometimes government gets a lot of help in this process. After pointing the finger at Islamic extremists, particularly those in Iraq, since the day Saddam Hussein invaded Kuwait in 1990, the biggest boost they could have asked for came on 11 September 2001, when a group of crazed terrorists hijacked planes and crashed them into New York's World Trade Center and the Pentagon. As real as the threat from terrorists may be, it does not alter the fact that governments must identify the bogey man hiding in the closet, and it really doesn't matter who the bogey man is or whether or not he presents any real danger. It would seem rather unlikely that Iraq had anything to do with 9/11 but that made no difference to the US propaganda machine. Before the Islamic extremists it was the Soviet Union, before them it was the Nazis and before them it was the Unions. In every case, members of this vast conspiracy were arrested and paraded before the public like penitents at one of the Spanish Inquisition's *auto-de-fes*. It is this turning of an otherwise invisible conspiracy into a tangible (but no longer acceptably human) object of ridicule that turns abstract fear into a very real object of hate and makes torture acceptable as official government policy.

Inevitably, to turn fear and paranoia into an institutionalised policy of torture, the enemy must be carefully chosen in such a way that they appear demonstrably unlike the rest of us. In medieval France, Spain and Germany it was Jews and heretics; in Hitler's Germany it was Jews, communists, Poles and Russians; in Stalin's Soviet Union it was Western Imperialists and counter-revolutionaries. In every case, a specific group was identified and demonised before the rack, burning post, gas chamber and firing squad were brought into action. Once a few heretics (or communists, or Jews, or terrorists) had been denounced as enemies of both God and man – that is to say, they no longer appeared to be quite human – then torturing them no longer seemed quite so horrible; in fact, it became everyone's duty to support the just punishment of such 'evil beings'. For an extended examination of just this kind of paranoia at work, read *Mein Kampf*, Adolf Hitler's political polemic and the book partially responsible for bringing him to power. If this is too much for you to bear, we offer the following extract from a speech by US Senator Joseph McCarthy, the man who started America's communist witch hunts in the early 1950s.

> How can we account for our present situation unless we believe that men high in this government are concerting to deliver us to disaster? This must be the product of a great conspiracy on a scale so immense as to dwarf any previous such venture in the history of man. A conspiracy of infamy so black that, when it is finally exposed, its principals shall forever be deserving of the maledictions of all honest men ...

Thanks to Senator McCarthy, and those who believed his rhetoric, hundreds of innocent men and women (from cleaning ladies to government clerks and movie stars) lost their jobs and were forever viewed with suspicion. Many went to prison and at least two (Julius and Ethel Rosenberg) were sent to the electric chair. Like all despots, McCarthy insisted that all he was doing was defending his country and helping to make it safe. Hitler said exactly the same thing, so did Thomas de Torquemada and dozens of others from the beginning of time until the present day. Inherent in any such propaganda campaign is the necessity for the leader to convince his people that the hunting down and torture of members of this 'invisible conspiracy' is the only acceptable, patriotic thing to do. Just as in the Middle Ages, those who continue to deny the existence of witches risk being branded a witch themselves.

Convincing the majority of the population that there is a 'clear and present danger' is always easier during times of political or economic distress. When things are bad, people are already looking for someone to blame their problems on and when the government hands them a scapegoat on a platter they are all too willing to accept it so long as it is: a) simple to understand and, b) the victim doesn't seem too much like one of their own family. Here too, propaganda plays a big part. During the Cold War, all Russians were portrayed in the Western media as being fat, dumpy and dressed in impossibly baggy, rumpled grey suits. How odd, then, that once the Cold War ended 200 million Russians instantly transformed themselves to look just like the rest of us.

Once the 'enemy' has been identified and the public has been convinced that they are not only an immediate threat to the survival of civilisation but are also, somehow, less than human, the single step from simmering hatred to institutionalised torture will inevitably be taken. When the former Yugoslavia descended into a self-devouring civil war in the late 1980s and early 1990s each side defined 'the enemy' by their religion. Christian and Islamic paramilitary groups spent nearly a decade destroying what had been by far the most stable and prosperous country in the old Communist Block. Each side, convinced that the other was to blame for whatever woes beset them, engaged in an orgy of beatings, rapes, murders, electric shock torture, physically damaging bondage, and heaven only knows what else. Since the 1960s similar situations of institutionalised torture have occurred in Vietnam, Rwanda, Zimbabwe, Palestine, Chile, Uganda, Malaysia, Iran, Iraq, Argentina, Sudan, Burundi and China. Sometimes the governments inflicted the madness on their own people – notably in Zimbabwe, Chile, Uganda and China – and other times it has been inflicted by invading powers as it was in Vietnam and, to a lesser extent, Iraq.

Like any bad habit, the use of torture increases with familiarity. As with alcohol, drugs, tobacco and so many other things which are bad for us, the more accustomed to torture a nation becomes the greater its tolerance for it. No one simply steps out of their car one day and decides to beat their neighbours to death. Depending upon your particular neighbour you might occasionally think about it, but you don't. Why? Because it is not acceptable behaviour of civilised people living in a civilised society. Even seriously contemplating such a thing is revolting. So how do people become so desensitised to the horrors of torture that they not only tacitly accept, but actively engage in, the physical mutilation and execution of other human beings? How long does it take to become a monster? Certainly the German people were just like the rest of us in 1930, but by 1939 those who were not directly engaged in the wholesale slaughter of millions upon millions of people gave their complete and (generally) unconditional support to those who did. Did they really know what was happening? While they might have turned a blind eye to those cattle-car-loads of Jews disappearing into the distance it would have been impossible to miss the decimation of Poland, Czechoslovakia, Hungary, Belgium, Denmark, Norway and the Netherlands. So how does such a thing happen? How do civilised people become so convinced that their neighbours are sub-human threats to all that is good and right, that they themselves descend to the state of ravening animals?

In search of an answer to this question, in 1963 Yale Professor of Psychology, Stanley Milgram, set up an experiment to see if the guards at Nazi concentration camps were 'only following orders' as they claimed at the Nuremburg War Crimes Trials in 1946 and '47, or

Stanley Milgram, pictured here with the 'electric generator' he used in the Interaction Laboratory at the University of Yale, in an experiment into human obedience.

if there was something far more sinister at work. Milgram's experiment involved a group of his students who were assigned to ask a series of questions to outside volunteers. When the volunteers gave a wrong answer the student examiner was told to administer a mild electrical shock. Each time the subject gave an incorrect answer the voltage was to be increased. Despite the subjects writhing and screaming in pain – some pleading that they had heart conditions and could die from the shocks – more than 50 per cent of the students continued to ask the entire slate of questions and administer the punishment as instructed. Only later were the students told that their victims were actually actors, and that the effects of the supposed electrical shocks had been faked. If the idea that such educated people as a group of Yale University students would knowingly threaten the health and lives of innocent people simply because they were ordered to do so is frightening, the results of a subsequent experiment had far more ominous implications.

In August 1971, social psychologist and Stanford University Professor Philip Zimbardo carried out what has since become known as the Stanford Prison Experiment. In the experiment, Zimbardo assigned a random group of student volunteers to play the parts of either prison guards or, alternatively, of prisoners. Under the carefully laid out parameters of the experiment the students were to live for several weeks in a simulated prison-like building fitted with all the standard accoutrements of any real prison. The 'guards' were given official-looking uniforms and mirror-finished sun glasses to mask their eyes. This same eye-disguising technique has long been used by American policemen and Highway Patrol officers. The prisoners were dressed in standard, bright orange, prison-style jumpsuits. Zimbardo's motive in setting up this experiment was to find out, in his own words, 'If you put good people in a bad place do the people triumph or does the place corrupt them?'

The outcome of the experiment not only flew in the face of reason, but was worse than anything either Zimbardo, or undoubtedly the student volunteers, could ever have imagined. At the end of the first week the experiment was terminated when, according to Zimbardo: 'I witnessed naked, shackled prisoners with bags over their heads, guards stepping on prisoners' backs as they did pushups, guards sexually humiliating prisoners.' Three decades later Zimbardo would recall: 'Some images from my experiment are practically interchangeable with those from Iraq.' What Zimbardo also found, as would be discovered in the aftermath of the Abu Ghraib fiasco, was that the incidences of abuse increased significantly at night, after those in authority had gone home.

From the disastrous outcome of the above two experiments we must conclude two things. First, people, no matter how benign and well educated they may be, are capable of horrible things when ordered to do so. Secondly, people will repeatedly commit singularly savage acts if they think they can get away with them; that is, when they believe they are not being watched.

Comparing the actions of nice, upper-middle-class students from Stanford and Yale with the atrocities committed by Spanish Inquisitors, witch hunters and Nazi concentration camp guards may seem shocking and far-fetched, but is it really? A terrifying example of just how cruel people can become when they believe they can get away with it comes from the archives of Nazi Germany. In June 1942, Heinrich Himmler, head of Hitler's secret police, the Gestapo, authorised the use of limited physical abuse during interrogations, 'where preliminary investigation had indicated that the person could give information on important matters such as subversive activities'. As in all cases where specific groups of 'enemies of the state' have been singled out this order was limited to 'communists, Marxists, Jehovah's Witnesses, saboteurs, terrorists, members of resistance movements and Polish or Soviet Russian loafers of slackers'. Beyond those specific limits Himmler gave strict orders that any member of the SS or Gestapo suspected of having sadistic tendencies should be severely reprimanded and punished. There is, however, no question that Nazi interrogation methods went far beyond the limits set by Himmler. SS and Gestapo interrogators and guards routinely whipped, beat, chained and starved their prisoners. Those subjected to particularly intense questioning were immersed in ice water, nearly drowned, subjected to electric shock and having their fingernails ripped out. There is nothing here that the Spanish Inquisition would not have immediately recognised and condoned. So why did the Nazis carry out such horrific tortures if they had not been ordered to do so? Because they had been indoctrinated into thinking of their prisoners as something less than human and they knew their actions, although not sanctioned by official policy, would go unpunished.

Equally frightening is the fact that an American Army report, compiled after the liberation of Paris in 1944, concluded that much of the Nazi torture was completely random and pointless. In the report we find this conclusion. 'The tortures were all the more horrible because the Germans, in many cases, had no clear idea of what information they wanted and just tortured haphazard[ly]'. This is truly a case of sadism for the sake of sadism but, as in all such instances of 'official' torture, the guilty parties actually believed their victims were somehow less than human and, of course, they could comfortably put the blame on some higher authority regardless of whether or not their actions bore official sanction. In the Middle Ages the torturers saw the Church as the sanctioning authority, the Church in turn, pointed to God. In Revolutionary France the approving authority was the Committee of Public Safety, in Nazi Germany it was Hitler and the High Command and at Yale and Stanford Universities it was Professors Milgram and Zimbardo. The point seems to be that so long as people actually have, or believe they have, someone to accept the blame for their actions, they will commit acts that they would never ordinarily contemplate.

In the instances of the Yale and Stanford experiments, the abuse ended when the experiments were ended or called off. The students involved suffered only a very limited exposure to the dark side of their own human nature. In instances of war – be it open, declared war or more subtle, undeclared wars like the Cold War, the War on Terrorism, or endless paramilitary in-fighting in Africa and the Middle East – the individuals involved experience year upon year of ever-increasing levels of brutality. The first time a (presumably normal) person beats a defenceless human being half to death must be a revolting experience; the second time is a lot easier and after ten, or twenty, or 100 such experiences it makes no impression at all. It is in this manner that brutality is so much like alcohol or drugs; slow but continuous exposure to the experience allows us to build up a tolerance and it is with complete knowledge of our tolerance-building capacity that governments slowly ratchet up the demonisation of target groups and the ever-increasing levels of brutality carried out against them.

In the aftermath of the 11 September 2001 attacks on the World Trade Center and Pentagon, US Vice President Dick Cheney appeared on NBC news. In his statement he obliquely referred to the fact that the US would: 'work the dark side, if you will. We have to spend time in the shadows'. Precisely what he may have meant by that is open to speculation, but undoubtedly a part of the dark side included what the CIA – in a master-stroke of obfuscation and double talk – now refers to as 'enhanced interrogation techniques'. In a December 2004 memorandum the US Justice Department stated that such enhanced techniques as prolonged, forced standing; forcing prisoners to wear hoods; subjecting them to loud noises and deprivation of sleep, food and drink might be considered inhumane but did not constitute torture. That point might be argued by the victims of England's seventeenth-century Witchfinder General, Matthew Hopkins, who were subjected to identical tortures to the point where they confessed to having engaged in intercourse with Satan himself. In an attempt to clarify the Justice Department's memorandum – but without actually saying anything at all – spokesman Erik Amblin refused to specify what specific interrogation techniques might be cruel and degrading but would still not qualify as torture. He did say, however, that: 'acting with the specific intent of causing prolonged mental harm' would be illegal under US and international law. Does this mean that causing a prisoner to have a mental breakdown is acceptable if it was unintentional? Does everyone have the same tolerance to torture? If not, then do US interrogators call in a psychologist to determine each individual's emotional and physical threshold to pain before torturing them?

In an eerie reflection of Heinrich Himmler's order specifying limits on when and how much torture could be inflicted on prisoners, US

Secretary of Defense Donald Rumsfeld approved the use of 'enhanced interrogation techniques' on a single prisoner who was being held at the US military base at Guantanamo Bay, Cuba, who was suspected of being involved in planning the 9/11 attacks on the World Trade Center and Pentagon. Once this genie was officially out of the bottle, and US interrogators realised that censure and punishment for inflicting torture were unlikely to be levelled against them, the practice quickly spread to US forces in both Afghanistan and Iraq.

In May 2004, pictures of American soldiers, inflicting a litany of torture and abuse on prisoners being held at the Abu Ghraib Correctional Facility near Baghdad, Iraq, appeared on almost every major television network in the world. Like something out of the Middle Ages we saw photos – taken by the perpetrators themselves – of prisoners being beaten, kicked and slapped; their bare feet being jumped on by soldiers in combat boots. In other pictures prisoners were stripped naked and arranged in decorative piles, forced to masturbate and simulate fellatio, dragged around on the end of a leash like dogs and threatened with unmuzzled, attack-trained dogs. When called to account for her troop's acts, the General in charge of Abu Ghraib at the time of the incident, Brigadier General Janis Karpinski, insisted it was all the fault of 'a few bad apples'. But was it? Or was it a case where the prisoners had been so dehumanised that no-one really cared how horribly they were abused? The ensuing investigation revealed that military interrogators came and went without even being asked to present identification. No authority figures checked on the prisoners' status or well-being. To complicate matters even more, the prisoners and their guards did not speak the same language. Unless there was an interpreter present the guards had no way of knowing what the prisoners were saying. This in itself made the prisoners seem alien and suspicious.

What is certainly not open to speculation is the later testimony of American military policemen Chip Frederick and Ken Davis; both of whom served at Abu Ghraib at the time of the incident. Frederick stated: 'It was clear that there was no accountability', and Davis added:

> As soon as we'd have prisoners come in, sandbags instantly (went over) their head. They would flexicuff them; throw them down to the ground; some would be stripped. It was told to all of us, 'they're nothing but dogs'. You start looking at these people as less than human and you start doing things to them that you would never dream of.

It would seem that MP Davis belatedly learned a lesson in propaganda techniques that was already well known during the Middle Ages and has been employed by despots ever since: identify an enemy, demonise him until people accept him as something less than human and torture is no longer objectionable.

As Professor Milgram discovered at the conclusion of his 1963 Yale experiment; given the right instruction and the correct circumstances almost anyone can be induced to cooperate in, participate in, and even enjoy the destruction of other human beings, even if only vicariously.

Of course, normal people in the normal circumstances of their daily lives would never enjoy seeing other people abused and humiliated. Or would they? Every day millions of people gloat over copies of tawdry 'fan magazines' that fill their pages with lurid accounts of movie stars' dissolving lives, drug problems and marital infidelities. Every evening tens of millions of viewers glue themselves to their television sets staring at 'reality' programs like *Big Brother*, *Survivor*, *Fear Factor*, *Jerry Springer* and dozens of similar shows around the world that focus on the ever-increasing levels of humiliation and degradation to which the contestants or participants subject each other. The readership and viewing audience has become the leering, jeering crowd gathered around Tyburn Tree and Madame Guillotine and the sanctioning authority has become the networks and sponsors. Like Pontius Pilate we wash our hands of the blood of the innocent and sit back and watch events follow their horrible course to an inevitable end. We are not the guilty party because someone else is sanctioning our actions. But then, how many people through history have ever accepted that they were the guilty party?

Let us leave you, then, with one final thought. Does turning a blind eye to the horrors and injustices of the world help perpetuate the inhumanity? Can it be interpreted as a sort of tacit approval or acceptance? Was Edmund Burke correct in his assessment that: 'All it takes for evil to triumph is for good men to do nothing'? If this is indeed so, dear reader (who has stayed by our side though every page of this gruesome topic), you have to ask yourself which side of the equation you wish to be on. You have to ask yourself, 'what sort of world do you want to live in?' And then, most difficultly, you have to ask yourself, 'what are you going to do about it?'

BIBLIOGRAPHY

BOOKS

Abbott, Geoffrey, *Lords of the Scaffold: A History of Execution*, Headline, 1991.

Abbott, Geoffrey, *Rack, Rope and Red-Hot Pincers: A History of Torture and Its Instruments*, Headline Books, 1993.

Abbott, Geoffrey, *The Book of Execution: An encyclopedia of methods of Judicial Executions*, Headline, 1994.

Abbott, Geoffrey, *The Who's Who of British Beheadings*, Andre Deutsch, 2000.

Andrews, William, *Old Time Punishments*, William Andrews and Co., 1890.

Andrews, William, *Bygone Punishments*, William Andrews and Co., 1899.

Anonymous, *Torture, Inquisition, and the Crime of Capital Punishment: An exhibition presented in various European and American cities since 1983*, Avon and Arno Publishers, 2001.

Burford, E.J. and Shulman, Sandra, *Of Bridles and Burnings, The Punishment of Women*, Robert Hale Ltd., 1992.

Byrne, Richard, *The London Dungeon Book of Crime and Punishment*, Little, Brown and Company, 1993.

Cameron, Joy, *Prisons and Punishment in Scotland from the Middle Ages to the Present*, Canongate Publishing Ltd., 1983.

Dawson, Ian, *Crime and Punishment Through Time*, John Murray (Publishers) Ltd., 1999.

Duff, Charles, *A Handbook on Hanging – the fine art of Execution*, The Bodley Head, 1928.

Earle, Alice Morse, *Curious Punishments of Bygone Days*, Loompanics Limited, Port Townsend Washington, 1896.

Hibbert, Christopher, *The Roots of Evil: A Social History of Crime and Punishment*, Weidenfeld and Nicholson, 1963.

Hroch, Miroslav/Skybova, Anna, *Ecclesia Militans: The Inquisition*, Dorset Press, 1988.

Hurwood, Bernhardt J., *Torture through the Ages*, Paperback Library, 1969.

Farrington, Karen, *Hamlyn History of Punishment and Torture: a journey through the dark side of justice*, Hamlyn, 1996.

Foxe, John, *Foxe's Booke of Martyrs*, Whitaker House, 1981.

Innes, Brian, *The History of Torture*, Brown Packaging Books, 1998.

Kerrigan, Michael, *The Instruments of Torture*, Spellmount, 2001.

Lane, Brian, *The Encyclopedia of Cruel and Unusual Punishment*, Virgin Publishing Ltd, 1993.

Laurence, John, *A History of Capital Punishment*, The Citadel Press, 1960.

Lee, Stephen, *Crime, Punishment and Protest 1450 to the Present Day*, Longman Group Limited, 1994.

Levinson, Sanford (ed.), *Torture: A Collection*, Oxford University Press, 2004.

Lyons, Lewis, *The History of Punishment*, Amber Books, 2003.

Mannix, Daniel P., *The History of Torture*, Sutton Publishing, 1964.

Oakley, Gilbert, *The History of the Rod and other Corporal Punishments*, The Walton Press, 1964.

Peters, Edward, *Torture*, Basil Blackwell, 1985.

Pettifer, Ernest W., *Punishments of Former Days*, Taylor and Colbridge, 1939.

Priestley, Philip, *Victorian Prison Lives*, Pimlico, 1999.

Ransford, Oliver, *The Slave Trade*, Readers Union, 1972.

Ruthven, Malise, *Torture: The Grand Conspiracy*, Weidenfeld and Nicolson, 1978.

Salgado, Gamini, *The Elizabethan Underworld*, JM Dent and Sons Ltd, 1977.

Scott, George Ryley, *The History of Capital Punishment*, Torchstream Books, 1950.

Scott, George Ryley, *The History of Corporal Punishment*, Torchstream Books, 1968.

Scott, George Ryley, *The History of Torture Through the Ages*, Torchstream Books, 1940.

Silverman, Lisa, *Tortured Subjects: Pain, Truth, and the Body in Early Modern France*, University of Chicago Press, 2001.

Sprenger, Jacobus/Kramer, Heinrich (Summers, Montague, Trans.), *Malleus Maleficarum – The Hammer of Witchcraft*, The Folio Society, 1968.

Swain, John, *The Pleasures of the Torture Chamber*, Noel Douglas Ltd., 1931.

Swain, John, *A History of Torture*, Tandem, 1931.

Tyldesley, Joyce, *Judgement of the Pharaoh: Crime and Punishment in Ancient Egypt*, Phoenix, 2000.

Van Yelyr, R.G., *The Whip and the Rod: An Account of Corporal Punishment among all Nations and for all Purposes*, Gerald G. Swan, 1942.

Walker, Peter N., *Punishment: an Illustrated History*, David and Charles, 1972.

Whiting, Roger, *Crime and Punishment: A Study Across Time*, Stanley Thornes (Publishers) Ltd., 1986.

Wilkinson, George Theodore, *The Newgate Calendar (Book 1)*, Panther Books, 1962.

Zimbardo, Philip, *The Lucifer Effect: Understanding How Good People Turn Evil*, Random House, 2007.

MAGAZINES AND JOURNALS

Brushfield, T.N., 'Notes on the Punishment known as the Drunkard's Cloak of Newcastle-on-Tyne', *Journal of the British Archaeological Association*, September 1888.

Rushkoff, Douglas, 'Peer Review: The reason we should loathe ourselves for watching reality TV', *Discover*, May 2007.

INDEX